Everyman, I will go with thee,
and be thy guide

THE EVERYMAN
LIBRARY

*The Everyman Library was founded by J. M. Dent
in 1906. He chose the name Everyman because he wanted
to make available the best books ever written in every
field to the greatest number of people at the cheapest possible
price. He began with Boswell's 'Life of Johnson';
his one-thousandth title was Aristotle's 'Metaphysics',
by which time sales exceeded forty million.*

*Today Everyman paperbacks remain true to
J. M. Dent's aims and high standards, with a wide range
of titles at affordable prices in editions which address
the needs of today's readers. Each new text is reset to give
a clear, elegant page and to incorporate the latest thinking
and scholarship. Each book carries the pilgrim logo,
the character in 'Everyman', a medieval mystery play,
a proud link between Everyman
past and present.*

Voltaire

SELECTED WRITINGS

Edited by
CHRISTOPHER THACKER

EVERYMAN
J. M. DENT · LONDON
CHARLES E. TUTTLE
VERMONT

Tim Mathews, University of London,
is Consultant Editor for the Everyman French series.

Introduction, critical apparatus and new translations © J. M. Dent 1995

All rights reserved

J. M. Dent
Orion Publishing Group
Orion House
5 Upper St Martin's Lane
London WC2H 9EA
and
Charles E. Tuttle Co. Inc.
28 South Main Street
Rutland, Vermont 05701, USA

Typeset by CentraCet Ltd, Cambridge
Printed in Great Britain by
The Guernsey Press Co. Ltd, Guernsey, C. I.

This book if bound as a paperback is subject to
the condition that it may not be issued on loan or otherwise
except in its original binding.

British Library Cataloguing-in-Publication Data
is available upon request.

ISBN 0 460 87624 4

CONTENTS

NOTE ON THE AUTHOR AND EDITOR

VOLTAIRE was born in 1694 and lived through the last twenty-one years of Louis XIV, throughout Louis XV's reign, and into the first four years of Louis XVI. He died in 1778. Eleven years later, the Bastille was stormed and the French Revolution began.

From the start, Voltaire's sharp pen and tongue made him admirers and enemies, and in 1717 he spent eleven months in the Bastille. Undeterred, he wrote plays, epic poetry, essays, pamphlets whilst imprisoned. In trouble again upon release, he went to England and wrote a book about the English, followed by more, and more publications . . .

Soon he was recognised as France's foremost living writer-poet, tragedian, historian and critic. In 1736 Frederick, the Crown Prince of Prussia, made contact, and a long, intense relationship began, lasting until Voltaire's death. After a period in Potsdam, in 1750–53, Voltaire escaped to Switzerland, buying properties near Geneva, staying at Ferney until the year of his death. From the mid-40s he had started to write *contes* or 'tales', culminating with *Candide* in 1759. He continued in politico-religious dispute, in the 1750s related to the fortunes of the *Encyclopédie*, in the 1760s and later related to questions of injustice – such as Calas' execution in 1762.

A giant of literature, he never stopped writing – and he is still read widely today.

CHRISTOPHER THACKER studied at Oxford, and later at Indiana University, taking a Ph.D. in Comparative Literature. After four years in Cyprus as secretary to a Greek millionaire he taught at university. In the mid-1980s he became Garden Historian with English Heritage, to compile England's first 'register' of historic gardens. He has written a dozen books, mostly related to eighteenth-century matters – literature, aesthetics, gardens – and to the history of gardens generally. They include an edited edition, in French, of Voltaire's *Candide*; a new translation of *Candide*; *The Wildness Pleases: the Origins of Romanticism*; *Masters of the Grotto: Joseph and Josiah Lane*; *The History of Gardens*; and *The Genius of Gardening: the History of Gardens in Britain and Ireland*.

CHRONOLOGY OF VOLTAIRE'S LIFE

Year	Age	Life
1694		Birth of François-Marie Arouet
1701	7	Death of Mme Arouet, his mother
1704	10	Attends Collège Louis-le-Grand in Paris until 1711
1712	18	Birth of Voltaire's niece, Marie-Louise Mignot
1713	19	Visits the Hague, first foreign journey
1716	22	Exiled, briefly, from Paris
1717	23	Imprisoned in the Bastille for eleven months
1718	24	Changes his names to Voltaire; *Oedipe*
1720	26	Visits Bolingbroke, at *La Source*, near Orleans
1722	28	Death of M. Arouet, his father. Travels in the Low Countries
1723	29	Surreptitious edition of *La Ligue*

CHRONOLOGY OF HIS TIMES

Year	Literary and Artistic Context	Historical Events
1696	Swift, *Tale of a Tub*, 1696–7 (published 1704)	
1697	Births of Mme du Deffand, Hogarth Bayle, *Dictionnaire*	
1701		Reign of Frederick I of Prussia begins, 1701–13. War of Spanish Succession, 1701–13
1702		Death of William III. Queen Anne reigns, 1702–14
1704	Birth of Boucher	Battle of Blenheim
1707	Birth of Fielding	Union of England and Scotland
1708	Swift, *Bickerstaff Papers* (1708–9)	
1709	Birth of Samuel Johnson	
1711	*The Spectator*, 1711–14	
1712	Births of Algarotti, Rousseau	Birth of Frederick the Great
1713	Birth of Diderot Addison, *Cato*	Reign of Frederick William I of Prussia begins, 1713–40
1714		Death of Queen Anne, George I reigns, 1714–27
1715		Death of Louis XIV. Louis XV reigns, 1715–74. First Jacobite rebellion
1716	Birth of David Garrick	
1717	Births of d'Alembert, Horace Walpole	
1720	Gay, *Collected Poems*	
1721	Montesquieu, *Lettres persanes* Death of Watteau	

Year	Age	Life
1725	31	Quarrels with chevalier de Rohan
1726	32	Imprisoned in the Bastille, goes to England, returns to Paris briefly in July; death of his sister, Mme Mignot, in September
1728	34	The *Henriade*
1729	35	End of 1728 or early '29, returns to France
1730	36	*Brutus*
1731	37	*Histoire de Charles XII*
1732	38	*Zaïre*
1733	39	*Letters Concerning the English Nation*
1734	40	*Lettres philosophiques*; to Cirey, 1734–43
1736	42	First letter from Frederick of Prussia
1738	44	Marie-Louise Mignot marries Nicolas-Charles Denis
1740	46	Tries to stop publication of the *Anti-Machiavel*; meets Frederick, goes to Berlin
1741	47	*Mahomet*
1743	49	Elected F.R.S.
1744	50	Death of N.-C. Denis
1745	51	Appointed *Historiographe du roi*
1746	52	Elected to the *Académie Française*
1747	53	*Memnon/Zadig*; Mme du Châtelet at the *jeu de la reine*
1748	54	To Lunéville with Mme du Châtelet; Saint-Lambert
1749	55	Death of Mme du Châtelet
1750	56	To Potsdam/Berlin
1752	58	*Micromégas*
1753	59	Leaves Berlin; to Frankfurt, Schwetzingen, Colmar
1754	60	To Geneva
1755	61	14 Feb., *Les Délices* until 1759; *Orphelin de la Chine*
1756	62	D'Alembert comes to *Les Délices*; *Essai sur les Moeurs*
1757	63	Mme d'Epinay visits Voltaire

Year	Literary and Artistic Context	Historical Events
1725		Death of Peter the Great
1726	Swift, *Gulliver's Travels* (26 Oct.)	
1727	Swift in England Death of Newton	Death of George I. George II reigns, 1722–60
1728	Gay, *Beggar's Opera*	
1730	Death of Mlle Lecouvreur	
1732	Births of Beaumarchais, Fragonard	
1733	Pope, *Essay on Man*	
1737	Birth of Edward Gibbon	
1740	Birth of Boswell	Death of Frederick William I. Frederick II reigns, 1740–86. The War of the Austrian Succession, 1741–8
1743		Battle of Dettingen
1744	Death of Pope	
1745	Death of Swift	Battle of Fontenoy. Second Jacobite rebellion
1746		Battle of Culloden
1748	Montesquieu, *Esprit des lois*	Excavations at Pompeii
1749	Fielding, *Tom Jones* Birth of Goethe	
1750	Johnson, *The Rambler*, 1750–52	
1751	Volume I of the *Encyclopédie*	
1752	Rousseau, *Le Devin du village*	
1754	Death of Fielding	
1755	Death of Montesquieu	Lisbon earthquake (1 Nov.)
1756	Edmund Burke, *Philosophical Enquiry*	Seven Years' War, 1756–63
1757	Volume VII of the *Encyclopédie*	Damiens attacks Louis XV Admiral Byng executed

Year	Age	Life
1758	64	To Schwetzingen; writing *Candide*; buys Ferney
1759	65	*Candide*; writes *Mémoires*
1760	66	'Écrasons l'infâme'
1761	67	Builds church at Ferney, *Deo erexit Voltaire*
1763	69	*Traité sur la tolérance*
1764	70	*Dictionnaire philosophique portatif*
1765	71	*Pot-pourri*
1767	73	*L'Ingénu*
1768	74	*La Princesse de Babylone*
1770	76	*Questions sur l'Encyclopédie* – until 1772
1778	84	To Paris, in Feb.; dies 30 May

Year	Literary and Artistic Context	Historical Events
1758	D'Alembert leaves the *Encyclopédie* Helvétius, *De l'Esprit* Death of Handel	Wolfe at Quebec
1759	Samuel Johnson, *Rasselas* Palissot, *Les Philosophes*	
1760	Sterne, *Tristram Shandy*	Death of George II. George III reigns, 1760–1820
1761	Rousseau, *La Nouvelle Héloïse*	
1762	Rousseau, *Émile* *Encyclopédie*, Volume I of plates	Calas executed. Jesuits banished from France. Catherine of Russia reigns, 1762–96
1763	Death of Marivaux First meeting of Johnson and Boswell	
1764	Death of Algarotti, Hogarth	
1766	Fragonard, *The Swing* *Encyclopédie*, Volume IV of plates and remaining text	
1767	*Encyclopédie*, Volumes V–XI of plates, 1767–72	
1768	First edition of *Encyclopaedia Britannica*	Beginning of Cook's first voyage
1769		Birth of Napoleon Bonaparte
1770	Death of Boucher Birth of Wordsworth	Cook at Botany Bay
1772	Birth of Coleridge	
1773		Boston Tea Party
1774	Goethe, *Werther*	Cook explores coast of New Zealand. Death of Louis XV, Louis XVI reigns, 1774–93
1775	Birth of Jane Austen Beaumarchais, *Barbier de Séville* Goethe, *Urfaust*	American War of Independence
1776	Gibbon, Volume I of the *Decline and Fall of the Roman Empire*	Declaration of Independence
1777	Rousseau writing the *Rêveries*	
1778	Death of Rousseau (2 July)	
1779	Death of Garrick	
1780	Death of Mme du Deffand	
1783	Death of d'Alembert	

Year   *Age* *Life*

1784   First publication of *Mémoires*; 'Kehl' edition of Voltaire's
                works, 70 volumes, 1784-9

Year	Literary and Artistic Context	Historical Events
1784	Deaths of Diderot, Johnson Production of Beaumarchais' *Mariage de Figaro*	
1786		Death of Frederick II, 'the Great'
1789		Fall of the Bastille

INTRODUCTION

In late December 1764 a young man – aged twenty-four – went to Ferney, just inside the French border with Switzerland, not far from Geneva. He was going to see Voltaire, who had acquired his Ferney estate in 1758, and had built a small church there in 1761. The young man was excited, and wrote in his journal: 'I was in true spirits; the earth was covered with snow; I surveyed wild nature with a noble eye. I called up all the grand ideas which I have ever entertained of Voltaire. The first object that struck me was his church with this inscription: "Deo erexit Voltaire MDCCLXI" ["Voltaire erected this to God 1761"].'

The young man – a Scot – was James Boswell, forty-six years younger than Voltaire. While full of admiration for the great writer, his interests were in part those of a later age – apparent in his first phrases, 'I surveyed wild nature with a noble eye'. Voltaire, truly classical in his concerns, would not have shared this enthusiasm – as became clear quite soon in their conversation. Boswell had met Dr Johnson the year before, and their long acquaintanceship was already well under way. To Voltaire, Boswell related 'that Mr Johnson and I intended to make a tour through the Hebrides ... He smiled, and cried, "Very well; but I shall remain here. You will allow me to stay here?" "Certainly." "Well then, go. I have no objections at all."'[1]

In their subsequent discussions, the subject of 'wild nature' was not touched upon, while the centre of Voltaire's concern, 'the men who dwell in the city', their beliefs and problems and ambitions and follies, received full and inspiring attention. Voltaire, then aged 70, was still at the height of his intellectual powers. A glance at the Contents page for this volume, in which the pieces by Voltaire are arranged in chronological order, shows how much he produced between 1759–60 – when he finished the *Memoirs* – and the early 1770s. In 1763, the year before Boswell's visit, there was, among the many items to do with the execution of Jean Calas, the vital *Treatise on Tolerance*. And in 1764 he published *The Portable Philosophical Dictionary*, which grew and evolved through several issues into the *Questions on the Encyclopaedia* of 1770–72. There were many volumes more – articles, tales, plays, dialogues – and over twenty-one thousand letters.

Voltaire is one of the giants of literature. Another giant (there are not so many of them) was Goethe, who wrote a breathless and unstinting list of Voltaire's qualities:

Profundity, Genius, Perceptivity, Sublimity, Spontaneity, Talent, Merit, Nobility, Spirit, beautiful Spirit, good Spirit, Feeling, Sensibility, Taste, good Taste, Understanding, Judgement, Tone, good Tone, courtly Tone, Diversity, Fullness, Richness, Fertility, Warmth, Magic, Charm, Grace, Courtesy, Agility, Liveliness, Refinement, Brilliance, Boldness, Sparkle, Savour, Delicacy, Ingenuity, Style, Versification, Harmony, Purity, Correctness, Elegance, Completeness.[2]

Not all commentators have seen Voltaire with such deep respect. Macaulay, writing his long essay *Frederick the Great*, published in 1855, perceived Voltaire's brilliance in satire as something doomed to bring him and Frederick into conflict when Voltaire at last agreed to stay as Frederick's guest at Potsdam, and these comments are quoted later in the introduction to the *Memoirs* (pp. 88–90 below). But Macaulay saw a more general negative quality in Voltaire which Voltaire's enemies and opponents, especially those in the Roman Catholic Church, would confirm: 'Voltaire could not build: he could only pull down: he was the very Vitruvius of ruin.' Macaulay's next phrases are, apparently, total in their condemnation: 'He has bequeathed to us not a single doctrine to be called by his name, not a single addition to the stock of our positive knowledge.' Happily, if illogically, Macaulay goes on to admit that 'the better part' of Voltaire's nature often experienced 'the pleasure of vindicating innocence which had no other helper, or repairing cruel wrongs, of punishing tyranny in high places'.[3]

This 'better part' is, we may hope, clearly apparent in the course of this edition. We need quote only one piece from Diderot, in his novel *Le Neveu de Rameau* (*Rameau's Nephew*). Yes, Voltaire was a great man of letters, but he was every bit as much a man of action: 'I would give everything I possess to have done one particular deed. Certainly Voltaire's *Mahomet* [produced in 1742] is a sublime work to have written, but I would prefer even more to have vindicated the memory of the Calas family.' (For this matter, *see* the 'Short Account of the Death of John Calas', pp. 141–52 below.)

Voltaire's life began in the last decades of Louis XIV's military, political and aesthetic ascendancy, and a part of his writing reflects and repeats this late-seventeenth century glory – his adherence to the 'aesthetic of Versailles', whether in his poetry (virtually all of it in rigid keeping with the rules of French classical versification), his tragedies (written as if Corneille and Racine were watching over his shoulder), and his general, and magisterial, use of the French language. At the same time, his social, political and religious views are in many respects synonymous with those of the Enlightenment – the thinkers and political writers of the mid- and later eighteenth century. In his twenties, Voltaire was already at odds with parts of the French establishment. First, with some of the aristocracy, for his bourgeois impertinence. (The son of a lawyer, of middle-class or peasant background, he had abandoned his original name, Arouet, in 1718, to call himself Voltaire – an anagram of AROUET LE J, 'Arouet the younger', and boldly prefixed this new name with a 'de', the 'particule nobiliare' or 'particle indicating noble birth', to which, as a commoner, he was in no way entitled.) Second, with the Church, for his criticisms of intolerance, and ecclesiastical interference in secular matters. These clashes led to his being exiled from Paris, and to his imprisonment – twice – in the Bastille. By his mid-twenties, he was thinking of a visit to England, to get his epic poem *La Ligue*, in honour of Henri IV – it was later renamed the *Henriade* – published, since it was not to be allowed in France, because of its many condemnations of religious fanaticism.[4] And in England, he found (or, possibly, chose to see) what he was looking for: a society, a government and attitudes which he could contrast with those in France.

Above all, Voltaire was interested in human beings. Man is the subject of his entire, and enormous, work. In his first sixty years, he travelled a fair amount – much in France, several times to the Low Countries (to Brussels, to The Hague), to England,

to Germany, to Switzerland.⁵ Yet in these travels his interest is
firmly concentrated on people – their attitudes, culture, politics,
religion – and hardly ever extends to the landscapes around
them. Though he passed some two years in England, almost all
his time was spent in or near London. His comments on the
places he visited are directed wholly to their *human* connections;
unlike the young Boswell, who in 1764 was looking forward to
showing the Hebrides to Dr Johnson . . .

The selections from Voltaire's prose works in this volume,
presented in chronological order, fall approximately into three
sections – first England, then his meetings with Frederick of
Prussia, and last, his retirement to Ferney, near Geneva, and his
happy and active cultivation of 'the Lord's vineyard'.

England

In England, Voltaire quickly plunged into literary matters. He
went to the theatre, saw Shakespeare's plays, met writers such
as Pope and Swift. From the start, his attitude was selective – he
saw, read, commented on *what he wanted*. So his later presen-
tations to the French of Shakespeare, Swift and Addison are not
in the least 'objective'. Shakespeare fascinated, yet repelled him,
and his early approval, or part-approval (as in Letter XVIII of
the *Letters Concerning the English Nation*) of *Hamlet* is later
restrained. By the 1770s, Shakespeare's reputation in France had
so increased – in competition with that of traditional French
dramatists, including Voltaire himself – that his erstwhile pride
in 'introducing' Shakespeare to the French was now an embar-
rassment. Indeed, his reading of Shakespeare was clearly limited
– ten or twelve tragedies, no comedies at all. In Letter XIX of the
Letters, 'On Comedy', there is no word of Shakespeare. His
interest seems to have been greatest in *Julius Caesar*. Here, in
1764, he produced a prose translation of Acts I, II, and III as far
as scene 1, l.118 – two-and-a-half acts out of five.⁶ The later and
distant action, away from Rome and with battles on the stage,
is ignored.

With Swift there is a comparable approach. His acquaintance
with Swift was slight – otherwise Voltaire's attitude might have
changed. Reading *Gulliver's Travels* (published in 1726, the
year Voltaire arrived in England), Voltaire chose to see Swift as

a satirist and unbeliever, happily employed within the Church of England.[7] Had he known Swift better, he would have been disabused, but this did not happen and, as late as 1759, he could write to Mme du Deffand of Swift and his *Tale of a Tub*, 'How I love that English daring! How I love people who say what they think! We're only half alive, if we dare think only a half of our thoughts.'[8]

Voltaire's selective presentation of English matters deserves fuller comment than it has received. He praises Addison for his tragedy *Cato*, as being within the form and limits of French classical tragedy, yet ignores Addison's strictures on French formal gardens, published in the same period. It is curious, that the conclusion of his piece on English tragedy (Shakespeare, then Addison) should state that English drama 'dies if you attempt to force its Nature, and to lop and dress it in the same Manner as the Trees of the Gardens of Marly'. Voltaire had clearly chosen to ignore what Shaftesbury, Pope and Addison had already said about the 'Trees of the Gardens of Marly' – that their artificial trimming was an abomination.[9]

Yet his time in England had been vital: English ways, trade, parliament, church and churches, philosophy and literature, all provided valuable contrasts with his earlier experiences in France. What he wrote, in the *Letters Concerning the English Nation*, was – according to Gustave Lanson in 1909 – the 'first bomb thrown at the *ancien régime*', the first shot fired in the French Revolution. Pedants may argue about this, but Voltaire's praise of English matters – and, therefore, oblique criticism of French matters – is influential until the end of his life.

Frederick of Prussia[10]

The *Memoirs* were written within a few months of Voltaire's tale *Candide* (completed at the end of 1758), and present vivid glimpses of life on the parade-ground and in the palaces of Berlin and Potsdam. They tell a great deal of Frederick's Germany which does not appear in *Candide* – where Candide, the hero, and a German, leaves his country by the end of Chapter 3, and never returns.

Ferney

Escaping from Frederick, Voltaire bought properties in Switzerland, including 'Les Délices', then – at Ferney – in France, to
secure his wished-for existence. He succeeded. In March 1755,
he wrote a long ecstatic poem on the qualities of 'Les Délices'.
Entitled 'The Author, arriving at his property, near to the lake
of Geneva', it begins

> 'Aristippus, behold your house! And, Epicurus, gardens fit for you!
> You who present me, in your various ways,
>   What lacks so often in my verse,
> The charms of art, in nature's charge,
> As seen in Pomona's and in Flora's realms,
>   Receive me as your owner now!'[11]

And then, in 1758, he bought his property at Ferney. He had in
fact become a 'monarch of all he surveyed', with an independence acquired through money. 'My orchards, my vineyards, I
myself, owe nothing to anyone',[12] he wrote in March 1757. And
his niece, Mme Denis, looked after him. A lucky man.

Within three years – in 1761 – he had built a small church in
the grounds of his Ferney estate. It is still there, with Voltaire's
tomb half in, half out of the wall of the church, and with the
dedication, DEO EREXIT VOLTAIRE over the doorway. Boswell
remarked on this in 1763, and countless visitors were to do so
thereafter. Voltaire was not a Christian, but he believed in a
supreme, all-powerful and benevolent deity and, at the crudest
level, he argued that belief in God was useful for the lower levels
of humanity. 'If there was no God', he said, 'we should invent
one.'[13]

Once he had settled in Switzerland, and later at Ferney, he
had innumerable visitors. He was, after all, the world's most
famous living writer. His visitors have recorded the details of
his household – the personalities, the furnishings and so forth –
in repeated letters or journal entries, from his first arrival in
Geneva until his death.[14] One of the earliest to comment was
Edward Gibbon, who had had a 'pre-publication' glimpse of the
poem whose first stanza is quoted above, and who then attended
several of the theatrical performances, at Monrion, which
Voltaire arranged in early 1757, again in 1758, and later at

Ferney in August 1763.[15] Voltaire's hospitality was lavish, his guests numerous, and the pattern of his existence so arranged that he did not 'emerge' from study and writing until the latter part of the day, to converse, and to take part in plays (usually his own!) with other members of the household, such as his niece Mme Denis.

Acting, and the recitation of poetry, were a part of Voltaire's nature – 'masks' which enabled him to be sociable, without necessarily revealing too much of his intimate thought. Another *persona* was that of the 'old man at death's door'; part true, part adopted as a useful shield against tedious or unwelcome people. Another, with English visitors, was to break into English, and to discuss aspects of English life – politics, Locke and Newton, Shakespeare – familiar to him from his stay in England long before. Another topic, which amused his English visitors, was the garden at Ferney, since – if the weather allowed – Voltaire would display it, exclaiming that it was all in the English manner. In May 1765, Thomas Pennant relates that Voltaire 'proposed a walk in his garden, which was extensive but in a wretched taste – with strait walks and espalier hedges, but as it was not inclosed with a wall he informed us that it was flung open in conformity to the English taste'.[16]

But in the forenoon he wrote – and wrote, 'cultivating the Lord's vineyard', striving to 'écraser l'infâme', 'to crush the infamous thing'. The latter phrase seems to have been coined first by Frederick, in 1759, to imply the frightfulness of *clerical* superstition, and quickly adopted by Voltaire to mean superstition of *any* kind, leading to unjust or fanatical conduct.[17] Early in his struggle to clear the memory of Jean Calas, he had persuaded no less a person than Mme de Pompadour of the injustice that had occurred, and she wrote on 27 August 1762, that 'the affair of this wretched man Calas makes one shudder [. . .] It seems impossible that he should have committed this crime [. . .] The King's kind heart has suffered much at the account of this strange procedure and all France cries for vengeance.'[18]

A year later, Voltaire's *Treatise on Religious Toleration* had appeared, its first chapter – printed below, pp. 141–52 – relating Calas' terrible story. Soon, all France, and much of western Europe, knew of this, through Voltaire's continued efforts. In

August 1765, John Wilkes visited him at Ferney, and wrote 'I think him the most universal genius, the most amiable as well as the wittiest of our species. He is a divine old man, born for the advancement of true philosophy and the polite arts, and to free mankind from the gloomy terrors of superstition [...] His conduct in the affair of the family of Calas is more meritorious than the whole life of most saints.'[19]

CHRISTOPHER THACKER

References

1. Quoted in Sir Gavin de Beer and André-Michel Rousseau, eds., *Voltaire's British Visitors*, in *Studies on Voltaire and the Eighteenth Century*, XLIX (1967), 85–6, and taken from Frederick A. Pottle, ed., *Boswell on the Grand Tour: Germany and Switzerland 1764* (1953), pp. 272–3.

2. From Goethe's notes on Diderot's *Le Neveu de Rameau*, in Goethe, *Werke* (1887–1912), XL, 216. Tr. C. T.

3. Thomas Babington Macaulay, *Frederick the Great* (1855), p. 74.

4. A small, 'surreptitious' edition was published in 1723. *See* Theodore Besterman, *Voltaire* (1969), pp. 91–9.

5. Though never to Italy, Spain, or anywhere in the Levant – a curious fact, since so many of his plays and tales have settings in these regions.

6. *See* Voltaire, *Oeuvres complètes*, ed. L. Moland, 52 volumes, 1877–85, VII, 431–86. Further references to this edition are to 'Moland'. *See also* T. Besterman, *Voltaire on Shakespeare* (*Studies*, LIV, 1967).

7. *See* Thacker, 'Swift and Voltaire', in *Hermathena*, CIV (1967), 51–66.

8. To Mme du Deffand, 13 October 1759. In Voltaire, *Correspondance*, ed. T. Besterman, 51 volumes 1968–77, letter D. 8533. Further references to letters in this edition are to 'D' followed by the number of the letter. Tr. C. T.

9. *See* Thacker, *The Wildness Pleases: the Origins of Romanticism* (1983), pp. 31–2.

10. It has been simpler to spell this name throughout as 'Frederick', rather than *Friedrich*, or – as he often signed himself – *Frédéric*.

11. Moland, X, 362–3. Tr. C. T.

12. Dated from Monrion, 27 March 1757, to F. A. P. de Moncrif, Moland, XXXIX, 199, and D. 7215.

13. Voltaire quotes this line from his *Epître à l'auteur du livre des Trois Imposteurs*, 'Epistle to the author of The Three Imposters' (1769. Moland, X, 402) in a letter to the Duc de Richelieu, 1 November 1770 (D. 16736). He precedes it with a cogent comment: 'in my view it is always a good thing to maintain the doctrine of the existence of a God who rewards and punishes, society needs such opinions'. Tr. C. T.

14. A useful collection of these records is in de Beer and Rousseau, *Voltaire's British Visitors*, though it is in a way misleading, since Voltaire had far more visitors from France and Switzerland, with whom other topics might well have been discussed.

15. *See* items 13, 17 and 49 in de Beer and Rousseau, *op. cit.*; Gibbon, *Memoirs of My Life*, ed. B. Radice, 1991, pp. 105–6, and *Private Letters of Edward Gibbon*, ed. R. E. Prothero, 2 volumes, 1896, I, 5, 43–4.

16. de Beer and Rousseau, *op. cit.*, item 72.

17. *See* T. Besterman, in *Voltaire*, pp. 396–8.

18. Letter to Charles, Duc de Fitzjames (D. 10677). Tr. C. T.

19. In de Beer and Rousseau, *op. cit.*, and taken from R. A. Davenport, *New Elegant Extracts* (1827), Part X, p. 350.

NOTE ON THE TEXTS

When possible, the English versions of Voltaire's writings in this volume are from texts published in his own lifetime, or soon afterwards. They have been modernised slightly to aid today's reader, but for the most part retain their original style of capitalisation and spelling. So, for example, the large selection from the *Letters Concerning the English Nation* is taken from the English text of 1733 (probably written for the most part by Voltaire himself), and 'A Short Account of the Death of John Calas' is taken from the English translation of 1764, a year after it was first published in French. In each instance the sources and dates, both French and English, are quoted at the beginning of the notes related to the different writings. A few later translations have been included, notably from the Morley edition of 1901, and from C. E. Vulliamy's translation of Voltaire's *The White Bull and Other Stories* of 1929. When English versions were not available, or only for a part of the writing, new translations have been made, and are indicated by 'Tr. C. T'.

SELECTED WRITINGS

CHAPTER I

Letters Concerning the English Nation

Published first in English, in 1733. French versions appeared in 1734; one, the Lettres Philosophiques, *augmented by a long section on Pascal.*

Voltaire was in England between 1726 and 1728 (see the Introduction pp. xx–xxi). His earlier contacts with Englishmen in France – notably Lord Bolingbroke, and the merchant Everard Fawkener – provided him with help on arrival in London. While in England, he undoubtedly learnt more English than Frenchmen generally learn; he wrote a fair part of his comments on England in English; and he met many people in the forefront of English society, thought and letters. It is, however, far from likely that he travelled much in England. Briefly, to Blenheim, north of Oxford; possibly to Eastbury in Dorset; but not further afield. From the Letters, *from his correspondence, and from the copious notebooks which he kept in this period, his interests were clearly directed to people and concerns which were centred in London – politics, religion, trade, philosophy, science, literature and the theatre. And one should add that these interests were again and again related to what would be thought of these people and these concerns in France.*

As early as December 1722, he had visited Lord Bolingbroke, exiled in France at La Source, near Orleans. On 2 January 1723 he writes to his friend Thieriot:

I must tell you of my delight, after visiting Milord Bolingbroke at
La Source ... In this illustrious Englishman I have encountered
all the learning of his country, and all the courtesy of ours. I've
never heard our language spoken with so much force and exactness ...*

After a few months in England in 1726, Voltaire's English was already as good, probably, as Bolingbroke's French. On 26

October 1726, he wrote, in English, to Thieriot*. His interests are clear – poetry, life in London (including the expense: his finances were in difficulties), his hopes of getting the Henriade *published, his admiration of English liberty – and, linked with his regret at his sister's death a month before, echoes of Hamlet's 'to be or not to be' speech:*

I intend to send you two or three poems of Mr Pope, the best poet of England, and at present of all the world. I hope you are acquainted enough with the English tongue, to be sensible of all the charms of his works. For my part I look on his poem called the *Essay upon Criticism* as superior to the *Art of Poetry* of Horace; and his *Rape of the Lock, la boucle de cheveux,* [that is a comical one] is in my opinion above the *Lutrin* of Despreaux*. I never saw so amiable an imagination, so gentle graces, so great varyety, so much wit, and so refined knowledge of the world, as in this little performance [. . .] An other London citizen* that I had seen but once in Paris, carried me to his own country house, where I lead an obscure and charming life since that time, without going to London, and quite given over to the pleasures of indolence and friendshipp. The true and generous affection of this man who sooths the bitterness of my life brings me to love you more and more. All the instances of friendshipp indear my friend Tiriot* to me. I have seen often mylord and mylady Bolinbroke. I have found their affection still the same, even increased in proportion to my unhappiness. They offered me all, their money, their house; but I refused all, because they are lords, and I have accepted all from Mr Faulknear, because he is a single gentleman.

I had a mind at first to print out poor Henry* at my own expenses in London, but the loss of my money is a sad stop to my design: I question if I shall try the way of subscriptions by the favour of the court. I am weary of courts, my Thiriot. All that is King, or belongs to a King, frights my republican philosophy, I won't drink the least draught of slavery in the land of liberty [. . .]

All that I wish for, is to see you one day in London. I am entertaining myself with this pleasant hope; if it is but a dream, let me enjoy it, don't deceive me, let me believe I shall have the pleasure to see you in London, [drawing up] the strong spirit of this unaccountable nation; you will translate their thoughts better, when you live among em. You will see a nation fond of their liberty, learned, witty, despising life and death, a nation of philosophers, not but that there are some fools in England, every country has its madmen; it may be French folly is pleasanter than English madness, but by God English Wisdom and English Honesty is above yours. One day I will acquaint you with the character of this strange people, but tis time to put an end to my English talkativeness [. . .]

I have written so much about the death of my sister to those who had writ to me on this account, that I had almost forgotten to speak to you of her. I have nothing to tell you on that accident but that you know my heart and my way of thinking. I have wept for her death, and I would be with her. Life is but a dream full of starts of folly and of fancied and true miseries. Death awakes us from this painful dream, and gives us, either a better existence or no existence at all. Farewell [. . .]

In this letter, Voltaire did not say, in as many words, 'and my experiences will surely lead to a book about the English', yet this was surely in his mind. There were several recent volumes of travels which were in part about England (by B. L. de Muralt (1723), and A. de la Motraye (1727) for example), and two works, the Espion Turc *or* Turkish Spy, *by G. P. Marana (in French, 1684–6, in English 1687–91), and Montesquieu's* Lettres Persanes *or* Turkish Letters *(French 1721, English 1722), which launched the genre of 'innocent' or 'naïve' commentary on the ways of a nation, or nations as seen through the eyes of an ignorant but observant foreigner. Voltaire would have encountered these books, and the following 'letter', written probably in mid-1728, represents a tentative, yet lengthy beginning of a work on the English, seen through the eyes of one who has just arrived in the country.*

Draft of a letter on the English *

To M——

[. . .] You want me to give you a general idea of the people among whom I live. Such general ideas are liable to too many exceptions; besides, a traveller only has, as a rule, a very imperfect knowledge of the country in which he finds himself. He sees only the front of the building; almost all the interior remains unknown to him. You might believe, perhaps, that an ambassador is a man who is always well-versed in the character of the country to which he is sent, and could tell you more about it than anyone. This might be true, as regards the foreign ministers who reside in Paris, since they all know the language of the country; they are dealing with a nation which displays itself freely: should they so desire, they may enter all sorts of society, all endeavouring to please them; they read our books, they visit our theatres. A French ambassador in England is quite another thing. Most commonly he doesn't know a word of English, he cannot address three-fourths of the nation except through an interpreter; he has not the slightest idea of the works written in the language; he cannot enjoy the plays which portray the manners of the nation. The restricted groups of society to which he may be admitted have ways which are the very opposite of French familiarity; they only gather together to play cards and to be silent. Besides, since the nation is almost always divided into two parties, the ambassador is not in a position to have any contact with those in the party opposed to the government, for fear of exciting suspicion; he is hardly free to see anyone apart from the ministers, rather like a tradesman who knows only his correspondents and his business – yet with this difference, that if he is to succeed, the merchant must perform with a good faith which is not always prescribed in the instructions given to His Excellency; so that it happens often enough that the ambassador is a kind of post-boy through whose hands political falsities and deceptions pass from one court to the other, and who, after having lied in ceremony in the name of his master the king for several years, leaves a nation for ever, not knowing it in the slightest.

It seems that you might gain more instruction from a private individual with enough leisure and determination to learn and speak the English tongue, who could converse freely with both Whigs and Tories, dine with a bishop, and sup with a Quaker, go to a synagogue on Saturday, to St Paul's on Sunday, listen to a sermon in the morning, and enjoy a comedy in the afternoon, and who could move between the court and the exchange, and, above all this, not be discouraged by the coldness, the disdainful, icy manner which English ladies display at first acquaintance – and which some of them never shake off; such a man as I've described would still tend to make mistakes, and to mislead you, especially if his opinions were formed, as commonly they are, from first impressions.

When I came ashore, not far from London, it was springtime; not a cloud in the sky, like a lovely day in the south of France; the air was freshened by a sweet western breeze, which added to nature's calm, and inclined one's feelings towards delight: are we not *machines*, so much are our spirits affected by bodily concerns! I arrived near Greenwich on the banks of the Thames. This lovely river, which never overflows, and whose banks are green and beautiful throughout the year, was covered six miles along by merchant vessels; they all had unfurled their sails in honour of the King and Queen,* who were proceeding down the river in a gilded barge, preceded by boats filled with musicians, and followed by a thousand little rowing boats; each had two oarsmen, all of them clothed like our pages in years past, with points and little doublets adorned with a great silver badge on the shoulder. Without exception these mariners declared, by their features, their dress and their sturdy figure, that they were free, and well-provided.

Close to the river, on a great stretch of turf extending for some four miles, I saw a prodigious number of handsome young people prancing on horseback round a kind of track, marked out with white posts, set in the ground at regular intervals. Then there were women on horseback, galloping here and there with so much grace; and above all, young girls on foot, mostly dressed in muslin. Among them, many were very beautiful, all were shapely; they had an air of cleanliness, and in their appearance there was a liveliness and contentment which made them all attractive.

Another, smaller course was enclosed within the large one; it was five hundred feet long, ending at a balustrade. I asked what all this was for. Quickly I was told that the large track was for horse races, the little one for racing on foot. Beside one of the posts on the large track was a mounted man, holding a kind of large, covered silver urn; at the balustrade of the inner track were two poles; at the top of one, you could see a large man's hat, on the other hung a lady's dress. Between the two poles a big fellow was standing, with a purse in his hand. The silver urn was the prize for the horse-race; the purse, for the race on foot;

but I was pleasantly surprised when I was told that there was also a race for the young women; and that, apart from the purse awarded to the winner, she was given, as a sign of honour, the dress which fluttered at the top of the pole, and that the hat was for the best runner among the men.

In the crowd I was happy to meet several merchants for whom I had letters of introduction. These gentlemen did me the honours of the festival, with the assiduity and friendliness of people who are happy, and who wish to share their happiness. They found me a horse, they sent for refreshments, and they were careful to set me at a point where I might easily enjoy the sight of all the races, and of the river, with the distant prospect of London.

I imagined that I had been wafted to the Olympic games; but the beauty of the Thames, the crowded ships, the vastness of the city of London, soon made me blush to have dared to confuse Elis with England. I learnt that at that very moment there was a combat of gladiators in London,* and at once I saw myself among the ancient Romans. A courier from Denmark, who had arrived that morning, and who went back happily that very evening, was close to me during the races. I could see that he was filled with joy and astonishment; he was convinced that the entire nation was always happy; that all the women were lovely and lively, and that the sky over England was always clear and calm; that pleasure was the sole concern; that each and every day was like the day he had seen; and he left without learning his mistake. As for myself, I was much more bewitched than the Dane. That evening, I was introduced to several ladies at court; I spoke only about the enchanting scene I had witnessed; I was sure they had been there, and that they had been among the ladies I had seen galloping so gracefully. After a while, I was mildly surprised to see that they did not have the lively look of people who have just enjoyed themselves; they were strained, cold, drank their tea, clattered with their fans, said nothing, or all exclaimed at once to slander their neighbour; some played quadrille, others were reading the gazette; in the end, one who was kinder than the others informed me that the *beau monde* did not condescend to these popular assemblies – which had so much charmed me – and that all those lovely creatures clothed in muslin were servants or village girls; that all the radiant young people, so well mounted and prancing round the course, were just a band of students and apprentices, riding hired horses. I felt deeply angry with the lady who told me all this. I tried not to believe any of it; and I went back to the City to find those merchants and aldermen who had done me the honours so cordially at my imagined Olympic games.

Next day, in a dirty, poorly furnished, poorly served and ill-lit café, I found most of these gentlemen, who had been so affable and good-humoured the day before; not one of them recognised me; I ventured to engage one or two in conversation; I received no answers, or at best a *yes* or a *no*; I reasoned with myself that I had caused them all some offence the day before. I racked my brains, trying to recall whether I had said that I preferred Lyons cottons to theirs; or that French cooks were better than English, that Paris was a much pleasanter city than London, that Versailles was more entertaining than St James, or something equally discourteous. I felt that I was in no way guilty, and so I took the liberty of asking one of them, in a lively tone which they found distinctly out of place, why they were all so glum: the fellow answered with a scowl that the east wind was blowing.* At that moment one of their friends arrived, who told them with an air of indifference: 'Molly cut her throat this morning. Her lover found her dead in her room, with a bloody razor at her side.' This Molly was a pretty young girl, and very rich, who was about to be married to the very man who had found her dead. These gentlemen – they were all Molly's friends – heard the news without raising an eyebrow. Just one of them asked, what had become of the lover? One of the company replied in a cold voice, he had purchased the razor.

For my part, horrified by so strange a death, and these gentlemen's indifference, I could not help enquiring what could have compelled a young lady, apparently so happy, to end her life so cruelly; their only answer was that the east wind was blowing. I was unable to comprehend at first what link there was between the east wind, these gentlemen's gloomy mood, and Molly's death. Without more ado I left the café, and I went to the court, filled with that fine French prejudice that a court is always a cheerful place. All was sad and dismal, even the maids of honour. In melancholy terms, they were discussing the east wind. Then I remembered the Dane I had met the day before. I was tempted to laugh at the vain idea he had of England; but the climate had taken its effect on me; to my astonishment, I could not laugh. A famous doctor at the court, to whom I confided my surprise, told me I was wrong to be astonished, that I should see far worse in the months of November and March; then, folk hanged themselves in dozens; practically everyone was seriously ill at those times, and a black melancholy spread over the entire nation; that's when, he said, the east wind blows most consistently. This wind is the ruin of us all. Even the animals suffer from it, and they all look dejected. Even those men who are sturdy enough to stay fit in this accursed wind lose their good humour. At these times, everyone looks grim, with a tendency towards desperate measures. Truly the east wind was blowing when Charles I was beheaded, and James II was dethroned. 'Should you have any favour to ask at court', he murmured in my ear, 'never consider it except when the wind blows from the west or south.'

Apart from these contradictions, bred by the elements in the English character, they have others born from party hatred; and this is which most bewilders a foreigner.

I have heard it said here, word for word, that the Duke of Marlborough was the greatest coward in the world, and that Mr Pope was a fool.

I came here convinced that a Whig was an ardent republican, an enemy of royalty; and a Tory, a supporter of passive disobedience. But I found that in parliament almost all the Whigs sided with the court, and the Tories were against.

One day, during an excursion on the Thames, one of the oarsmen, who saw I was French, began to boast in the proudest terms of his country's liberty, and swore to me, by God, that he'd rather be a waterman on the Thames than an archbishop in France. The following day I saw this very man in a prison I was passing; his feet were in irons, and he stretched his hand through the bars to the passers-by. I asked him if he still thought so poorly of an archbishop in France; he recognised me. 'Oh, sir, what a vile government this is! I've been taken by force to serve on one of the King's ships in Norway; I've been torn from my wife and children, and they've thrown me in jail, with my feet in irons, until the ship sets sail, for fear I should escape.'

This man's misfortune, and such a crying injustice, moved me profoundly. A Frenchman who was with me admitted that he felt a malicious delight to see that the English, who accuse us so loudly of being slaves, were in just as sorry a state as ourselves. My own feelings were more human, I was grieved that liberty had vanished from the earth.

I had written a long, gloomy lecture on this topic, when an Act of Parliament put an end to the abuse of enrolling sailors by force, and so I threw my letter on the fire.* To give you an even stronger idea of the contradictions I have described, I have seen four most learned treatises* disputing the reality of the miracles of Jesus Christ, printed here with impunity, at the same time as a wretched bookseller was pilloried for publishing *The Nun in Her Shift*, a translation of *La Religieuse en Chemise*.

They had promised me that I would discover the Olympic games once again at Newmarket. 'Twice each year', they told me, 'all the nobility are gathered there; the King himself some-times goes with the royal family. You'll find an amazing number of the fastest horses in Europe, bred from Arab sires and English mares, which fly round a course of green turf extending as far as you can see. Their riders are little jockeys, dressed in silk, and they are watched by all the court.' I went to witness this noble sight, and I saw fancy touts, betting against each other, and who employed infinitely more dishonesty than nobility in this solemn business.

Might I move from little matters to great things? I would ask, if you think it is easy to describe a nation which beheaded Charles I, because he wished to introduce the use of surplices in Scotland,* and because he insisted on a tribute which the judges declared was his right – while this very nation watched without a murmur as Cromwell expelled both parliaments, lords and bishops, and destroyed the law.

A sense of enthusiasm, and a mad superstition had taken hold of the entire nation throughout the civil wars; in the reign of Charles II, these troubled times were followed by mild and slothful impiety.

So. Things change, and contradictions abound. Truth in one age is error in another. The Spaniards have a saying, that a man 'was brave yesterday'. We should judge nations more or less like this – above all the English; we should say to them: 'They were like this in such and such a year, in such and such a month.'

This letter remained unpublished for many years, set aside, it has been thought, because of Voltaire's other literary activities, and because he may have wished to tackle a book about England in a less anecdotal and more 'philosophic' way. Late in 1728, he returned to France, and re-entered Parisian life in early 1729. He did not ever go back to England, and his contacts were from then onwards to be either by letter or through the many, many meetings with travellers from the British Isles who came to visit him – most often at his later residences at and near Geneva.

Among his written contacts is a letter in English to Mrs Charlotte Clayton, thanking her for her kindness to him. Mrs Clayton was a friend of Lady Bolingbroke and the Duchess of Marlborough, and a lady of the bedchamber to Queen Caroline, consort of George II. She eventually became Mistress of the Robes, and, when her husband was raised to the peerage as Viscount Sundon, she became Viscountess Sundon.

To Mrs Clayton*

Paris, 18 April 1729

Madam,

Though I am out of London, the favours your ladyship has honoured me with, are not, nor ever will be, out of my memory. I will remember as long as I live, that the most respectable lady who waits and is a friend of the most truly great Queen in the world, has vouchsafed to protect me, and receive me with kindness, while I was in London. I am just now arrived in Paris, and I pay my respects to your Court before I see my own. I wish, for the honour of Versailles, and for the improvement of virtue and letters, we could have here some ladies like you. You see my wishes are unbounded; so is the respect and gratitude I am with,

Madam,

your most humble obedient servant

Voltaire

It was to Mrs Clayton's mistress Queen Caroline that Voltaire's Henriade was dedicated, and in the following two or three years – until 1732 – a part of his Parisian activity lay in polishing and completing a book of letters on England, which was first published in England, in English, in 1733, entitled Letters concerning the English Nation. *It is thought nowadays that Voltaire himself wrote well over half of these letters in English himself, that he may have written parts of others in English, and parts in French, and only seven of the original twenty-four letters in French.* Who polished Voltaire's English, and translated the French parts into English, remains uncertain.*

In the following year, 1734, the volume was published in French, augmented by a long twenty-fifth letter on the Pensées *of Pascal. This addition, though in most senses unconnected with England, is not wholly irrelevant in the framework of Voltaire's lifelong concern with the varieties of religious persuasion – like the views of the Quakers, discussed in the first four of the following* Letters.

Letter 1: On the Quakers*

I was of opinion, that the doctrine and history of so extraordinary a people, were worthy the attention of the curious. To acquaint myself with them, I made a visit* to one of the most eminent Quakers in England, who after having traded thirty years, had the wisdom to prescribe limits to his fortune and to his desires, and was settled in a little solitude not far from London. Being come into it, I perceived a small, but regularly built house, vastly neat, but without the least pomp of furniture. The Quaker who owned it, was a hale ruddy complexioned old man, who had never been afflicted with sickness, because he had always been insensible to passions, and a perfect stranger to intemperance. I never in my life saw a more noble or a more engaging aspect than his. He was dressed like those of his persuasion, in a plain coat, without pleats in the sides, or buttons on the pockets and sleeves; and had on a beaver, the brims of which were horizontal, like those of our clergy. He did not uncover himself when I appeared, and advanced towards me without once stooping his body; but there appeared more politeness in the open, humane air of his countenance, than in the custom of drawing one leg behind the other, and taking that from the head, which is made to cover it. Friend, says he to me, I perceive thou* art a stranger, but if I can do any thing for thee, only tell me. Sir, says I to him, bending forwards, and advancing as is usual with us, one leg towards him, I flatter myself that my just curiosity will not give you the least offence, and that you'll do me the honour to inform me of the particulars of your religion. The people of thy country, replied the Quaker, are too full of their bows and compliments, but I never yet met with one of them who had so much curiosity as thy self. Come in, and let us first dine together. I still continued to make some very unseasonable ceremonies, it not being easy to disengage one's self at once from habits we have been long used to; and after taking part of a frugal meal, which began and ended with a prayer to God, I began to question my courteous host. I opened with that which good Catholicks have more than once made to Huguenots. My dear sir, says I, were you ever baptised?* I never was, replied the Quaker, nor any of my brethren. Zouns, says I to him, you are not Christians then. Friend, replies the old man in a soft tone of voice, swear not; we are Christians, and endeavour to be good Christians, but we are not of opinion, that the sprinkling water on a child's head makes him a Christian. Heavens! says I, shocked at his impiety, you have then forgot that Christ was baptised by St John. Friend, replies the mild Quaker once again, swear not. Christ indeed was baptised by John, but he himself never baptised anyone. We are the disciples of Christ, not of John. I pitied very much the sincerity of my worthy Quaker, and was absolutely for forcing him to get himself christened. Were that all, replied he very gravely, we would submit cheerfully to baptism, purely in compliance with thy weakness, for we don't condemn any person who uses it; but then we think, that those who profess a religion of so holy, so spiritual a nature as that of Christ, ought to abstain to the utmost of their power from the Jewish ceremonies. O unaccountable! says I, what! baptism a Jewish ceremony? Yes, my friend says he, so truly Jewish, that a great many Jews use the baptism of John to this day. Look into ancient authors, and thou wilt find that John only revived this practice; and that it had been used by the Hebrews, long before his time, in like manner as the Mahometans imitated the Ishmaelites in their pilgrimages to Mecca. Jesus indeed submitted to the baptism of John, as he had suffered himself to be circumcised; but circumcision and the washing with water ought to be abolished by the baptism of Christ, that baptism of the spirit, that ablution of the soul, which is the salvation of mankind. Thus the forerunner said, *I indeed baptise you with water unto repentance; but he that cometh after me, is mightier than I, whose shoes I am not worthy to bear: he shall baptise you with the Holy Ghost and with fire.*[1] Likewise Paul the great apostle of the Gentiles, writes as follows to the Corinthians; *Christ sent me not to baptise, but to preach the Gospel;*[2] and indeed Paul never baptised but two persons with water, and that very much against his inclinations. He circumcised his disciple Timothy, and the other disciples likewise circumcised all who were willing to submit to that carnal ordinance. But art thou circumcised, added he? I have not the honour to be so, says I. Well, friend, continues the Quaker, thou art a Christian without being circumcised, and I am one without being baptised. Thus did this pious man make a wrong, but very specious application, of four or five texts of scripture which seemed to favour the tenets of his sect; but at the same time forgot very sincerely an hundred texts which made directly against them. I had more sense than to contest with him, since there is no possibility of convincing an enthusiast. A man should never pretend to inform a lover of his mistress's faults, no more than one who is at law, of the badness of his cause; nor attempt to win over a fanatic by strength of reasoning. Accordingly I waived the subject.

Well, says I to him, what sort of a communion have you? We have none like that thou hintest at among us, replied he. How! no communion, says I? Only that spiritual one, replied he, of hearts. He then began again to throw out his texts of scripture; and preached a most eloquent sermon against that ordinance. He harangued in a tone as though he had been inspired, to prove that the sacraments were merely of human invention, and that the word sacrament, was not once mentioned in the gospel. Excuse, says he, my ignorance, for I have not employed an hundredth part of the arguments which might be brought, to prove the truth of our religion, but these thou thy self mayest peruse in the *Exposition of our Faith* written by Robert Barclay.* 'Tis one of the best pieces that ever was penned by man; and as our adversaries confess it to be of dangerous tendency,

[1] St Matthew iii:11.
[2] I Cor. i:17.

the arguments in it must necessarily be very convincing. I promised to peruse this piece, and my Quaker imagined he had already made a convert of me. He afterwards gave me an account in few words, of some singularities which make this sect the contempt of others. Confess, says he, that 'twas very difficult for thee to refrain from laughter, when I answered all thy civilities without uncovering my head, and at the same time said *Thee* and *Thou* to thee. However, thou appearest to me too well read, not to know that in Christ's time no nation was so ridiculous as to put the plural number for the singular. Augustus Caesar himself was spoke to in such phrases as these, *I love thee, I beseech thee, I thank thee*; but he did not allow any person to call him Domine, Sir. 'Twas not till many ages after, that men would have the word *You*, as though they were double, instead of *Thou* employed in speaking to them; and usurped the flattering titles of lordship, of eminence, and of holiness, which mere worms bestow on other worms, by assuring them that they are with a most profound respect, and an infamous falsehood, their most obedient, humble servants. 'Tis to secure our selves more strongly from such a shameless traffick of lies and flattery, that we *thee* and *thou* a king with the same freedom as we do a beggar, and salute no person; we owing nothing to mankind but charity, and to the laws respect and obedience.

Our apparel is also somewhat different from that of others, and this purely, that it may be a perpetual warning to us not to imitate them. Others wear the badges and marks of their several dignities, and we those of christian humility. We fly from all assemblies of pleasure, from diversions of every kind, and from places where gaming is practised; and indeed our case would be very deplorable, should we fill with such levities as those I have mentioned, the heart which ought to be the habitation of God. We never swear, not even in a court of justice, being of opinion that the most holy name of God ought not to be prostituted in the miserable contests betwixt man and man. When we are obliged to appear before a magistrate upon other people's account (for lawsuits are unknown among the friends) we give evidence to the truth by sealing it with our *yea* and *nay*; and the judges believe us on our bare affirmation, whilst so many other Christians forswear themselves on the holy Gospels. We never war or fight in any case; but 'tis not that we are afraid, for so far from shuddering at the thoughts of death, we on the contrary bless the moment which unites us with the Being of Beings; but the reason of our not using the outward sword is, that we are neither wolves, tigers, nor mastiffs, but men and Christians. Our God, who has commanded us to love our enemies, and to suffer without repining, would certainly not permit us to cross the seas, merely because murtherers clothed in scarlet, and wearing caps two foot high enlist citizens by a noise made with two little sticks on an ass's skin extended. And when, after a victory is gained, the whole city of London is illuminated; when the sky is in a blaze with fireworks, and a noise is heard in the air of thanksgivings, of bells, of organs, and of the cannon, we groan in silence, and are deeply affected with sadness of spirit and brokenness of heart, for the sad havock which is the occasion of those public rejoycings.

Letter II: On the Quakers

Such was the substance of the conversation I had with this very singular person; but I was greatly surprised to see him come the Sunday following, and take me with him to the Quaker's meeting. There are several of these in London, but that which he carried me to stands near the famous pillar called the monument.* The brethren were already assembled at my enter-ing it with my guide. There might be about four hundred men and three hundred women in the meeting. The women hid their faces behind their fans, and the men were covered with their broad-brimmed hats; all were seated, and the silence was universal. I passed through them, but did not perceive so much as one lift up his eyes to look at me. This silence lasted a quarter of an hour, when at last one of them rose up, took off his hat, and after making a variety of wry faces, and groaning in a most lamentable manner, he partly from his nose, and partly from his mouth, threw out a strange, confused jumble of words, (bor-rowed as he imagined from the Gospel) which neither himself nor any of his hearers understood. When this distorter had ended his beautiful soliloquy, and the stupid, but greatly edified, congregation were separated, I asked my friend how it was possible for the judicious part of their assembly to suffer such a babbling. We are obliged, says he, to suffer it, because no one knows when a man rises up to hold forth, whether he will be moved by the spirit or by folly. In this doubt and uncertainty we listen patiently to every one, we even allow our women to hold forth; two or three of these are often inspired at one and the same time, and 'tis then that a most charming noise is heard in the Lord's house. You have then no priests, says I to him. No, no, friend, replies the Quaker, to our great happiness. Then opening one of the friend's books, as he called it, he read the following words in an emphatic tone: God forbid we should presume to ordain any one to receive the holy spirit on the Lord's day, to the prejudice of the rest of the brethren. Thanks to the almighty, we are the only people upon earth that have no priests. Wouldst thou deprive us of so happy a distinction? Why should we abandon our babe to mercenary nurses, when we our selves have milk enough for it? These mercenary creatures would soon domineer in our houses, and destroy both the mother and the babe. God has said, freely you have received, freely give. Shall we after these words cheapen, as it were, the Gospel; sell the Holy Ghost, and make of an assembly of Christians a mere shop of traders. We don't pay a set of men clothed in black, to assist our poor, to bury our dead, or to preach to the brethren; these offices are all of too tender a nature, for us ever to entrust them to others. But how is it possible for you, says I, with some warmth, to know whether your discourse is really inspired by the Almighty? Whosoever, says he, shall implore Christ to enlighten him, and shall publish the Gospel truths he may feel inwardly, such an one may be assured that he is inspired by the Lord.* He then poured forth a numberless multitude of Scripture-texts, which proved, as he imagined, that there is no such thing as Christianity without an immediate revelation, and added these remarkable words: When thou movest one of thy limbs, is it moved by thine own power? Certainly not, for this limb is often sensible to involuntary motions; consequently he who created thy body, gives motion to this earthly tabernacle. And are the several ideas of which thy soul receives the impression formed by thy self? Much less are they, since these pour in upon thy mind whether thou wilt or no; consequently thou receivest thine ideas from him who created thy soul: But as he leaves thine affections at full liberty, he gives thy mind such ideas as thine affections may deserve; if thou livest in God, thou actest, thou thinkest in God. After this thou needest only but open thine eyes to that light which enlightens all mankind, and 'tis then thou wilt perceive the truth, and make others perceive it. Why this, says I, is Malbranche's* doctrine to a tittle. I am acquainted with thy Malbranche, says he; he had something of the *friend* in him, but was not enough so. These are the most considerable particulars I learnt concerning the doctrine of the Quakers; in my next letter I shall acquaint you with their history, which you will find more singular than their opinions.

Letter III: *On the Quakers*

You have already heard that the Quakers date from Christ, who according to them was the first Quaker. Religion, say these, was corrupted, a little after his death, and remained in that state of corruption about 1600 Years. But there were always a few Quakers concealed in the world, who carefully preserved the sacred fire, which was extinguished in all but themselves, 'till at last this light spread it self in England in 1642.

'Twas at the time when Great Britain was torn to pieces by the intestine wars, which three or four sects had raised in the name of God, that one George Fox,* born in Leicestershire, and son to a silk-weaver, took it into his head to preach; and, as he pretended, with all the requisites of a true apostle, that is, without being able either to read or write. He was about twenty-five[1] years of age, irreproachable in his life and conduct, and a holy mad-man. He was equipped in leather from head to foot, and travelled from one village to another, exclaiming against war and the clergy. Had his invectives been levelled against the soldiery only, he would have been safe enough, but he inveighed against ecclesiasticks. Fox was seized at Derby, and being carried before a justice of peace; he did not once offer to pull off his leathern hat; upon which an officer gave him a great box o'th' ear, and cried to him, Don't you know you are to appear uncovered before his worship? Fox presented his other cheek to the officer, and begged him to give him another box for God's sake. The justice would have had him sworn before he asked

---

[1] Fox could read at that age.

him any questions: Know, friend, says Fox to him, that I never swear. The justice observing he *Thee'd* and *Thou'd* him, sent him to the house of correction in Derby, with orders that he should be whipped there. Fox praised the Lord all the way he went to the house of correction, where the justice's order was executed with the utmost severity. The men who whipped this enthusiast, were greatly surprised to hear him beseech them to give him a few more lashes for the good of his soul. There was no need of intreating these people; the lashes were repeated, for which Fox thanked them very cordially, and began to preach. At first, the spectators fell a laughing, but they afterwards listened to him; and as enthusiasm is an epidemical distemper, many were persuaded, and those who scourged him became his first disciples. Being set at liberty, he ran up and down the country with a dozen proselytes at his heels, still declaiming against the clergy, and was whipped from time to time. Being one day set in the pillory, he harangued the crowd in so strong and moving a manner, that fifty of the auditors became his converts; and he won the rest so much in his favour, that his head being freed tumultuously from the hole where it was fastened, the populace went and searched for the church of England clergyman, who had been chiefly instrumental in bringing him to this punishment, and set him on the same pillory where Fox had stood.

Fox was bold enough to convert some of Oliver Cromwell's Soldiers, who thereupon quitted the service and refused to take the oaths. Oliver having as great a contempt for a sect which would not allow its members to fight, as *Sixtus Quintus* had for another sect, *Dove non si chiavava,** began to persecute these new converts. The prisons were crowded with them, but persecution seldom has any other effect than to increase the number of proselytes. These came therefore from their confinement, more strongly confirmed in the principles they had imbibed, and followed by their gaolers whom they had brought over to their belief. But the circumstances which contributed chiefly to the spreading of this sect were as follows. Fox thought himself inspired, and consequently was of opinion, that he must speak in a manner different from the rest of mankind. He thereupon began to writhe his body, to screw up his face, to hold in his breath, and to exhale it in a forcible manner, insomuch that the priestess of the Pythian God at Delphos could not have acted her part to better advantage. Inspiration soon became so habitual to him, that he could scarce deliver himself in any other manner. This was the first gift he communicated to his disciples. These aped very sincerely their master's several grimaces, and shook in every limb the instant the fit of inspiration came upon them, whence they were called Quakers. The vulgar attempted to mimick them, they trembled, they spake through the nose; they quaked and fancied themselves inspired by the Holy Ghost. The only thing now wanting was a few miracles, and accordingly they wrought some.

Fox, this modern patriarch, spoke thus to a justice of peace, before a large assembly of people. Friend, take care what thou dost: God will soon punish thee for persecuting his saints. This magistrate being one who besotted himself every day with bad beer and brandy, died of an apoplexy two days after, the moment he had signed a *mittimus* for imprisoning some Quakers. The sudden death with which this justice was seized, was not ascribed to his intemperance, but was universally looked upon as the effect of the holy man's predictions; so that this accident made more converts to Quakerism, than a thousand sermons and as many shaking fits could have done. Oliver finding them increase daily was desirous of bringing them over to his party, and for that purpose attempted to bribe them by money. However, they were incorruptible, which made him one day declare, that this religion was the only one he had ever met with that had resisted the charms of gold.

The Quakers were several times persecuted under Charles the second, not upon a religious account, but for refusing to pay the tythes, for *Thee-ing* and *Thou-ing* the magistrates, and for refusing to take the oaths enacted by the laws.

At last Robert Barclay, a native of Scotland, presented to the king in 1675, his apology for the Quakers, a work as well drawn up as the subject could possibly admit. The dedication to Charles the second is not filled with mean, flattering encomiums; but abounds with bold touches in favour of truth, and with the wisest counsels. 'Thou has tasted,' says he to the king at the close of his epistle dedicatory, 'of prosperity and adversity; thou knowest what it is to be banished thy native country; to be over-ruled as well as to rule, and sit upon the throne; and being oppressed, thou hast reason to know how hateful the oppressor is both to God and man: If after all these warnings and advertisements, thou dost not turn unto the Lord with all thy heart; but forget him who remembered thee in thy distress, and give up thy self to follow lust and vanity, surely great will be thy condemnation.

Against which snare, as well as the temptation of those, that may or do feed thee, and prompt thee to evil, the most excellent and prevalent remedy will be, to apply thy self to that light of Christ, which shineth in thy conscience, which neither can nor will flatter thee, nor suffer thee to be at ease in thy sins; but doth and will deal plainly and faithfully with thee, as those, that are followers thereof have plainly done—— *Thy faithful friend and subject*, Robert Barclay.'

A more surprising circumstance is, that this epistle, written by a private man of no figure, was so happy in its effects as to put a stop to the persecution.

Letter IV: On the Quakers

About this time[1] arose the illustrious William Pen,* who established the power of the Quakers in America, and would have made them appear venerable in the eyes of the Europeans, were it possible for mankind to respect virtue, when revealed in a ridiculous light. He was the only son of vice-admiral Pen, favourite to the duke of York, afterwards king James the second.

William Pen at twenty years of age happening to meet with a Quaker in Cork,[2] whom he had known at Oxford, this man made a proselyte of him; and William being a sprightly youth, and naturally eloquent, having a winning aspect, and a very engaging carriage, he soon gained over some of his Intimates. He carried matters so far that he formed by insensible degrees a society of young Quakers who met at his house; so that he was at the head of a sect when a little above twenty.

Being returned, after his leaving Cork, to the vice-admiral his father, instead of falling upon his knees to ask him blessing, he went up to him with his hat on, and said, Friend, I'm very glad to see thee in good health. The vice-admiral imagined his son to

[1] 1666.
[2] Thomas Loe.

be crazy; but soon finding he was turned Quaker, he employed all the methods that prudence could suggest, to engage him to behave and act like other people. The youth made no other answer to his father, than by exhorting him to turn Quaker also. At last his father confined himself to this single request, *viz* that he should wait upon the king and the duke of York with his hat under his arm, and should not *Thee* and *Thou* them. William answered, that he could not do these things for conscience sake, which exasperated his father to such a degree, that he turned him out of doors. Young Pen gave God thanks, for permitting him to suffer so early in his cause, after which he went into the city, where he held forth,[3] and made a great number of converts.

The church of England clergy found their congregations dwindle away daily; and Pen being young, handsome, and of a graceful stature, the court as well as the city ladies flocked very devoutly to his meeting. The patriarch George Fox hearing of his great reputation, came to London, (though the journey was very long) purely to see and converse with him. Both resolved to go upon missions into foreign countries, and accordingly they embarked for Holland, after having left labourers sufficient to take care of the London vineyard.

Their labours were crowned with success in Amsterdam; but a circumstance which reflected the greatest honour on them, and at the same time put their humility to the greatest trial, was the reception they met with from Elizabeth* the princess of Palatine, aunt to George the first of Great Britain, a lady conspicuous for her genius and knowledge, and to whom Descartes had dedicated his *Philosophical Romance.**

She was then retired to the Hague, where she received these friends, for so the Quakers were at that time called in Holland. This princess had several conferences with them in her palace, and she at last entertained so favourable an opinion of Quakerism, that they confessed she was not far from the kingdom of heaven. The friends sowed likewise the good seed in Germany, but reaped very little fruit; for the mode of *Thee-ing* and *Thou-ing* was not approved of in a country, where a man is perpetually obliged to employ the titles of highness and excellency. William Pen returned soon to England upon hearing of his father's

[3] About 1668, and the 24th year of his age.

sickness, in order to see him before he died. The vice-admiral was reconciled to his son, and though of a different persuasion, embraced him tenderly. William made a fruitless exhortation to his father not to receive the sacrament, but to die a Quaker; and the good old man intreated his son William to wear buttons on his sleeves, and a crape hatband in his beaver, but all to no purpose.

William Pen inherited very large possessions, part of which consisted in crown-debts due to the vice-admiral for sums he had advanced for the sea-service. No monies were at that time more secure than those owing from the king. Pen was obliged to go more than once, and *Thee* and *Thou* king Charles and his ministers, in order to recover the debt; and at last instead of specie, the government invested him with the right and sovereignty of a province of America, to the south* of Maryland. Thus was a Quaker raised to sovereign power. Pen set sail for his new dominions with two ships freighted with Quakers, who followed his fortune. The country was then called Pensilvania from William Pen, who there founded Philadelphia,* now the most flourishing city in that country. The first step he took was to enter into an alliance with his American neighbours; and this is the only treaty between those people and the Christians that was not ratified by an oath, and was never infringed. The new sovereign was at the same time the legislator of Pensilvania, and enacted very wise and prudent laws, none of which have ever been changed since his time. The first is, to injure no person upon a religious account, and to consider as brethren all those who believe in one God.

He had no sooner settled his government, but several American merchants came and peopled this colony. The natives of the country instead of flying into the woods, cultivated by insensible degrees a friendship with the peaceable Quakers. They loved these foreigners as much as they detested the other Christians who had conquered and laid waste America. In a little time, a great number of these savages (falsely so called) charmed with the mild and gentle disposition of their neighbours, came in crowds to William Pen, and besought him to admit them into the number of his vassals. 'Twas very rare and uncommon for a sovereign to be *Thee'd* and *Thou'd* by the meanest of his subjects, who never took their hats off when they came into his presence; and as singular for a government to be without one priest in it, and for a people to be without arms, either offensive or defensive; for a body of citizens to be absolutely undistinguished but by the publick employments, and for neighbours not to entertain the least jealousy one against the other.

William Pen might glory in having brought down upon earth the so much boasted golden age, which in all probability never existed but in Pensilvania. He returned to England to settle some affairs relating to his new dominions. After the death of king Charles the second, king James, who had loved the father, indulged the same affection to the son, and no longer considered him as an obscure Sectary, but as a very great man. The king's politicks on this occasion agreed with his inclinations. He was desirous of pleasing the Quakers, by annulling the laws made against Nonconformists,* in order to have an opportunity, by this universal toleration, of establishing the *Romish* religion. All the sectarists in England saw the snare that was laid for them, but did not give into it; they never failing to unite when the Romish religion, their common enemy, is to be opposed. But Pen did not think himself bound in any manner to renounce his principles, merely to favour Protestants to whom he was odious, in opposition to a king who loved him. He had established an universal toleration with regard to conscience in America, and would not have it thought that he intended to destroy it in Europe; for which reason he adhered so inviolably to king James, that a report prevailed universally of his being a Jesuit. This calumny affected him very strongly and he was obliged to justify himself in print. However, the unfortunate king James the second, in whom, as in most princes of the Stuart family, grandeur and weakness were equally blended; and who, like them, as much overdid some things as he was short in others, lost his kingdom in a manner that is hardly to be accounted for.

All the English sectarists accepted from William the third and his parliament, the toleration and indulgence which they had refused when offered by king James. 'Twas then the Quakers began to enjoy, by virtue of the laws, the several privileges they possess at this time. Pen having at last seen Quakerism firmly established in his native country, went back to Pensilvania. His own people and the Americans received him with tears of joy, as though he had been a father who was returned to visit his children. All the laws had been religiously observed in his absence, a circumstance in which no legislator had ever been happy but himself. After having resided some years in Pensilvania, he left it, but with great reluctance, in order to return to England, there to solicit some matters in favour of the commerce of Pensilvania. But he never saw it again, he dying in Ruscomb in Berkshire, *anno* 1718.

I am not able to guess what fate Quakerism may have in America, but I perceive it dwindles away daily in England. In all countries where liberty of conscience is allowed, the established religion will at last swallow up all the rest. Quakers are disqualified from being members of parliament; nor can they enjoy any post or preferment, because an oath must always be taken on these occasions, and they never swear. They are therefore reduced to the necessity of subsisting upon traffick.* Their children, whom the industry of their parents has enriched, are desirous of enjoying honours, of wearing buttons and ruffles; and quite ashamed of being called Quakers, they become converts to the Church of England, merely to be in the fashion.

Letter v: On the Church of England

England is properly the country of sectarists. *Multæ sunt mansiones in domo patris mei* (in my father's house are many mansions).* An Englishman, as one to whom liberty is natural, may go to heaven his own way.

Nevertheless, though everyone is permitted to serve God in whatever mode or fashion he thinks proper, yet their true religion, that in which a man makes his fortune, is the sect of Episcoparians or Churchmen, called the Church of England, or simply the Church, by way of eminence. No person can possess an employment either in England or Ireland, unless he be ranked among the faithful, that is, professes himself a member of the Church of England. This reason (which carries mathematical evidence with it) has converted such numbers of dissenters of all persuasions, that not a twentieth part of the nation is out of the pale of the established church.* The English clergy have retained a great number of the Romish ceremonies, and especially that of receiving, with a most scrupulous attention, their tithes. They also have the pious ambition, to aim at superiority.

Moreover, they inspire very religiously their flock with a holy zeal against Dissenters of all denominations. This zeal was pretty violent under the Tories, in the last four years of queen Anne; but was productive of no greater mischief than the breaking the windows of some meeting-houses, and the demolishing of a few of them. For religious rage ceased in England with the civil wars; and was no more under queen Anne, than the hollow noise of a sea whose billows still heaved, though so long after the storm, when the Whigs and Tories laid waste their native country, in the same manner as the Guelphs and Gibelins* formerly did theirs. 'Twas absolutely necessary for both parties to call in religion on this occasion; the Tories declared for episcopacy, and the Whigs, as some imagined, were for abolishing it; however, after these had got the upper hand, they contented themselves with only abridging its power.

At the time when the earl of Oxford* and the lord Boling-broke* used to drink healths to the Tories, the Church of England considered those noblemen as the defenders of its holy privileges. The lower house of Convocation (a kind of house of Commons) composed wholly of the clergy, was in some credit at that time; at least the members of it had the liberty to meet, to dispute on ecclesiastical matters, to sentence impious books from time to time to the flames, that is, books written against themselves. The ministry, which is now composed of Whigs, does not so much as allow those gentlemen to assemble, so that they are at this time reduced (in the obscurity of their respective parishes) to the melancholy occupation of praying for the prosperity of the government, whose tranquillity they would willingly disturb. With regard to the bishops, who are twenty-six in all, they still have seats in the house of lords in spite of the Whigs, because the ancient abuse of considering them as Barons subsists to this day. There is a clause however in the oath which the government requires from these gentlemen, that puts their christian patience to a very great trial, *viz* that they shall be of the Church of England as by law established. There are few bishops, deans, or other dignitaries, but imagine they are so *jure divino**; 'tis consequently a great mortification to them to be obliged to confess, that they owe their dignity to a pitiful law enacted by a sett of profane laymen [...] The lord B——* observed, that this notion of divine right would only make so many tyrants in lawn-sleeves, but that the laws made so many citizens.

With regard to the morals of the English clergy, they are more regular than those of France, and for this reason. All the clergy (a very few excepted) are educated in the universities of Oxford or Cambridge, far from the depravity and corruption which reign in the capital. They are not called to dignities till very late, in an Age when men are sensible of no other passion but avarice, that is, when their ambition craves a supply. Employments are here bestowed both in the church and the army, as a reward for long services; and we never see youngsters made bishops or colonels immediately upon their laying aside the academical gown; and besides, most of the clergy are married. The stiff and awkward air contracted by them at the university, and the little familiarity the men of this country have with the ladies, commonly oblige a bishop to confine himself to, and rest contented with his own. Clergymen sometimes take a glass at the tavern, custom giving them a sanction on this occasion; and if they fuddle themselves 'tis in a very serious manner, and without giving the least scandal.

That sable mixed being (not to be defined) who is neither of the clergy nor of the laity; in a word, the thing called *Abbé** in France, is a species quite unknown in England. All the clergy here are very much upon the reserve, and most of them pedants. When these are told, that in France, young fellows famous for their dissoluteness and raised to the highest dignities of the church by female intrigues, address the fair publickly in an amorous way, amuse themselves in writing tender love-songs, entertain their friends very splendidly every night at their own houses, and after the banquet is ended, withdraw to invoke the assistance of the Holy Ghost, and call themselves boldly the successors of the apostles, they bless God for their being Protestants. But, these are shameless Hereticks, who deserve to be blown hence through the flames to old Nick, as Rabelais says*, and for this reason I don't trouble my self about them.

Letter VI: *On the Presbyterians*

The Church of England is confined almost to the kingdom whence it received its name, and to Ireland, for Presbyterianism is the established religion in Scotland. This Presbyterianism is directly the same with Calvinism, as it was established in France, and is now professed at Geneva. As the priests of this sect receive but very inconsiderable stipends from their churches, and consequently cannot emulate the splendid luxury of bishops, they exclaim very naturally against honours which they can never attain to. Figure to yourself the haughty Diogenes,* trampling under foot the pride of Plato. The Scotch Presbyterians are not very unlike that proud, though tattered reasoner. Diogenes did not use Alexander half so impertinently as these treated king Charles the second; for when they took up arms in his cause, in opposition to Oliver, who had deceived them, they forced that poor monarch to undergo the hearing of three or four sermons every day; would not suffer him to play, reduced him to a state of penitence and mortification; so that Charles soon grew sick of these pedants, and accordingly eloped from them with as much joy as a youth does from school.

A Church of England minister appears as another Cato* in presence of a juvenile, sprightly French graduate, who bawls for a whole morning together in the divinity schools, and hums a song in chorus with ladies in the evening: But this Cato is a very spark, when before a Scotch Presbyterian. The latter affects a serious gait, puts on a sour look, wears a vastly broad-brimmed hat, and a long cloak over a very short coat; preaches through the nose, and gives the name of the whore of Babylon to all churches, where the ministers are so fortunate as to enjoy an annual revenue of five or six thousand pounds; and where the people are weak enough to suffer this, and to give them the titles of my lord, your lordship, or your eminence.

These gentlemen, who have also some churches in England, introduced there the mode of grave and severe exhortations. To them is owing the sanctification of Sunday in the three kingdoms. People are there forbid to work or take any recreation on that day, in which the severity is twice as great as that of the Romish church. No operas, plays or concerts are allowed in London on Sundays; and even cards are so expressly forbid, that none but persons of quality and those we call the genteel, play on that day; the rest of the nation go either to church, to the tavern, or to see their mistresses.

Though the Episcopal and Presbyterian sects are the two

prevailing ones in Great Britain, yet all others are very welcome to come and settle in it, and live very sociably together, though most of their preachers hate one another almost as cordially as a Jansenist damns a Jesuit.

Take a view of the Royal Exchange* in London, a place more venerable than many courts of justice, where the representatives of all nations meet for the benefit of mankind. There the Jew, the Mahometan, and the Christian transact together as though they all professed the same religion, and give the name of Infidel to none but bankrupts. There the Presbyterian confides in the Anabaptist, and the Churchman depends on the Quaker's word. At the breaking up of this pacific and free assembly, some withdraw to the synagogue, and others to take a glass. This man goes and is baptised in a great tub, in the name of the Father, Son, and Holy Ghost: That man has his son's foreskin cut off, whilst a set of Hebrew words (quite unintelligible to him) are mumbled over his child. Others retire to their churches, and there wait for the inspiration of heaven with their hats on, and all are satisfied.

If one religion only were allowed in England, the government would very possibly become arbitrary; if there were but two, the people would cut one another's throats; but as there are such a multitude, they all live happy and in peace.

Letter VII: On the Socinians, or Arians, or Antitrinitarians

There is a little sect here composed of clergymen, and of a few very learned persons among the laity, who, though they don't call themselves Arians or Socinians,* do yet dissent entirely from St Athanasius, with regard to their notions of the Trinity, and declare very frankly, that the Father is greater than the Son [. . .]

The celebrated Sir Isaac Newton* honoured this opinion so far as to countenance it. This philosopher thought that the Unitarians argued more mathematically than we do. But the most sanguine stickler for Arianism is the illustrious Dr Clark.* This man is rigidly virtuous, and of a mild disposition; is more fond of his tenets than desirous of propagating them; and absorbed so entirely in problems and calculations, that he is a mere reasoning machine.

'Tis he who wrote a book which is much esteemed and little understood, on the existence of God; and another more intelligible, but pretty much contemned, on the truth of the Christian religion.

He never engaged in scholastic disputes, which our friend calls venerable trifles. He only published a work containing all the testimonies of the primitive ages, for and against the Unitarians, and leaves to the reader the counting of the voices, and the liberty of forming a judgment. This book won the doctor a great number of partisans, and lost him the See of Canterbury: But in my humble opinion, he was out in his calculation, and had better have been Primate of all England, than merely an Arian parson.

You see that opinions are subject to revolutions as well as Empires. Arianism after having triumphed during three centuries, and then forgot twelve, rises at last out of its own ashes; but it has chose a very improper season to make its appearance in, the present age being quite cloyed with disputes and Sects. The members of this Sect are, besides, too few to be indulged the liberty of holding public assemblies, which however they will doubtless be permitted to do, in case they spread considerably. But people are now so very cold with respect to all things of this kind, that there is little probability any new religion, or old one that may be revived, will meet with favour. Is it not whimsical enough that Luther, Calvin and Zuinglius,* all of 'em wretched authors, should have founded Sects which are now spread over a great part of Europe; that Mahomet, though so ignorant, should have given a religion to Asia and Africa; and that Sir Isaac Newton, Dr Clark, Mr Locke, Mr Le Clerc* etc. the greatest philosophers, as well as the ablest writers of their ages, should scarce have been able to raise a little flock, which even decreases daily.

This it is to be born at a proper period of time. Were Cardinal de Retz* to return again into the world, neither his eloquence nor his intrigues would draw together ten women in Paris.

Were Oliver Cromwell, he who beheaded his Sovereign and seized upon the kingly dignity, to rise from the dead, he would be a wealthy city trader, and no more.

Letter VIII: *On the Parliament*

The Members of the English Parliament are fond of comparing themselves to the old Romans.

Not long since, Mr Shippen* opened a speech in the house of Commons with these words, *The Majesty of the People of* England *would be wounded.* The singularity of the expression occasioned a loud laugh; but this Gentleman, so far from being disconcerted, repeated the same words with a resolute tone of voice, and the laugh ceased. In my opinion, the Majesty of the people of England has nothing in common with that of the people of Rome, much less is there any affinity between their governments. There is in London a Senate, some of the members whereof are accused, (doubtless very unjustly) of selling their voices on certain occasions, as was done in Rome; this is the only resemblance. Besides, the two nations appear to me quite opposite in character, with regard both to good and evil. The Romans never knew the dreadful folly of religious Wars, an abomination reserved for devout Preachers of patience and humility. Marius and Sylla, Caesar and Pompey, Anthony and Augustus, did not draw their swords and set the world in a blaze, merely to determine whether the Flamen* should wear his shirt over his robe, or his robe over his shirt; or whether the sacred Chickens should eat and drink, or eat only, in order to take the augury. The English have hanged one another by law, and cut one another to pieces in pitch battles, for quarrels of as trifling a nature. The Sects of the Episcoparians and Presbyterians quite distracted these very serious Heads for a time. But I fancy they'll hardly ever be so silly again, they seeming to be grown wiser at their own expence; and I don't perceive the least inclination in them to murther one another merely about syllogisms, as some Zealots among them once did.

But here follows a more essential difference between Rome and England, which gives the advantage entirely to the latter, *viz* that the civil wars of Rome ended in slavery, and those of the English in liberty. The English are the only people upon earth who have been able to prescribe limits to the power of Kings by resisting them; and who, by a series of struggles, have at last established that wise Government, where the Prince is all powerful to do good, and at the same time is restrained from committing evil; where the Nobles are great without insolence, though there are no Vassals; and where the People share in the government without confusion.

The House of Lords and that of the Commons divide the legislative power under the King, but the Romans had no such balance [. . .]

The English are not fired with the splendid folly of making conquests, but would only prevent their neighbours from conquering. They are not only jealous of their own Liberty, but even of that of other nations. The English were exasperated against Lewis the Fourteenth, for no other reason but because he was ambitious; and declared war against him merely out of levity, not from any interested motives.*

The English have doubtless purchased their Liberties at a very high price, and waded through seas of blood to drown the Idol of arbitrary Power. Other nations have been involved in as great calamities, and have shed as much blood; but then the blood they spilt in defence of their Liberties, only enslaved them the more.

That which rises to a Revolution in England is no more than a Sedition in other countries. A city in Spain, in Barbary, or in Turkey, takes up arms in defence of its Privileges, when immediately, 'tis stormed by mercenary Troops, 'tis punished by Executioners, and the rest of the Nation kiss the chains they are loaded with. The French are of opinion, that the government of this Island is more tempestuous than the sea which surrounds it, which indeed is true; but then 'tis never so but when the King raises the storm; when he attempts to seize the Ship of which he is only the chief Pilot. The civil wars of France lasted longer; were more cruel, and productive of greater evils than those of England: But none of these civil Wars had a wise and prudent Liberty for their object [. . .]

That for which the French chiefly reproach the English Nation, is, the murther of King Charles the First, whom his subjects treated exactly as he would have treated them, had his Reign been prosperous. After all, consider on one side, Charles the first defeated in a pitched battle, imprisoned, tryed, sentenced to die in Westminster-hall, and then beheaded: And on the other, the Emperor Henry the seventh, poisoned by his chaplain at his receiving the sacrament; Henry the third stabbed by a Monk; thirty assassinations projected against Henry the fourth;* several of them put in execution, and the last bereaving that great Monarch of his life. Weigh, I say, all these wicked attempts, and then judge.

Letter IX: On the Government

That mixture in the English government, that harmony between King, Lords and Commons, did not always subsist. England was enslaved for a long series of years by the Romans, the Saxons, the Danes, and the French successively. William the Conqueror particularly ruled them with a rod of iron. He disposed as absolutely of the lives and fortunes of his conquered subjects as an eastern Monarch; and forbid, upon pain of death, the English both fire or candle in their houses after eight o'clock; whether he did this to prevent their nocturnal meetings, or only to try, by this odd and whimsical prohibition, how far it was possible for one Man to extend his power over his fellow Creatures. 'Tis true indeed that the English had Parliaments before and after William the Conqueror; and they boast of them, as though these assemblies then called Parliaments, composed of ecclesiastical Tyrants, and of plunderers entitled Barons, had been the guardians of the publick liberty and happiness.

The Barbarians who came from the shores of the Baltick, and settled in the rest of Europe, brought with them the form of government called States or Parliaments, about which so much noise is made, and which are so little understood.* Kings indeed were not absolute in those days, but then the people were more wretched upon that very account, and more completely enslaved. The Chiefs of these savages who had laid waste France, Italy, Spain and England, made themselves Monarchs. Their generals divided among themselves the several countries they had conquered, whence sprung those Margraves, those Peers, those Barons, those petty Tyrants, who often contested with their Sovereigns for the spoils of whole nations. These were birds of prey, fighting with an Eagle for Doves, whose blood the Victorious was to suck. Every nation, instead of being governed by one Master, was trampled upon by an hundred Tyrants. The priests soon played a part among them. Before this, it had been the fate of the Gauls, the Germans and the Britons, to be always governed by their Druids, and the Chiefs of their villages, an ancient kind of Barons, not so tyrannical as their successors. These Druids pretended to be mediators between God and man. They enacted laws, they fulminated their excommunications, and sentenced to death. The Bishops succeeded, by insensible degrees, to their temporal authority in the Goth and Vandal government. The Popes set themselves at their head, and armed with their Briefs, their Bulls, and reinforced by Monks, they made even Kings tremble; deposed and assassinated them at pleasure, and employed every artifice to draw into their own purses, monies from all parts of Europe. The weak Ina, one of the tyrants of the Saxon Heptarchy* in England, was the first Monarch that submitted, in his pilgrimage to Rome, to pay St Peter's penny (equivalent very near to a French crown) for every house in his dominions. The whole Island soon followed his example; England became insensibly one of the Pope's provinces, and the holy Father used to send from time to time his Legates thither to levy exorbitant taxes. At last King John* delivered up by a public instrument, the Kingdom of England to the Pope, who had excommunicated him; but the Barons not finding their account in this resignation, dethroned the wretched King John and seated Lewis, father to St Lewis King of France in his place. However they were soon weary of their new Monarch, and accordingly obliged him to return back to France.

Whilst that the Barons, the Bishops, and the Popes, all laid waste England, where all were for ruling; the most numerous, the most useful, even the most virtuous, and consequently the most venerable part of mankind, consisting of those who study the laws and the sciences; of traders, of artificers, in a word, of all who were not tyrants; that is, those who are called the people; these, I say, were by them looked upon as so many animals beneath the dignity of the human species. The Commons in those ages were far from sharing in the government, they being Villains* or Peasants whose labour, whose blood were the property of their Masters who entitled themselves the Nobility. The major part of men in Europe were at that time what they are to this day in several parts of the world, they were Villains or Bondsmen of Lords, that is, a kind of cattle bought and sold with the land. Many ages passed away before justice could be done to human nature; before mankind were conscious,

that 'twas abominable numbers should sow, and but few reap:
And was not France very happy, when the power and authority
of those petty Robbers was abolished by the lawful authority of
Kings and of the People?

Happily in the violent shocks which the divisions between
Kings and the Nobles gave to empires, the chains of Nations
were more or less heavy. Liberty, in England, sprung from the
quarrels of Tyrants. The Barons forced King John and King
Henry the third, to grant the famous Magna Carta, the chief
design of which was indeed to make Kings dependent on the
Lords, but then the rest of the nation were a little favoured in it,
in order that they might join, on proper occasions, with their
pretended Masters. This great Charter which is considered as
the sacred origin of the English Liberties, shows in itself how
little Liberty was known.

The Title alone proves, that the King thought he had a just
right to be absolute; and that the Barons, and even the Clergy
forced him to give up that pretended right, for no other reason
but because they were the most powerful.

Magna Carta begins in this style, *We grant, of our own free
will, the following Privileges to the Archbishops, Bishops, Priors
and Barons of our Kingdom,* etc.

The House of Commons is not once mentioned in the Articles
of this Charter, a Proof that it did not yet exist, or that it existed
without Power. Mention is therein made, by name, of the
Freemen of England, a melancholy Proof that some were not so.
It appears by the thirty second Article, that these pretended
Freemen owed Service to their Lords. Such a Liberty as this, was
not many removes from Slavery.

By Article XXI, the King ordains that his Officers shall not
henceforward seize upon, unless they pay for them, the Horses
and Carts of Freemen. The people considered this Ordinance as
a real Liberty, though it was* a greater Tyranny. Henry the
seventh, that happy Usurper and great Politician, who pretended
to love the Barons, though he in reality hated and feared them,
got their Lands alienated. By this means the Villains, afterwards
acquiring Riches by their Industry, purchased the Estates and
Country-Seats of the illustrious Peers who had ruined themselves
by their Folly and Extravagance, and all the Lands got by
insensible Degrees into other Hands.

The Power of the House of Commons increased every Day. The Families of the ancient Peers were at last extinct; and as Peers only are properly noble in England, there would be no such thing in strictness of Law, as Nobility in that Island, had not the Kings created new Barons from Time to Time, and preserved the Body of Peers, once a Terror to them, to oppose them to the Commons since become so formidable.

All these new Peers who compose the higher House, receive nothing but their Titles from the King, and very few of them have Estates in those Places whence they take their Titles. One shall be Duke of D—— though he has not a Foot of Land in Dorsetshire; and another is Earl of a Village, though he scarce knows where it is situated. The Peers have Power, but 'tis only in the Parliament House.

There is no such thing here, as[1] *haute, moyenne, & basse justice*, that is, a Power to judge in all Matters civil and criminal; nor a Right or Privilege of Hunting in the Grounds of a Citizen, who at the same time is not permitted to fire a Gun in his own field.

No one is exempted in this Country from paying certain Taxes, because he is a Nobleman or a Priest.* All Duties and Taxes are settled by the House of Commons, whose Power is greater than that of the Peers, though inferior to it in dignity. The spiritual as well as temporal Lords have the Liberty to reject a Money Bill brought in by the Commons, but they are not allowed to alter any thing in it, and must either pass or throw it out without Restriction. When the Bill has passed the Lords and is signed by the King, then the whole Nation pays, every Man in proportion to his Revenue or Estate, not according to his Title, which would be absurd. There is no such thing as an arbitrary Subsidy or Poll-Tax, but a real Tax on the Lands, of all which an Estimate was made in the Reign of the famous King William the Third.

The Land-Tax continues still upon the same foot, though the

---

[1] *La haute justice*, is that of a Lord, who has Power to sentence capitally, and to judge of all Causes civil and criminal, those of the Crown excepted. *La moyenne justice*, is empowered to judge of Actions relating to Guardianships, and Offences. *La basse justice* takes Cognizance of the Fees due to the Lord, of the Havock of Beasts, and of Offences. The *moyenne justice* is imaginary, and there is perhaps no Instance of its ever being put in Execution.

Revenue of the Lands is increased. Thus no one is tyrannised over, and every one is easy. The Feet of the Peasants are not bruised by wooden Shoes; they eat white Bread, are well clothed, and are not afraid of increasing their Stock of Cattle, nor of tiling their Houses, from any Apprehensions that their Taxes will be raised the Year following. The annual Income of the Estates of a great many Commoners in England, amounts to two hundred thousand Livres; and yet these don't think it beneath them to plough the Lands which enrich them, and on which they enjoy their Liberty.

Letter x: On Trade

As Trade enriched the Citizens in England, so it contributed to their Freedom, and this Freedom on the other Side extended their Commerce, whence arose the Grandeur of the State. Trade raised by insensible Degrees the naval Power, which gives the English a Superiority over the Seas, and they are now Masters of very near two hundred Ships of War. Posterity will very possibly be surprised to hear that an Island whose only Produce is a little Lead, Tin, Fuller's Earth and coarse Wood, should become so powerful by its Commerce, as to be able to send in 1723,* three Fleets at the same Time to three different and far distanced Parts of the Globe. One before Gibraltar, conquered and still possessed by the English; a second to Porto Bello, to dispossess the King of Spain of the Treasures of the West Indies; and a third into the Baltick, to prevent the Northern Powers from coming to an Engagement.

At the Time when Lewis XIV made all Italy tremble, and that his Armies, which had already possessed themselves of Savoy and Piedmont, were upon the Point of taking Turin; Prince Eugene* was obliged to march from the Middle of Germany in order to succour Savoy. Having no Money, without which Cities cannot be either taken or defended, he addressed himself to some English Merchants. These, at an Hour and half's Warning, lent him five Millions, whereby he was enabled to deliver Turin, and to beat the French; after which he wrote the following short Letter to the Persons who had disbursed him the above mentioned Sums: 'Gentlemen, I have received your Money, and flatter myself that I have laid it out to your Satisfaction.' Such a

Circumstance as this raises a just Pride in an English Merchant, and makes him presume (not without some Reason) to compare himself to a Roman Citizen; and indeed a Peer's Brother does not think Traffic beneath him. When the Lord Townshend was Minister of State, a Brother of his was content to be a City Merchant; and at the Time that the Earl of Oxford governed Great Britain, his younger Brother was no more than a Factor in Aleppo*, where he chose to live, and where he died. This Custom, which begins however to be laid aside, appears monstrous to Germans, vainly puffed up with their Extraction. These think it morally impossible that the Son of an English Peer should be no more than a rich and powerful Citizen, for all are Princes in Germany. There have been thirty Highnesses of the same Name, all whose Patrimony consisted only in their Escutcheons* and their Pride.

In France the Title of Marquis is given *gratis* to any one who will accept it; and whosoever arrives at Paris from the midst of the most remote Provinces with Money in his Purse, and a Name terminating in *ac* or *ille*, may strut about, and cry, such a Man as I! A Man of my Rank and Figure! And may look down upon a Trader with sovereign Contempt; whilst the Trader on the other Side, by thus often hearing his Profession treated so disdainfully, is Fool enough to blush at it. However, I cannot say which is most useful to a Nation; a Lord, powdered in the tip of the Mode, who knows exactly at what a Clock the King rises and goes to bed; and who gives himself Airs of Grandeur and State, at the same Time that he is acting the Slave in the Anti-chamber of a prime Minister; or a Merchant, who enriches his Country, dispatches Orders from his Compting-House to Surat and Grand Cairo, and contributes to the Felicity of the World.

Letter XI: *On Inoculation*

It is inadvertently affirmed in the Christian Countries of Europe, that the English are Fools and Madmen. Fools, because they give their Children the Small-Pox to prevent their catching it; and Madmen, because they wantonly communicate a certain and dreadful Distemper to their Children, merely to prevent an uncertain Evil. The English, on the other Side, call the rest of the Europeans cowardly and unnatural. Cowardly, because they are afraid of putting their Children to a little Pain; unnatural, because they expose them to die one Time or other of the Small-Pox. But that the Reader may be able to judge, whether the English or those who differ from them in opinion, are in the right, here follows the History of the famed Inoculation,* which is mentioned with so much Dread in France.

The Circassian Women have, from Time immemorial, communicated the Small-Pox to their Children when not above six Months old, by making an Incision in the arm, and by putting into this Incision a Pustle, taken carefully from the Body of another Child. This Pustle produces the same Effect in the arm it is laid in, as Yest* in a Piece of Dough: It ferments, and diffuses through the whole Mass of Blood, the Qualities with which it is impregnated. The Pustles of the Child, in whom the artificial Small-Pox has been thus inoculated, are employed to communicate the same Distemper to others. There is an almost perpetual Circulation of it in Circassia; and when unhappily the Small-Pox has quite left the Country, the Inhabitants of it are in as great Trouble and Perplexity, as other Nations when their Harvest has fallen short.

The Circumstance that introduced a Custom in Circassia, which appears so singular to others, is nevertheless a Cause common to all Nations, I mean maternal Tenderness and Interest.

The Circassians are poor, and their Daughters are beautiful, and indeed 'tis in them they chiefly trade. They furnish with Beauties, the Seraglios of the Turkish Sultan, of the Persian Sophi, and of all those who are wealthy enough to purchase and maintain such precious Merchandise. These Maidens are very honourably and virtuously instructed to fondle and caress Men; are taught Dances of a very polite and effeminate kind; and how to heighten by the most voluptuous Artifices, the Pleasures of their disdainful Masters for whom they are designed. These unhappy Creatures repeat their Lesson to their Mothers, in the same manner as little Girls among us repeat their Catechism, without understanding one Word they say.

Now it often happened, that after a Father and Mother had taken the utmost Care of the Education of their Children, they were frustrated of all their Hopes in an Instant. The Small-Pox getting into the Family, one Daughter died of it, another lost an Eye, a third had a great Nose at her Recovery, and the unhappy Parents were completely ruined. Even frequently, when the Small-Pox became epidemical, Trade was suspended for several Years, which thinned very considerably the Seraglios of Persia and Turkey.

A trading Nation is always watchful over its own Interests, and grasps at every Discovery that may be of Advantage to its Commerce. The Circassians observed, that scarce one Person in a Thousand was ever attacked by a Small-Pox of a violent kind. That some indeed had this Distemper very favourably three or four Times, but never twice so as to prove fatal; in a Word, that no one ever had it in a violent Degree twice in his Life. They observed farther, that when the Small-Pox is of the milder Sort, and the Pustles have only a tender, delicate Skin to break through, they never leave the least Scar in the Face. From these natural Observations they concluded, that in case an Infant of six Months or a Year old, should have a milder Sort of Small-Pox, he would not die of it, would not be marked, nor be ever afflicted with it again.

In order therefore to preserve the Life and Beauty of their Children, the only Thing remaining was, to give them the Small-Pox in their infant Years. This they did, by inoculating in the Body of a Child, a Pustle taken from the most regular, and at the same Time the most favourable Sort of Small-Pox that could be procured.

The Experiment could not possibly fail. The Turks, who are People of good Sense, soon adopted this Custom, insomuch that at this Time there is not a Bassa* in Constantinople, but communicates the Small-Pox to his Children of both Sexes, immediately upon their being weaned.

Some pretend, that the Circassians borrowed this Custom anciently from the Arabians; but we shall leave the clearing up of this Point of History to some learned Benedictine, who will not fail to compile a great many Folios on this Subject, with the several Proofs or Authorities. All I have to say upon it, is, that in the beginning of the Reign of King George the First, the Lady Wortley Mountague,* a Woman of as fine a Genius, and endued with as great a Strength of Mind, as any of her Sex in the British Kingdoms, being with her Husband who was Ambassador at the Port, made no scruple to communicate the Small-Pox to an Infant of which she was delivered in Constantinople. The Chaplain represented to his Lady, but to no purpose, that this was an unchristian Operation, and therefore that it could succeed with none but Infidels. However, it had the most happy Effect upon the Son of the Lady Wortley Mountague, who, at her Return to England, communicated the Experiment to the Princess of Wales, now Queen of England.* It must be confessed that this Princess, abstracted from her Crown and Titles, was born to encourage the whole Circle of Arts, and to do good to Mankind. She appears as an amiable Philosopher on the Throne, having never let slip one Opportunity of improving the great Talents she received from Nature, nor of exerting her Beneficence. 'Tis she, who being informed that a Daughter of Milton* was living, but in miserable Circumstances, immediately sent her a considerable Present. 'Tis she who protects the learned Father Courayer. 'Tis she who condescended to attempt a Reconciliation between Dr Clark and Mr Leibnitz. The Moment this Princess heard of Inoculation, she caused an Experiment of it to be made on four Criminals sentenced to die, and by that means preserved their Lives doubly; for she not only saved them from the Gallows, but by means of this artificial Small-Pox, prevented their ever having that Distemper in a natural Way, with which they would very probably have been attacked one Time or other, and might have died of in a more advanced Age.

The Princess being assured of the Usefulness of this Operation, caused her own Children to be inoculated. A great Part of the Kingdom followed her Example, and since that Time ten thousand Children, at least, of Persons of Condition owe in this Manner their Lives to her Majesty, and to the Lady Wortley Mountague; and as many of the Fair Sex are obliged to them for their Beauty.*

Upon a general Calculation, threescore Persons in every hundred have the Small-Pox. Of these threescore, twenty die of it in the most favourable Season of Life, and as many more wear the disagreeable Remains of it in their Faces as long as they live. Thus, a fifth Part of Mankind either die, or are disfigured by this Distemper. But it does not prove fatal to so much as one, among those who are inoculated in Turkey or in England, unless the Patient be infirm, or would have died had not the Experiment been made upon him. Besides, no one is disfigured, no one has the Small-Pox a second Time, if the Inoculation was perfect. 'Tis therefore certain, that had the Lady of some French Ambassador brought this Secret from Constantinople to Paris, the Nation would have been for ever obliged to her. Then the Duke de Villequier, Father to the Duke d'Aumont, who enjoys the most vigorous Constitution, and is the healthiest Man in France, would not have been cut off in the Flower of his Age.

The Prince of Soubise, happy in the finest Flush of Health, would not have been snatched away at five and twenty; nor the Dauphin, Grandfather to Lewis the Fifteenth, have been laid in his Grave in his fiftieth Year.* Twenty thousand Persons whom the Small-Pox swept away at Paris in 1723, would have been alive at this Time. But are not the French fond of Life, and is Beauty so inconsiderable an Advantage as to be disregarded by the Ladies! It must be confessed that we are an odd kind of People. Perhaps our Nation will imitate, ten Years hence, this Practice of the English, if the Clergy and the Physicians will but give them Leave to do it: Or possibly our Country Men may introduce Inoculation three Months hence in France out of mere whim, in case the English should discontinue it through Fickleness.

I am informed that the Chinese have practised Inoculation these hundred Years, a Circumstance that argues very much in its Favour, since they are thought to be the wisest and best governed People in the World. The Chinese indeed don't communicate this Distemper by Inoculation, but at the Nose, in the same Manner as we take Snuff. This is a more agreeable way, but then it produces the like Effects; and proves at the same Time, that had Inoculation been practised in France, 'twould have saved the Lives of Thousands.

Letter XII: On the Lord Bacon

Not long since, the trite and frivolous Question following was debated in a very polite and learned Company, *viz* who was the greatest Man, Caesar, Alexander, Tamerlane, Cromwell, etc.

Somebody answered, that Sir Isaac Newton excelled them all. The Gentleman's Assertion was very just; for if true Greatness consists in having received from Heaven a mighty Genius, and in having employed it to enlighten our own Minds and that of others; a Man like Sir Isaac Newton, whose equal is hardly found in a thousand Years, is the truly great Man. And those Politicians and Conquerors, (and all ages produce some) were generally so many illustrious wicked Men. That Man claims our Respect, who commands over the Minds of the rest of the World by the Force of Truth, not those who enslave their Fellow Creatures; He who is acquainted with the Universe, not They who deface it.

Since therefore you desire me to give you an Account of the famous Personages which England has given birth to, I shall begin with Lord Bacon, Mr Locke, Sir Isaac Newton, etc. [. . .]

I must begin with the celebrated Viscount Verulam, known in Europe by the Name of Bacon,* which was that of his Family. His Father had been Lord Keeper, and himself was a great many Years Lord Chancellor under King James the First. Nevertheless, amidst the Intrigues of a Court, and the Affairs of his exalted Employment, which alone were enough to engross his whole Time, he yet found so much Leisure for Study, as to make himself a great Philosopher, a good Historian, and an elegant Writer; and a still more surprising Circumstance is, that he lived in an Age in which the Art of writing justly and elegantly was little known, much less true Philosophy. Lord Bacon, as is the Fate of Man, was more esteemed after his Death than in his Life-time. His Enemies were in the British Court, and his Admirers were Foreigners [. . .]

I shall therefore confine myself to those Things which so justly gained Lord Bacon the Esteem of all Europe [. . .]

He is the Father of experimental Philosophy. It must indeed be confessed, that very surprising Secrets had been found out before his Time. The Sea-Compass, Printing, engraving on Copper Plates, Oil-Painting, Looking-Glasses; the Art of restoring, in some Measure, old Men to their Sight by Spectacles; Gun-Powder, etc. had been discovered. A new World had been sought for, found, and conquered. Would not one suppose that these sublime Discoveries had been made by the greatest Philosophers, and in Ages much more enlightened than the present? But 'twas far otherwise; all these great Changes happened in the most stupid and barbarous Times. Chance only gave Birth to most of those Inventions; and 'tis very probable that what is called Chance, contributed very much to the Discovery of America; at least it has been always thought, that Christopher Columbus undertook his Voyage, merely on the Relation of a Captain of a Ship, which a Storm had drove as far Westward as the Caribee Islands. Be this as it will, Men had sailed round the World, and could destroy Cities by an artificial Thunder more dreadful than the real one: But, then they were not acquainted with the Circulation of the Blood, the Weight of the Air, the Laws of Motion, Light, the Number of our Planets, etc. And a Man who maintained a Thesis on Aristotle's Categories; on the universals *a parte rei*,* or such like Nonsense, was looked upon as a Prodigy.

The most astonishing, the most useful Inventions, are not those which reflect the greatest Honour on the human Mind. 'Tis to a mechanical Instinct, which is found in many Men, and not to true Philosophy, that most Arts owe their Origin.

The discovery of Fire, the Art of making Bread, of melting and preparing Metals, of building Houses, and the Invention of the Shuttle, are infinitely more beneficial to Mankind than Printing or the Sea-Compass: And yet these Arts were invented by uncultivated, savage Men.

What a prodigious use the Greeks and Romans made afterwards of Mechanicks! Nevertheless, they believed that there were crystal Heavens; that the Stars were small Lamps which sometimes fell into the Sea; and one of their greatest Philosophers,* after long Researches found that the Stars were so many Flints which had been detached from the Earth.

In a Word, no one, before the Lord Bacon, was acquainted with experimental Philosophy, nor with the several physical Experiments which have been made since his Time. Scarce one of them but is hinted at in his Work, and he himself had made several. He made a kind of pneumatic Engine, by which he guessed the elasticity of the Air. He approached, on all Sides as it were, to the Discovery of its Weight, and had very near attained it, but some Time after Toricelli* seized upon this Truth. In a little Time experimental Philosophy began to be cultivated on a sudden in most Parts of Europe. 'Twas a hidden Treasure which the Lord Bacon had some Notion of, and which all the Philosophers, encouraged by his Promises, endeavoured to dig up.

But that which surprised me most was to read in his Work, in express Terms, the new Attraction, the Invention of which is ascribed to Sir Isaac Newton.

We must search, says Lord Bacon, whether there may not be a kind of magnetic Power, which operates between the Earth and heavy Bodies, between the Moon and the Ocean, between the Planets, etc. In another Place he says, either heavy Bodies must be carried towards the Centre of the Earth, or must be reciprocally attracted by it; and in the latter Case 'tis evident, that the nearer Bodies, in their falling, draw towards the Earth, the stronger they will attract one another. We must, says he, make an Experiment to see whether the same Clock will go faster on the Top of a Mountain or at the Bottom of a Mine. Whether the Strength of the Weights decreases on the Mountain, and increases in the Mine. 'Tis probable that the Earth has a true attractive Power.

This Fore-runner in Philosophy was also an elegant Writer, an Historian and a Wit.

His moral *Essays** are greatly esteemed, but they were drawn up in the View of instructing rather than of pleasing: And as they are not a Satyr upon Mankind, like Rochefoucaults's Maxims, nor written upon a sceptical Plan, like Montaigne's *Essays*, they are not so much read as those two ingenious Authors [. . .]

Letter XIII: *On Mr Locke*

Perhaps no Man ever had a more judicious or more methodical Genius, or was a more acute Logician than Mr Locke,* and yet he was not deeply skilled in the Mathematicks. This great Man could never subject himself to the tedious Fatigue of Calculations, nor to the dry Pursuit of Mathematical Truths, which do not at first present any sensible Objects to the Mind; and no one has given better Proofs than he, that 'tis possible for a Man to have a geometrical Head without the Assistance of Geometry. Before his Time, several great Philosophers had declared, in the most positive Terms, what the Soul of Man is; but as these absolutely knew nothing about it, they might very well be allowed to differ entirely in opinion from one another [. . .]

Such a Multitude of Reasoners having written the Romance

of the Soul, a Sage at last arose, who gave, with an Air of the greatest Modesty, the History of it. Mr Locke has displayed the human Soul, in the same Manner as an excellent Anatomist explains the Springs of the human Body. He everywhere takes the Light of Physicks for his Guide. He sometimes presumes to speak affirmatively, but then he presumes also to doubt. Instead of concluding at once what we know not, he examines gradually what we would know. He takes an Infant at the Instant of his Birth; he traces, Step by Step, the Progress of his Understanding; examines what Things he has in common with Beasts, and what he possesses above them. Above all he consults himself; the being conscious that he himself thinks.

I shall leave,* says he, to those who know more of this Matter than my self, the examining whether the Soul exists before or after the Organisation of our Bodies. But I confess that 'tis my Lot to be animated with one of those heavy Souls which do not think always; and I am even so unhappy as not to conceive, that 'tis more necessary the Soul should think perpetually, than that Bodies should be for ever in Motion.

With regard to my self, I shall boast that I have the Honour to be as stupid in this Particular as Mr Locke. No one shall ever make me believe, that I think always; and I am as little inclined as he could be, to fancy that some Weeks after I was conceived, I was a very learned Soul; knowing at that Time a thousand Things which I forgot at my Birth; and possessing when in the Womb, (though to no Manner of Purpose), Knowledge which I lost the Instant I had occasion for it; and which I have never since been able to recover perfectly.

Mr Locke after having destroyed innate Ideas; after having fully renounced the Vanity of believing that we think always; after having laid down, from the most solid Principles, that Ideas enter the Mind through the Senses; having examined our simple and complex Ideas; having traced the human Mind through its several Operations; having showed that all the Languages in the World are imperfect, and the great Abuse that is made of Words every Moment; he at last comes to consider the Extent or rather the narrow Limits of human Knowledge. 'Twas in this Chapter he presumed to advance, but very modestly, the following Words, 'We shall, perhaps, never be capable of knowing, whether a Being, purely material, thinks or not.'* This sage Assertion was, by more Divines than one, looked upon as a scandalous Declaration that the Soul is material and mortal. Some Englishmen, devout after their Way, sounded an Alarm. The Superstitious are the same in Society as Cowards in an Army; they themselves are seized with a panic Fear, and communicate it to others. 'Twas loudly exclaimed, that Mr Locke intended to destroy Religion; nevertheless, Religion had nothing to do in the Affair, it being a Question purely Philosophical, altogether independent of Faith and Revelation. Mr Locke's Opponents needed but to examine, calmly and impartially, whether the declaring that Matter can think, implies a Contradiction; and whether God is able to communicate Thought to Matter. But Divines are too apt to begin their Declarations with saying, that God is offended when People differ from them in Opinion; in which they too much resemble the bad Poets, who used to declare publickly that Boileau spake irreverently of Lewis the Fourteenth, because he ridiculed their stupid Productions. Bishop Stillingfleet* got the Reputation of a calm and unprejudiced Divine, because he did not expressly make use of injurious Terms in his Dispute with Mr Locke. That Divine entered the Lists against him, but was defeated; for he argued as a Schoolman, and Locke as a Philosopher, who was perfectly acquainted with the strong as well as the weak Side of the human Mind, and who fought with Weapons whose Temper he knew. If I might presume to give my Opinion on so delicate a Subject after Mr Locke, I would say, that Men have long disputed on the Nature and the Immortality of the Soul. With regard to its Immortality, 'tis impossible to give a Demonstration of it, since its Nature is still the Subject of Controversy; which however must be thoroughly understood, before a Person can be able to determine whether it be immortal or not. Human reason is so little able, merely by its own Strength, to demonstrate the Immortality of the Soul, that 'twas absolutely necessary Religion should reveal it to us. 'Tis of Advantage to Society in general, that Mankind should believe the Soul to be immortal; Faith commands us to do this; nothing more is required, and the Matter is cleared up at once. But 'tis otherwise with respect to its Nature; 'tis of little Importance to Religion, which only requires the Soul to be virtuous, what Substance it may be made of. 'Tis a Clock which is given us to regulate, but the Artist has not told us what Materials the Spring of this Clock is composed.*

I am a Body and, I think, that's all I know of the Matter. Shall I ascribe to an unknown Cause, I can so easily impute to the only second Cause I am acquainted with? Here all the School Philosophers interrupt me with their Arguments, and declare that there is only Extension and Solidity in Bodies, and that there they can have nothing but Motion and Figure. Now Motion, Figure, Extension and Solidity cannot form a Thought, and consequently the Soul cannot be Matter. All this, so often repeated, mighty Series of Reasoning, amounts to no more than this; I am absolutely ignorant what Matter is; I guess but imperfectly, some Properties of it; now, I absolutely cannot tell whether these Properties may be joyned to Thought. As I therefore know nothing, I maintain positively that Matter cannot think. In this Manner do the Schools reason.

Mr Locke addressed these Gentlemen in the candid, sincere Manner following. At least confess your selves to be as ignorant as I. Neither your Imaginations nor mine are able to comprehend in what manner a Body is susceptible of Ideas; and do you conceive better in what manner a Substance, of what kind soever, is susceptible of them? As you cannot comprehend either Matter or Spirit, why will you presume to assert any thing?

The superstitious Man comes afterwards, and declares, that all those must be burnt for the Good of their Souls, who so much as suspect that 'tis possible for the Body to think without any foreign Assistance. But what would these People say should they themselves be proved irreligious? And indeed, what Man can presume to assert, without being guilty at the same time of the greatest Impiety, that 'tis impossible for the Creator to form Matter with Thought and Sensation? Consider only, I beg you, what a Dilemma you bring yourselves into; you who confine in this Manner the Power of the Creator. Beasts have the same Organs, the same Sensations, the same Perceptions as we; they have Memory, and combine certain Ideas. In case it was not in the Power of God to animate Matter, and inform it with Sensation, the Consequence would be, either that Beasts are mere Machines, or that they have a spiritual Soul.

Methinks 'tis clearly evident that Beasts cannot be mere Machines, which I prove thus. God has given them the very same Organs of Sensation as to us: If therefore they have no Sensation, God has created a useless Thing; now according to your own Confession God does nothing in vain; he therefore did not create so many Organs of Sensation, merely for them to be uninformed with this Faculty; consequently Beasts are not mere Machines. Beasts, according to your Assertion, cannot be animated with a spiritual Soul; you will therefore, in spite of your self, be reduced to this only Assertion, *viz* that God has endued the Organs of Beasts, who are mere Matter, with the Faculties of Sensation and Perception, which you call Instinct in them. But why may not God if he pleases, communicate to our more delicate Organs, that Faculty of feeling, perceiving, and thinking, which we call human Reason? To whatever Side you turn, you are forced to acknowledge your own Ignorance, and the boundless Power of the Creator. Exclaim therefore no more against the sage, the modest Philosophy of Mr Locke, which so far from interfering with Religion, would be of use to demonstrate the Truth of it, in case Religion wanted any such Support. For what Philosophy can be of a more religious Nature than that, which affirming nothing but what it conceives clearly; and conscious of its own Weakness, declares that we must always have recourse to God in our examining of the first Principles.

Besides, we must not be apprehensive, that any philosophical Opinion will ever prejudice the Religion of a Country. Though our Demonstrations clash directly with our Mysteries, that's nothing to the Purpose, for the latter are not less revered upon that Account by our Christian Philosophers, who know very well that the Objects of Reason and those of Faith are of a very different Nature. Philosophers will never form a religious Sect, the Reason of which is, their Writings are not calculated for the Vulgar, and they themselves are free from Enthusiasm. If we divide Mankind* into twenty Parts, 'twill be found that nineteen of these consist of Persons employed in manual Labour, who will never know that such a Man as Mr Locke existed. In the remaining twentieth Part how few are Readers? And among such as are so, twenty amuse themselves with Romances to one who studies Philosophy. The thinking Part of Mankind are confined to a very small Number, and these will never disturb the Peace and Tranquillity of the World.

Neither Montaigne, Locke, Bayle, Spinoza, Hobbes, the Lord

Shaftesbury, Collins nor Toland lighted up the Firebrand of Discord in their Countries;* this has generally been the Work of Divines, who being at first puffed up with the Ambition of becoming Chiefs of a Sect, soon grew very desirous of being at the Head of a Party. But what do I say? All the Works of the modern Philosophers put together will never make so much Noise as even the Dispute which arose among the Franciscans, merely about the Fashion of their Sleeves and of their Cowls.

Letter XIV: On Descartes and Sir Isaac Newton*

A Frenchman who arrives in London, will find Philosophy, like every Thing else, very much changed there. He had left the World a plenum, and he now finds it a vacuum.* At Paris the Universe is seen, composed of Vortices of subtile Matter; but nothing like it is seen in London. In France, 'tis the Pressure of the Moon that causes the Tides; but in England 'tis the Sea that gravitates towards the Moon; so that when you think that the Moon should make it Flood with us, those Gentlemen fancy it should Ebb, which, very unluckily, cannot be proved. For to be able to do this, 'tis necessary the Moon and the Tides should have been enquired into, at the very instant of the Creation.

You'll observe farther, that the Sun, which in France is said to have nothing to do in the Affair, comes in here for very near a quarter of its Assistance. According to your Cartesians, every Thing is performed by an Impulsion, of which we have very little Notion; and according to Sir Isaac Newton, 'tis by an Attraction, the Cause of which is as much unknown to us. At Paris you imagine that the Earth is shaped like a Melon, or of an oblique Figure; at London it has an oblate one. A Cartesian declares that Light exists in the Air; but a Newtonian asserts that it comes from the Sun in six Minutes and a half. The several Operations of your Chemistry are performed by Acids, Alkalies and subtile Matter; but Attraction prevails even in Chemistry among the English.

The very Essence of Things is totally changed. You neither are agreed upon the Definition of the Soul, nor on that of Matter. Descartes, as I observed in my last, maintains that the Soul is the same Thing with Thought, and Mr Locke has given a pretty good Proof of the contrary.

Descartes asserts farther, that Extension alone constitutes Matter, but Sir Isaac adds Solidity to it.

How furiously contradictory are these Opinions!

Non nostrum inter vos tantas componere lites.

Virgil, *Eclog.* III

'Tis not for us to end such great Disputes.

This famous Newton, this Destroyer* of the Cartesian System, died in March *Anno* 1727. His Countrymen honoured him in his Life-Time, and interred him* as though he had been a King who had made his People happy [. . .]

'Twas his peculiar Felicity, not only to be born in a Country of Liberty, but in an Age when all scholastic Impertinencies were banished from the World. Reason alone was cultivated, and Mankind could only be his Pupil, not his Enemy.

One very singular Difference in the Lives of these two great Men is, that Sir Isaac, during the long Course of Years he enjoyed, was never sensible to any Passion, was not subject to the common Frailties of Mankind, nor ever had any Commerce with Women; a Circumstance which was assured me by the Physician and Surgeon who attended him in his last Moments.

We may admire Sir Isaac Newton on this Occasion, but then we must not censure Descartes.

The Opinion that generally prevails in England with regard to these two Philosophers is, that the latter was a Dreamer, and the former a Sage.

Very few People in England read Descartes, whose Works indeed are now useless. On the other Side, but a small Number peruse those of Sir Isaac, because to do this the Student must be deeply skilled in the Mathematicks, otherwise those Works will be unintelligible to him. But notwithstanding this, these great Men are the Subject of every One's Discourse. Sir Isaac Newton is allowed every Advantage, whilst Descartes is not indulged a single one. According to some, 'tis to the former that we owe the Discovery of a Vacuum, that the Air is a heavy Body, and the Invention of Telescopes. In a Word, Sir Isaac Newton is here as the Hercules of fabulous Story, to whom the Ignorant ascribed all the Feats of ancient Heroes [. . .]

Letter XV: On Attraction

[... Newton] despaired* of ever being able to discover, whether there is a secret Principle in Nature which, at the same Time, is the Cause of the Motion of all celestial Bodies, and that of Gravity on the Earth. But being retired in 1666, upon Account of the Plague, to a Solitude near Cambridge; as he was walking one Day in his Garden, and saw some Fruits fall from a Tree, he fell into a profound Meditation on that Gravity, the Cause of which had so long been sought, but in vain, by all the Philosophers, whilst the Vulgar think there is nothing mysterious in it. He said to himself, that from what height soever, in our Hemisphere, those Bodies might descend, their Fall would certainly be in the Progression discovered by Galileo;* and the Spaces they run through would be as the Square of the Times. Why may not this Power which causes heavy Bodies to descend, and is the same without any sensible Diminution at the remotest Distance from the Centre of the Earth, or on the Summits of the highest Mountains; Why, said Sir Isaac, may not this Power extend as high as the Moon? And in Case, its Influence reaches so far, is it not very probable that this Power retains it in its Orbit, and determines its Motion? But in case the Moon obeys this Principle (whatever it be) may we not conclude very naturally, that the rest of the Planets are equally subject to it? In case this Power exists (which besides is proved) it must increase in an inverse Ratio of the Squares of the Distances. All therefore that remains is, to examine how far a heavy Body, which should fall upon the Earth from a moderate height, would go; and how far in the same time, a Body which should fall from the Orbit of the Moon, would descend. To find this, nothing is wanted but the Measure of the Earth, and the Distance of the Moon from it.

Thus Sir Isaac Newton reasoned [...]

Letter XVIII: On Tragedy

The English as well as the Spaniards were possessed of Theatres, at a Time when the French had no more than moving, itinerant Stages. Shakespear,* who was considered as the Corneille* of the first mentioned Nation, was pretty near Cotemporary with

Lopez de Vega,* and he created, as it were, the English Theatre. Shakespear boasted a strong, fruitful Genius: He was natural and sublime, but had not so much as a single Spark of good Taste, or knew one Rule of the Drama. I will now hazard a random, but, at the same Time, true Reflection, which is, that the great Merit of this Dramatic Poet has been the Ruin of the English Stage. There are such beautiful, such noble, such dreadful Scenes in this Writer's monstrous Farces, to which the Name of Tragedy is given, that they have always been exhibited with great Success. Time, which only gives Reputation to Writers, at last makes their very Faults venerable. Most of the whimsical, gigantic Images of this Poet, have, through Length of Time (it being an hundred and fifty Years since they were first drawn) acquired a Right of passing for sublime. Most of the modern dramatic Writers have copied him; but the Touches and Descriptions which are applauded in Shakespear, are hissed at in these Writers; and you'll easily believe that the Veneration in which this Author is held, increases in Proportion to the Contempt which is shown to the Moderns. Dramatic Writers don't consider that they should not imitate him; and the ill Success of Shakespear's Imitators, produces no other Effect, than to make him be considered as inimitable. You remember that in the Tragedy of *Othello* Moor of Venice, (a most tender Piece) a Man strangles his Wife on the Stage; and that the poor Woman, whilst she is strangling, cries aloud, that she dies very unjustly. You know that in *Hamlet* Prince of Denmark, two Grave-Diggers made a Grave, and are all the Time drinking, singing Ballads, and making humourous Reflexions, (natural indeed enough to Persons of their Profession) on the several Skulls they throw up with their Spades; but a Circumstance which will surprise you is, that this ridiculous Incident has been imitated. In the Reign of King Charles the Second, which was that of Politeness, and the Golden Age of the Liberal Arts; Otway,* in his *Venice Preserved*, introduces Antonio the Senator, and Naki his Curtezan, in the Midst of the Horrors of the Marquis of Bedemar's Conspiracy. Antonio, the superannuated Senator plays, in his Mistress's Presence, all the apish Tricks of a lewd, impotent Debauchee who is quite frantic and out of his Senses. He mimicks a Bull and a Dog; and bites his Mistress's Leg, who kicks and whips him. However, the Players have struck these

Buffooneries (which indeed were calculated merely for the Dregs of the People) out of Otway's Tragedy; but they have still left in Shakespear's *Julius Cæsar*, the Jokes of the Roman Shoemakers and Cobblers, who are introduced in the same Scene with Brutus and Cassius. You will undoubtedly complain that those who have hitherto discoursed with you on the English Stage, and especially on the celebrated Shakespear, have taken Notice only of his Errors; and that no one has translated any of those strong, those forcible Passages which atone for all his Faults. But to this I will answer, that nothing is easier than to exhibit in Prose all the silly Impertinencies which a Poet may have thrown out; but that 'tis a very difficult Task to translate his fine Verses. All your junior academical Sophs,* who set up for Censors of the eminent Writers, compile whole Volumes; but methinks two Pages which display some of the Beauties of great Geniuses, are of infinitely more Value than all the idle Rhapsodies of those Commentators; and I will join in Opinion with all Persons of good Taste in declaring, that greater Advantage may be reaped from a Dozen Verses of Homer or Virgil, than from all the Critiques put together which have been made on those two great Poets.

I have ventured to translate some Passages of the most celebrated English Poets, and shall now give you one from Shakespear. Pardon the Blemishes of the Translation for the Sake of the Original; and remember always that when you see a Version, you see merely a faint Print of a beautiful Picture. I have made Choice of Part of the celebrated Soliloquy in *Hamlet*, which you may remember is as follows.

> *To be, or not to be! that is the Question!*
> *Whether 'tis nobler in the Mind to suffer*
> *The Slings and Arrows of outrageous Fortune,*
> *Or to take Arms against a Sea of Troubles,*
> *And by opposing, end them? To dye! to sleep!*
> *No more! and by a Sleep to say we end*
> *The Heart-ach, and the thousand natural Shocks*
> *That Flesh is Heir to! 'Tis a Consummation*
> *Devoutly to be wish'd. To die! to sleep!*
> *To sleep, perchance to dream! Ay, there's the Rub;*
> *For in that Sleep of Death, what Dreams may come*
> *When we have shuffled off this mortal Coyle,*

> *Must give us Pause. There's the respect*
> *That makes Calamity of so long Life:*
> *For who wou'd bear the Whips and Scorns of Time*
> *Th' Oppressor's Wrong, the poor Man's contumely,*
> *The Pangs of despis'd Love, the Laws Delay,*
> *The Insolence of Office, and the Spurns*
> *That patient Merit of th' unworthy takes,*
> *When by himself might his Quietus make*
> *With a bare Bodkin? Who would these Fardles bear*
> *To groan and sweat under a weary Life,*
> *But that the Dread of something after Death,*
> *The undiscover'd Country, from whose Bourn*
> *No traveller returns, puzzles the Will,*
> *And makes us rather bear those Ills we have,*
> *Than fly to others that we know not of?*
> *Thus Conscience does make Cowards of us all;*
> *And thus the native Hue of Resolution*
> *Is sicklied o'er with the pale Cast of Thought;*
> *And Enterprizes of great Weight and Moment*
> *With this Regard their Currents turn away,*
> *And lose the Name of Action——*

My Version of it runs thus:

> *Demeure, il faut choisir & passer à l'instant*
> *De la vie, à la mort, ou de l'Etre au neant.*
> *Dieux cruels, s'il en est, éclairez mon courage.*
> *Faut-il vieillir courbé sous la main qui m'outrage,*
> *Supporter, ou finir mon malheur & mon sort?*
> *Qui suis je? Qui m'arrete! & qu'est ce que la Mort?*
> *C'est la fin de nos maux, c'est mon unique Azile*
> *Après de long transports, c'est un sommeil tranquile.*
> *On s'endort, & tout meurt, mais un affreux reveil*
> *Doit succeder peut etre aux douceurs du sommeil!*
> *On nous menace, on dit que cette courte Vie,*
> *De tourmens éternels est aussi-tôt-suivie.*
> *O Mort! moment fatal! affreuse Eternité!*
> *Tout cœur à ton seul nom se glace épouvanté.*
> *Eh! qui pourroit sans Toi supporter cette vie,*
> *De nos Prêtres menteurs benir l'hypocrisie;**
> *D'une indigne Maitresse encenser les erreurs,*

Ramper sous un Ministre, adorer ses hauteurs;
Et montrer les langueurs de son âme abattue,
A des Amis ingrats qui detournent la vue?
La Mort seroit trop douce en ces extrémitez,
Mais le scrupule parle, & nous crie, Arrêtez;
Il defend à nos mains cet heureux homicide
Et d'un Heros guerrier, fait un Chrétien timide, &c.

Don't imagine that I have translated Shakespear in a servile Manner. Woe to the Writer who gives a literal Verison; who by rendering every Word of his Original, by that very means enervates the Sense, and extinguishes all the Fire of it. 'Tis on such an Occasion one may justly affirm, that the Letter kills, but the Spirit quickens [. . .]

'Tis in these detached Passages that the English have hitherto excelled. Their dramatic Pieces, most of which are barbarous and without Decorum, Order or Verisimilitude, dart such resplendent Flashes, through this Gloom, as amaze and astonish. The Style is too much inflated, too unnatural, too closely copied from the Hebrew Writers, who abound so much with the Asiatic Fustian.* But then it must be also confessed, that the Stilts of the figurative Style on which the English Tongue is lifted up, raises the Genius at the same Time very far aloft, though with an irregular Pace. The first English Writer who composed a regular Tragedy and infused a Spirit of Elegance through every Part of it, was the illustrious Mr Addison. His *Cato** is a Masterpiece both with regard to the Diction, and to the Beauty and Harmony of the Numbers. The Character of Cato is, in my Opinion, vastly superior to that of Cornelia in the *Pompey* of Corneille: For Cato is great without any Thing like Fustian, and Cornelia, who besides is not a necessary Character, tends sometimes to bombast. Mr Addison's Cato appears to me the greatest Character that was ever brought upon any Stage, but then the rest of them don't correspond to the Dignity of it: And this dramatic Piece so excellently well writ, is disfigured by a dull Love-Plot, which spreads a certain Languor over the whole, that quite murders it.

The Custom of introducing Love at random and at any rate in the Drama, passed from Paris to London about 1660, with our Ribbons and our Perruques. The Ladies who adorn the Theatrical Circle, there, in like Manner as in this City, will suffer Love only to be the Theme of every Conversation. The judicious Mr Addison had the effeminate Complaisance to soften the Severity of his dramatic Character so as to adapt it to the Manners of the Age; and from an Endeavour to please, quite ruined a Masterpiece in its kind. Since his Time, the Drama is become more regular, the Audience more difficult to be pleased, and Writers more correct and less bold. I have seen some new Pieces that were written with great Regularity, but which at the same Time were very flat and insipid. One would think that the English had been hitherto formed to produce irregular Beauties only. The shining Monsters of Shakespear, give infinite more Delight than the judicious Images of the Moderns. Hitherto the poetical Genius of the English resembles a tufted Tree planted by the Hand of Nature, that throws out a thousand Branches at random, and spreads unequally, but with great Vigour. It dies if you attempt to force its Nature, and to lop and dress it in the same Manner as the Trees of the Garden of Marli.*

Letter XIX: On Comedy

I am surprised that the judicious and ingenious Mr de Muralt, who has published some Letters on the English and French Nations, should have confined himself, in treating of Comedy, merely to censure Shadwell* the comic Writer. This Author was had in pretty Contempt in Mr de Muralt's Time, and was not the Poet of the polite Part of the Nation. His dramatic Pieces which pleased some Time in acting, were despised by all Persons of Taste and might be compared to many Plays which I have seen in France, that drew Crowds to the Playhouse, at the same Time that they were intolerable to read; and of which it might be said, that the whole City of Paris exploded them, and yet all flocked to see 'em represented on the Stage. Methinks Mr de Muralt should have mentioned an excellent comic Writer (living when he was in England) I mean Mr Wycherley,* who was a long Time known publickly to be happy in the good Graces of the most celebrated Mistress of King Charles the Second. This Gentleman who passed his Life among Persons of the highest

Distinction, was perfectly well acquainted with their Lives and their Follies, and painted them with the strongest Pencil, and in the truest Colours. He has drawn a Misantrope or Man-hater, in Imitation of that of Molière. All Wycherley's Strokes are stronger and bolder than those of our Misantrope, but then they are less delicate, and the Rules of Decorum are not so well observed in this Play. The English Writer has corrected the only Defect that is in Molière's Comedy, the Thinness of the Plot, which also is so disposed that the Characters in it do not enough raise our Concern. The English Comedy affects us, and the Contrivance of the Plot is very ingenious, but at the same Time 'tis too bold for the French Manners. The Fable is this.— A Captain of a Man of War, who is very brave, open-hearted, and enflamed with a Spirit of Contempt for all Mankind, has a prudent, sincere Friend whom he yet is suspicious of, and a Mistress that loves him with the utmost Excess of Passion. The Captain so far from returning her Love, will not even conde- scend to look upon her; but confides entirely in a false Friend, who is the most worthless Wretch living. At the same Time he has given his Heart to a Creature who is the greatest Coquet, and the most perfidious of her Sex, and is so credulous as to be confident she is a Penelope, and his false Friend a Cato. He embarks on board his Ship in order to go and fight the Dutch, having left all his Money, his Jewels and every Thing he had in the World to this virtuous Creature, whom at the same Time he recommends to the Care of his supposed faithful Friend. Never- theless the real Man of Honour whom he suspects so unaccount- ably, goes on board the Ship with him; and the Mistress on whom he would not bestow so much as one Glance, disguises herself in the Habit of a Page, and is with him the whole Voyage, without his once knowing that she is of a Sex different from that she attempts to pass for, which, by the Way, is not over natural.

The Captain having blown up his own Ship in an Engagement, returns to England abandoned and undone, accompanied by his Page and his Friend, without knowing the Friendship of the one, or the tender Passion of the other. Immediately he goes to the Jewel among Women, who he expected had preserved her Fidelity to him, and the Treasure he had left in her Hands. He meets with her indeed, but married to the honest Knave in whom he had reposed so much Confidence; and finds she had acted as treacherously with regard to the Casket he had entrusted her with. The Captain can scarce think it possible, that a Woman of Virtue and Honour can act so vile a Part; but to convince him still more of the Reality of it, this very worthy Lady falls in Love with the little Page, and will force him to her Embraces. But as it is requisite Justice should be done, and that in a dramatick Piece Virtue ought to be rewarded and Vice punished; 'tis at last found that the Captain takes his Page's Place, and lyes with his faithless Mistress, cuckolds his treacherous Friend, thrusts his Sword through his Body, recovers his Casket and marries his Page. You'll observe that this Play is also larded with a petulant, litigious old Woman (a Relation of the Captain) who is the most comical Character that was ever brought upon the Stage.

Wycherley has also copied from Molière another Play, of as singular and bold a Cast, which is a kind of *École des Femmes*, or, *School for married Women*.

The principal Character in this Comedy is one Horner, a sly Fortune-Hunter, and the Terror of all the City Husbands. This Fellow in order to play a surer Game, causes a Report to be spread, that in his last Illness, the Surgeons had found it necessary to have him made an Eunuch. Upon his appearing in this noble Character, all the Husbands in Town flock to him with their Wives, and now poor Horner is only puzzled about his Choice. However, he gives the Preference particularly to a little female Peasant; a very harmless, innocent Creature, who enjoys a fine Flush of Health, and cuckolds her Husband with a Simplicity that has infinitely more Merit than the witty Malice of the most experienced Ladies. This Play cannot indeed be called the School of good Morals, but 'tis certainly the School of Wit and true Humour.

Sir John Vanbrugh* has writ several Comedies which are more humourous than those of Mr Wycherley, but not so ingenious. Sir John was a Man of Pleasure, and likewise a Poet and an Architect. The general Opinion is, that he is as sprightly in his Writings as he is heavy in his Buildings. 'Tis he who raised the famous Castle of Blenheim, a ponderous and lasting Monument of our unfortunate Battle of Hockstet. Were the Apartments but as spacious as the Walls are thick, this Castle would be commodious enough. Some Wag, in an Epitaph he made on Sir John Vanbrugh, has these Lines:

> Earth lye light on him, for he
> Laid many a heavy Load on thee.

Sir John having taken a Tour into France before the glorious War that broke out in 1701, was thrown into the Bastile, and detained there for some Time, without being ever able to discover the Motive which had prompted our Ministry to indulge him this Mark of their Distinction. He writ a Comedy during his Confinement; and a Circumstance which appears to me very extraordinary is, that we don't meet with so much as a single satyrical Stroke against the Country in which he had been so injuriously treated.

The late Mr Congreve* raised the Glory of Comedy to a greater Height than any English Writer before or since his Time. He wrote only a few Plays, but they are all excellent in their kind. The Laws of the Drama are strictly observed in them; they abound with Characters all which are shadowed with the utmost Delicacy, and we don't meet with so much as one low, or coarse Jest. The Language is everywhere that of Men of Honour, but their Actions are those of Knaves; a Proof that he was perfectly well acquainted with human Nature, and frequented what we call polite Company. He was infirm, and come to the Verge of Life when I knew him. Mr Congreve had one Defect, which was, his entertaining too mean an Idea of his first Profession, (that of Writer) though 'twas to this he owed his Fame and Fortune. He spoke of his Works as of Trifles that were beneath him; and hinted to me in our first Conversation, that I should visit him upon no other Foot than that of a Gentleman, who led a Life of Plainness and Simplicity. I answered, that had he been so unfortunate as to be a mere Gentleman I should never have come to see him; and I was very much disgusted at so unseasonable a Piece of Vanity.

Mr Congreve's Comedies are the most witty and regular, those of Sir John Vanbrugh most gay and humourous, and those of Mr Wycherley have the greatest Force and Spirit. It may be proper to observe, that these fine Geniuses never spoke disadvantageously of Molière; and that none but the contemptible Writers among the English have endeavoured to lessen the

Character of that great comic Poet. Such Italian Musicians as despise Lully* are themselves Persons of no Character or Ability; but a Buononcini* esteems that great Artist, and does Justice to his Merit.

The English have some other good comic Writers living, such as Sir Richard Steele,* and Mr Cibber,* who is an excellent Player, and also Poet Laureat, a Title which how ridiculous soever it may be thought, is yet worth a thousand Crowns a Year, (besides some considerable Privileges) to the Person who enjoys it. Our illustrious Corneille had not so much.

To conclude. Don't desire me to descend to Particulars with regard to these English Comedies, which I am so fond of applauding; nor to give you a single smart Saying, or humourous Stroke from Wycherley or Congreve. We don't laugh in reading a Translation. If you have a Mind to understand the English Comedy, the only way to do this will be for you to go to England, to spend three Years in London, to make your self Master of the English Tongue, and to frequent the Playhouse every Night. I receive but little Pleasure from the Perusal of Aristophanes and Plautus, and for this Reason, because I am neither a Greek nor a Roman. The Delicacy of the Humour, the Allusion, the *à propos*, all these are lost to a Foreigner.

But 'tis different with respect to Tragedy, this treating only of exalted Passions and heroical Follies, which the antiquated Errors of Fable or History have made sacred. Oedipus, Electra and such like Characters, may with as much Propriety, be treated of by the Spaniards, the English, or Us, as by the Greeks. But true Comedy is the speaking Picture of the Follies and ridiculous Foibles of a Nation; so that he only is able to judge of the Painting, who is perfectly acquainted with the People it represents.

Letter XXII: *On Mr Pope, and some other Famous Poets*

I intended to treat of Mr Prior,* one of the most amiable English Poets, whom you saw Plenipotentiary and Envoy Extraordinary at Paris in 1712. I also designed to have given you some Idea of the Lord Roscommon's* and the Lord Dorset's* Muse; but I find that to do this I should be obliged to write a large Volume, and that after much Pains and Trouble you would have but an imperfect Idea of all those Works. Poetry is a kind of Music, in which a Man should have some Knowledge before he pretends to judge of it. When I gave you a Translation of some Passages from those foreign Poets, I only prick down,* and that imperfectly, their Music; but then I cannot express the Taste of their Harmony.

There is one English Poem especially which I should despair of ever making you understand, the Title whereof is *Hudibras*.* The Subject of it is the Civil War in the Time of the Grand Rebellion; and the Principles and Practice of the Puritans are therein ridiculed [...] I never found so much Wit in one single Book as in that, which at the same Time is the most difficult to be translated. Who would believe that a Work which paints in such lively and natural Colours the several Foibles and Follies of Mankind, and where we meet with more Sentiments than Words, should baffle the Endeavours of the ablest Translator? But the Reason of this is; almost every Part of it alludes to particular Incidents. The Clergy are there made the principal Object of Ridicule, which is understood but by few among the Laity. To explain this a Commentary would be requisite, and Humour when explained is no longer Humour. Whoever sets up for a Commentator of smart Sayings and Repartees, is himself a Blockhead. This is the reason why the Works of the ingenious Dean Swift,* who has been called the English Rabelais, will never be well understood in France. This Gentleman has the Honour (in common with Rabelais) of being a Priest, and like him laughs at every Thing. But in my humble Opinion, the Title of the English Rabelais which is given the Dean, is highly derogatory to his Genius. The former has interspersed his unaccountably-fantastic and unintelligible Book, with the most gay Strokes of Humour, but which at the same Time has a greater Proportion of Impertinence. He has been vastly lavish of Erudition, of Smut, and insipid Raillery. An agreeable Tale of two Pages is purchased at the Expense of whole Volumes of Nonsense. There are but few Persons, and those of a grotesque Taste, who pretend to understand, and to esteem this Work; for as to the rest of the Nation, they laugh at the pleasant and diverting Touches which are found in Rabelais and despise his Book. He is looked upon as the Prince of Buffoons. The Readers are vexed to think that a Man who was Master of so much Wit should have made so wretched a Use of it. He is an intoxicated Philosopher, who never writ but when he was in Liquor.

Dean Swift is Rabelais in his Senses, and frequenting the politest Company. The former indeed is not so gay as the latter, but then he possesses all the Delicacy, the Justness, the Choice, the good Taste, in all which Particulars our giggling rural Vicar Rabelais is wanting. The poetical Numbers of Dean Swift are of a singular and almost inimitable Taste; true Humour whether in Prose or Verse, seems to be his peculiar Talent, but whoever is desirous of understanding him perfectly, must visit the Island* in which he was born.

'Twill be much easier for you to form an Idea of Mr Pope's Works. He is in my Opinion the most elegant, the most correct Poet; and at the same Time the most harmonious (a Circumstance which redounds very much to the Honour of this Muse) that England ever gave Birth to. He has mellowed the harsh Sounds of the English Trumpet to the soft Accents of the Flute. His Compositions may be easily translated, because they are vastly clear and perspicuous; besides, most of his Subjects are general, and relative to all Nations*[. . .]

Methinks I now have given you Specimens enough* from the English Poets. I have made some transient mention of their Philosophers, but as for good Historians among them, I don't know of any; and indeed a French Man was forced to write their History.* Possibly the English Genius, which is either languid or impetuous, has not yet acquired that unaffected Eloquence, that plain but majestic Air which History requires. Possibly too, the Spirit of Party which exhibits Objects in a dim and confused Light, may have sunk the Credit of their Historians. One half of the Nation is always at Variance with the other half. I have met with People who assured me that the Duke of Marlborough was a Coward, and that Mr Pope was a Fool; just as some Jesuits in France declare Pascal to have been a Man of little or no Genius; and some Jansenists affirm Father Bourdaloüe to have been a mere Babbler. The Jacobites consider Mary Queen of Scots as a pious Heroine, but those of an opposite Party look upon her as a Prostitute, an Adulteress, a Murtherer. Thus the English have Memorials of the several Reigns, but no such Thing as a History. There is indeed now living, one Mr Gordon, (the Publick are obliged to him for a

Translation of Tacitus) who is very capable of writing the History of his own Country, but Rapin de Thoyras got the Start of him. To conclude, in my Opinion, the English have not such good Historians as the French, have no such Thing as a real Tragedy, have several delightful Comedies, some wonderful Passages in certain of their Poems, and boast of Philosophers that are worthy of instructing Mankind. The English have reaped very great Benefit from the Writers of our Nation, and therefore we ought, (since they have not scrupled to be in our Debt) to borrow from them. Both the English and we came after the Italians, who have been our Instructors in all the Arts, and whom we have surpassed in some. I cannot determine which of the three Nations ought to be honoured with the Palm; but happy the Writer who could display their various Merits.

Letter XXIII: On the Regard that ought to be shown to Men of Letters

Neither the English, nor any other People have Foundations established in favour of the polite Arts like those in France. There are Universities in most Countries, but 'tis in France only that we meet with so beneficial an Encouragement for Astronomy, and all Parts of the Mathematicks, for Physick, for Researches into Antiquity, for Painting, Sculpture and Architecture. Lewis the Fourteenth has immortalised his Name by these several Foundations,* and this Immortality did not cost him two hundred thousand Livres a Year.

I must confess that one of the Things I very much wonder at, is, that as the Parliament of Great Britain have promised a Reward of twenty thousand Pounds Sterling to any Person who may discover the Longitude, they should never have once thought to imitate Lewis the Fourteenth in his Munificence with regard to the Arts and Sciences.

Merit indeed meets in England with Rewards of another kind, which redound more to the Honour of the Nation. The English have so great a Veneration for exalted Talents, that a Man of Merit in their Country is always sure of making his Fortune. Mr Addison in France would have been elected a Member of one of the Academies, and, by the Credit of some Women, might have obtained a yearly Pension of twelve hundred Livres; or else might have been imprisoned in the Bastile, upon Pretence that certain Strokes in his Tragedy of *Cato* had been discovered, which glanced at the Porter of some Man in Power. Mr Addison was raised to the Post of Secretary of State in England. Sir Isaac Newton was made Warden of the Royal Mint. Mr Congreve had a considerable[1] Employment. Mr Prior was Plenipotentiary. Dr Swift is Dean of St Patrick in Dublin, and is more revered in Ireland than the Primate himself. The Religion which Mr Pope professes* excludes him indeed from Preferments of every kind, but then it did not prevent his gaining two hundred Thousand Livres by his excellent Translation of Homer [. . .]

But the Circumstance which mostly encourages the Arts in England, is the great Veneration which is paid them. The Picture of the prime Minister hangs over the Chimney of his own Closet, but I have seen that of Mr Pope in twenty Noblemen's Houses. Sir Isaac Newton was revered in his Life-time, and had a due respect paid to him after his Death; the greatest Men in the Nation disputing who should have the Honour of holding up his Pall. Go into Westminster-Abbey, and you'll find that what raises the Admiration of the Spectator is not the Mausoleums of the English Kings, but the Monuments which the Gratitude of the Nation has erected, to perpetuate the Memory of those illustrious Men who contributed to its Glory. We view their Statues in that Abbey in the same Manner, as those of Sophocles, Plato and other immortal Personages were viewed in Athens; and I am persuaded, that the bare Sight of those glorious Monuments has fired more than one Breast, and been the Occasion of their becoming great Men.

The English have even been reproached with paying too extravagant Honours to mere Merit, and censured for interring the celebrated Actress Mrs Oldfield in Westminster-Abbey, with almost the same Pomp as Sir *Isaac Newton*. Some pretend that the English had paid her these great Funeral Honours, purposely to make us more strongly sensible of the Barbarity and Injustice which they object to us, for having buried Mademoiselle le Couvreur* ignominiously in the Fields.

But be assured from me, that the English were prompted by no other Principle, in burying Mrs Oldfield in Westminster-

---

[1] Secretary for Jamaica

Abbey, than their good Sense. They are far from being so ridiculous as to brand with Infamy an Art which has immortalised an Euripides and a Sophocles; or to exclude from the Body of their Citizens a Set of People whose Business is to set off with the utmost Grace of Speech and Action, those Pieces which the Nation is proud of.

Under the Reign of Charles the First, and in the Beginning of the Civil Wars raised by a Number of rigid Fanaticks, who at last were the Victims to it; a great many Pieces were published against Theatrical and other Shows, which were attacked with the greater Virulence, because that Monarch and his Queen, Daughter to Henry the Fourth of France, were passionately fond of them.

One Mr Prynne,* a Man of most furiously scrupulous Principles, who would have thought himself damned had he wore a Cassock instead of a short Cloak, and have been glad to see one half of Mankind cut the other to Pieces for the Glory of God, and the *Propaganda Fide*; took it into his Head to write a most wretched Satyr against some pretty good Comedies, which were exhibited very innocently every Night before their Majesties. He quoted the Authority of the Rabbis, and some Passages from St Bonaventure, to prove that the *Œdipus* of Sophocles was the Work of the evil Spirit; that Terence was excommunicated *ipso facto*; and added, that doubtless Brutus, who was a very severe Jansenist, assassinated Julius Caesar, for no other Reason, but because he, who was Pontifex Maximus, presumed to write a Tragedy the Subject of which was *Œdipus*. Lastly, he declared that all who frequented the Theatre were excommunicated, as they thereby renounced their Baptism. This was casting the highest Insult on the King and all the Royal Family; and as the English loved their Prince at that Time, they could not bear to hear a Writer talk of excommunicating him, though they themselves afterwards cut his Head off. Prynne was summoned to appear before the Star-Chamber; his wonderful Book, from which Father Le Brun* stole his, was sentenced to be burnt by the Common Hangman, and himself to lose his Ears. His Tryal is now extant.

The Italians are far from attempting to cast a Blemish on the Opera, or to excommunicate Signor Senesino or Signora Cuzzoni.* With regard to my self, I could presume to wish that the

Magistrates would suppress I know not what contemptible Pieces, written against the Stage. For when the English and Italians hear that we brand with the greatest Mark of Infamy an Art in which we excell; that we excommunicate Persons who receive Salaries from the King; that we condemn as impious a Spectacle exhibited in Convents and Monasteries; that we dishonour Sports in which Lewis the Fourteenth, and Lewis the Fifteenth performed as Actors; that we give the Title of the Devil's Works to Pieces which are received by Magistrates of the most severe Character, and represented before a virtuous Queen; when, I say, Foreigners are told of this insolent Authority, and this Gothic Rusticity which some presume to call Christian Severity; what an Idea must they entertain of our Nation? And how will it be possible for 'em to conceive, either that our Laws give a Sanction to an Art which is declared infamous, or that some Persons dare to stamp with Infamy an Art which receives a Sanction from the Laws, is rewarded by Kings, cultivated and encouraged by the greatest Men, and admired by whole Nations? And that Father Le Brun's impertinent Libel against the Stage, is seen in a Bookseller's Shop, standing the very next to the immortal Labours of Racine, of Corneille, of Molière, etc.

By 1733–4, when the Letters and their French translation had appeared, Voltaire had been out of England for several years. He never returned. But his interest in English matters continued till his death in 1778. He recalls the oddities and extremes in articles on 'Fanaticism', 'Quakers' and even on 'Cannibals', quoted here among the selections from The Portable Philosophical Dictionary.

He remains in – sporadic – contact with his friends across the Channel, such as Bubb Dodington, and he is visited by a stream of British travellers (see the Introduction, p. xxii), often with recommendations from his earlier acquaintances, or in fact related to them. One moving meeting was in January 1774, when William Augustus Fawkener and his brother visited the old man at Ferney. They were the sons of Everard Fawkener (1684–1758), who had welcomed Voltaire to his house in Wandsworth at the beginning of his stay in England. Fawkener had later been British Ambassador to the Sublime Porte, and was knighted in 1735.

Voltaire welcomed them 'with great cordiality. Seated at table between the two brothers, M. de Voltaire took them by the hand and exclaimed with emotion: "Dear God, how happy I am to be here between two Falkeners!"'*

Another contact, by letter, was renewed by tragic circumstances – the trial of Admiral Byng. In 1756 John Byng (1704–57) commanded the British fleet defending the island of Minorca, which was threatened by a French fleet commanded by La Gallissonnière. The wind, and the relative positions of the two fleets, prevented his engaging the enemy. There was no battle, Minorca was captured by the French – and Byng was accused of cowardice, court-martialled and condemned to death.

Voltaire had known him, slightly, when in England. He was appalled at the treatment Byng had received, and wrote several letters – particularly to the Duc de Richelieu – asking for help, and he wrote also, in English, to Byng, on 2 January 1757, enclosing a copy of a reply Richelieu had sent him:

> Sir, Tho' I am almost unknown to you, I think 'tis my duty to send you the copy of the letter which I have just received from the Marshal Duke de Richelieu. Honour, Humanity, and Equity order me to convey it into your hands. This noble and unexpected Testimony from one of the most candid, as well as the most generous of my countrymen, makes me presume your Judges will do you the same justice.
>
>   I am with respect.
> Sir Yr most humble obt servant,
>   Voltaire*

In vain. Admiral Byng* was executed 14 March 1757 – 'to encourage the others', as Voltaire wrote, bitterly, in Candide, *Ch. 23.*

CHAPTER 2

Fragment of a Letter on a Very Useful Custom which prevails in Holland*
(Fragment d'une lettre sur un usage très-utile établi en Hollande)

First published in 1739. Voltaire's faith in Dutch good sense was to be shaken a year later when the difficulties with the Dutch publisher Van Duren occurred (see Memoirs, p. 99).

It is to be wished that those who govern nations would imitate artists. As soon as it is known in London that a new stuff is made in France, they are sure to counterfeit it. Why is not a statesman equally desirous to establish in his own country a salutary law taken from a foreign nation? We have arrived, at length, at the secret of making chinaware of an equal goodness to that made in China. Let us learn the secret of imitating the good we observe practised among our neighbours, and let our neighbours profit by what they see excellent among us.

There are private persons who raise in their gardens the fruits which nature had appointed only to ripen under the line. We have a thousand wise laws, and a thousand excellent customs at our very doors; these are the fruits we ought to raise in our country; these are the trees we ought to transplant: they will thrive in every climate, and will prosper in every soil. The most salutary law, the most excellent custom, and the most useful I have ever seen is in Holland. When two persons are about to enter on a lawsuit, they are first obliged to go before a tribunal of reconciling judges, called the Peacemakers. If the parties happen to bring with them a lawyer and a counsellor, the first thing done is to send those gentlemen about their business, as we take off the wood from a fire we want to extinguish. The Peacemakers tell the parties: 'You are certainly great fools to spend your money to procure your own ruin; we will bring you to an agreement without costing you one farthing.' If the rage of chicane happens to be too violent in our parties, they put them off to another day, in order that time may soften and mitigate the symptoms of their disorder; after the expiration of which time the judges summon them before them a second and a third time. If their folly is of the incurable sort, they promise them they will consent to their having their cause tried in a court of justice, in the same manner as we abandon an incurable member to the surgeon; and then the law has its course.

There is no necessity to make long declamations, or to calculate how much it would be for the advantage of humanity, were this law universally adopted. And besides, I am by no means desirous to follow the footsteps of the Abbé* de Saint-Pierre, whose projects a certain minister, and a man of sense, called 'The dreams of a worthy man'. I know that if a private person of integrity and good sense offers a proposal for the public good, it too often happens that he is abused or laughed at for his pains. 'What meddling fellow is this,' some will say, 'who pretends to make us happier than we choose to be, and goes about to reform abuses by which so many people get their living?' What reply can be made to this? For my part, I know of none.

CHAPTER 3

A Dramatic Balderdash*
(*Galimatias dramatique*)

First published in 1756, this 'philosophic dialogue' may have been written as early as 1757. Its message is strikingly similar to that of Ch. 12, 'Le Souper' or The Supper, added to Voltaire's tale Zadig in 1748. There (in a pre-Christian setting) several merchants, each with a different religion, discuss their beliefs. At the end the Egyptian, the Indian, the Greek, the Celt, the Chaldean and the others all agree that their God is universal. 'You are then all of the same opinion,' said Zadig, 'and there is nothing in this for you to quarrel about.' Yet in A Dramatic Balderdash, a decade later, Voltaire underlines, not the universal nature of God, but the divisive and hurtful effects of men's varying interpretations. See also the last paragraphs of Letter VI in the Letters Concerning the English Nation.

A JESUIT, *preaching to the Chinese:*
I tell you this, my dear brethren, Our Lord wishes to make all men his chosen vessels; it rests with you to become vessels: you have only to believe here and now what I declare to you; you are masters of your mind, your heart, your thoughts, your feelings. Jesus Christ died for all men, as is known, and grace is given to all. If you lack contrition, you have attrition; if you do not have attrition, you have your own strength and mine.

A JANSENIST, *arriving.*
In this you lie, you child of Escobar* and perdition; your preaching is error and deceit. No, Jesus died only for certain of us; grace is granted to few; attrition is foolishness; the strength of the Chinese is a nothing, and your prayers are blasphemy; for Augustine and Paul . . .

THE JESUIT
Be silent, you heretic; leave us, you enemy of St Peter. My brethren, do not heed this innovator, who quotes Augustine and Paul; come now, let me baptise you all.

THE JANSENIST

Beware of that, my brethren; do not let yourselves be baptised by the hand of a Molinist* – you will be damned to hell. In a year's time, at the soonest, I shall baptise you, when I have taught you the nature of grace.

THE QUAKER

Ah, my brethren, let yourselves not be baptised, either by this fox's paw, or this tiger's claw. Believe me, it is better not to be baptised at all; this is our custom. Baptism has its merits; but one can well do without. All that you need, is for the Spirit to inspire you; only wait, and it will come, and in an instant you will understand more than these charlatans could tell you in a lifetime.

THE ANGLICAN

Ah, my flock, what monsters are here to devour you! My dear lambs, do you not know that the Anglican Church is the only one that is pure? Have these chaplains of ours, who came to drink punch in Canton, not told you this?

THE JESUIT

The Anglicans are renegades; they disowned our pope and the pope is infallible.

THE LUTHERAN

Your pope is an ass, as Luther declared. My dear Chinamen, scorn the pope, and the Anglicans, the Molinists, the Jansenists, the Quakers, and believe only the Lutherans: just repeat these words, *in, cum, sub,** and drink with the best of us.

THE PURITAN

We are saddened, my brethren, by the blindness of all these people, and by yours. But, thank the Lord, the Eternal Spirit has ordained that I should come to Peking on this appointed day to confound these babblers; that you should listen to me, and that we should sup together in the morning – for you will be aware that in the fourth century of the era of Dionysius the Little . . .

THE MUSLIM

Eh, death of Mahomet, what a lot of talk! If just one of these dog tries to bark again, I'll cut the ears off the lot of them; as for their foreskins, I'll not bother: you're the ones, my dear

Chinamen, whom I shall circumcise; I give you a week to prepare yourselves, and if any one of you, after that, thinks of drinking wine, he'll have to deal with me.

THE JEW
Ah, my children, if you wish to be circumcised, give me the preference: I'll let you drink as much wine as you wish; but if you are so ungodly as to eat a hare – which, as you know, chews the cud but doesn't have cloven feet* – I'll put you to the sword when I'm the strongest, or if you prefer I'll have you stoned; for . . .

THE CHINESE
Ah! by Confucius and the five Kings, have they all lost their senses? Master-keeper of the mad-houses of China, kindly lock up all these poor fools, each in his cell.

CHAPTER 4

Wives, Submit Yourselves unto Your Husbands*
(*Femmes, soyez soumises à vos maris*)

This piece was probably first published in 1756, near the beginning of Voltaire's long and admiring correspondence with the Empress Catherine II of Russia. While we may see the German princess who rises at five in the morning as a flattering reference to Catherine and her way of life as a ruler, it is a considerable anachronism. The Abbé François de Châteauroux (1645–1709), who refers to the princess, was Voltaire's godfather, and the Maréchale de Grancey died in 1694, the year of Voltaire's birth. The Abbé's brother, Pierre, Marquis de Châteauneuf (1644–1728) was a French diplomat. Voltaire went with him to the Hague in 1713 – Voltaire's first foreign journey.

The Abbé de Châteauneuf told me one day that Madame La Maréchale de Grancey was a very imperious woman; for all that, she had remarkable qualities. Her chief pride lay in respecting herself; in doing nothing of which she might have cause to blush in secret. She preferred rather to confess a dangerous truth than to make use of some ready dissimulation; she said that dissimulation was always a sign of cowardice. Her life was marked by a thousand generous deeds; but when she was praised for them, she thought herself insulted; she used to say: 'You think, then, that such actions cost me an effort?' Her lovers adored her, her friends made much of her, and her husband respected her.

She spent forty years in that dissipation and in that circle of amusements which form the serious occupations of women, having read nothing besides the letters she received, and having thought of nothing except the news of the day, the follies of her neighbours and the interests of her heart. At length, seeing that she had reached the age when, as they say, women who have both wit and beauty do but pass from one throne to another, she had a desire to read. She began with the tragedies of Racine, and was astonished to find, in reading them, an even greater pleasure than she had felt when she saw them acted: the good taste which was being formed in her mind showed her that this man spoke only of things which were true and of interest, that they were always in their right place, that he was noble and simple, without declamation, without anything forced, without striving after brilliance; that his plots, like his thoughts, were all founded on nature: she found again in her reading the history of her sentiments and the picture of her life.

They persuaded her to read Montaigne: she was charmed to find a man who seemed to converse with her, and who doubted everything. Then they gave her the great men of Plutarch: she asked why it was that he had not written the history of great women.

One day the Abbé de Châteauneuf discovered her all red with indignation. 'What is the trouble, madam?' said he. 'I opened by hazard,' she replied, 'a book which was lying about in my cabinet; it is, I believe, a certain collection of letters. Therein I saw these words: *Wives, submit yourselves unto your husbands.** I threw the book away.'

'How, madam? Do you not know that these are the Epistles of St Paul?'

'I care not who wrote them; the author is very impolite. Monsieur le Maréchal would never have written to me in such a style; I am persuaded that your St Paul was a very difficult man to live with. Was he married?'

'Yes, madam.'

'His wife must have been a good-natured creature indeed: if I had been the wife of such a fellow, I would have made him see a thing or two. "*Submit yourselves to your husbands!*" Now, if he had contented himself with saying: "*Be gentle, complaisant, attentive, thrifty*", I should have said, That's a man who understands life; and why *submit yourselves*, if you please? When I married Monsieur de Grancey, we promised to be faithful to each other: I have not kept my vows too exactly, nor he his; but neither he nor I promised obedience. Are we, then, slaves? Is it not enough that a man, after having married me, has the right to give me a nine-months' illness, which is sometimes mortal? Is it not enough that I should bring forth with bitter pains a child who may plead at law against me when he is of age? Is it not enough that I should be subjected each month to inconveniences which are mighty distasteful to a woman of quality, and that, to crown all, the suppression of one of these dozen-a-year maladies may cause my death, without any one coming, in addition, to say to me: *Obey*?

'Certainly nature has said no such thing; she has given us organs which differ from those of men; but, in making us necessary to each other, she has never pretended that our union should become a state of slavery. I remember well enough that Molière has said:

All power is on the side of the beard.*

But that is a quaint reason, truly, for giving me a master! What! because a man's chin is covered with a nasty rough skin which he is obliged to shave closely, whereas my chin is born shaven, it is necessary that I should very humbly obey him? I know quite well that men generally have muscles which are stronger than ours, and acquit themselves at fisticuffs better than we do: truly, I fear lest this be the origin of their superiority.

'They pretend also that their minds are better organised, and, in consequence, they boast that they are more capable of governing; but I could show them queens who have been worth more than many a king. I heard some days ago of a German princess who rises at five in the morning to work for the well-being of her subjects, who directs the affairs of State, answers all letters, encourages all the arts, and who dispenses benefits as numerous as her own talents. Her courage equals her knowledge; so she has not been brought up in a convent by idiots who teach us what we ought not to know, and who prevent us from knowing what we ought to know. For my part, if I had a state to govern, I feel that I should be bold enough to follow her example.'

The Abbé de Châteauneuf, who was a very courtly man, took care not to contradict Madame la Maréchale.

'By the way,' said she, 'is it true that Mahomet despised us so much that he pretended we were not worthy to enter Paradise, and that we should not be allowed beyond the portals?' 'In that case,' said the Abbé, 'the men would be always near the door. But comfort yourself; there is not one word of truth in all that they say here about the Mahometan faith. Our ignorant and wicked monks have thoroughly deceived us, as my brother, who was ambassador at the Porte for twelve years, has affirmed.'

'What! it is not true, sir, that Mahomet invented the plurality of wives in order to get a better hold on the men? It is not true that we are slaves in Turkey, and that we are forbidden to pray to God in a mosque?' – 'Not a word of truth in all that, madam. Mahomet, far from having invented polygamy, suppressed or restrained it. The wise Solomon had seven hundred wives. Mahomet reduced this number to four only. Ladies may go to Paradise, just the same as gentlemen; and, beyond doubt, they will make love there, but in a fashion different from that in which it is made here; for you perceive well enough that we know love but very imperfectly in this world of ours.'

'Alas, you are right,' said the Maréchale; 'man is truly of little account!

'But tell me, did your Mahomet command wives to submit themselves to their husbands?'

'No, madam; that is nowhere to be found in the *Alcoran*.'

'Then why are they slaves in Turkey?'

'They are by no means slaves; they have their property; they can make testaments; they are able to request a divorce on occasion; they go to the mosque at their proper time, and to their rendezvous at other times: one may see them in the streets with their veils over their noses, just as you wore your mask some years ago. It is true that they are not seen at the opera or the comedy, but that is because there is neither the one nor the other. Can you doubt that, if ever there was an opera in Constantinople – the land of Orpheus – the ladies of Turkey would not fill the front boxes?'

'*Wives, submit yourselves unto your own husbands!*' said the Maréchale between her teeth. 'This Paul was a perfect boor.'

'He was a bit hard,' replied the Abbé, 'and he was fond of being the master: he made short work of St Peter, who was really quite a good fellow. However, it would be very wrong to take all that he said too literally. He has been taxed with strong leanings towards the Jansenists.' – 'I suspected all along that he was a heretic,' said the Maréchale; and she went on with her toilet.

CHAPTER 5

How Far Should We Impose on the People?*
(*Jusqu'à quel point on doit tromper le peuple*)

*A gentle piece, first published in 1756, poking fun at the illogicalities
of the 'popular press' – the journals whose interests were directed to
trivial and ephemeral events, and not to more serious matters – or, if
mentioning them, approached them in a trivialising way. Whatever
would Voltaire have said about the press today?*

It is a question of great importance, however little regarded,
how far the people, i.e., nine-tenths of the human race, ought to
be treated like apes. The deceiving party have never examined
this problem with sufficient care; and, for fear of being mistaken
in the calculation, they have heaped up all the visionary notions
they could in the heads of the party deceived.

The good people who sometimes read Virgil, or the *Provincial
Letters*,* do not know that there are twenty times more copies
of the Almanac of Liège and of the *Courrier Boiteux* printed
than of all the ancient and modern books together. No one,
surely, has a greater veneration than myself for the illustrious
authors of these almanacs and their brethren. I know, that ever
since the time of the ancient Chaldeens, there have been fixed
and stated days for taking physic, paring our nails, giving battle,
and cutting wood. I know that the best part of the revenue of an
illustrious academy consists in the sale of such almanacs. May I
presume to ask, with all possible submission and a becoming
diffidence as to my own judgment, what harm it would do to
the world were some powerful astrologer to assure the peasants
and the good inhabitants of the little villages that they might
safely pare their nails when they please, provided it be done
with a good intention? The people, I shall be told, would not
buy the almanacs of this new astrologer. On the contrary, I will
venture to affirm, that there would be found among your great
geniuses many who would make a merit in following this
novelty. Should it be alleged that these geniuses would form

factions, and kindle a civil war, I have nothing further to say on the subject, but readily give up, for the sake of peace, my too dangerous opinion.

Everybody knows the King of Boutan.* He is one of the greatest princes in the universe. He tramples under his feet the thrones of the earth; and his shoes – if he has any – are provided with sceptres instead of buckles. He adores the devil, as is well known, and his example is followed by all his courtiers. He, one day, sent for a famous sculptor of my country, and ordered him to make a beautiful statue of Beelzebub. The sculptor succeeded to admiration. Never was there such a handsome devil. But, unhappily, our Praxiteles had only given five clutches* to his animal, whereas the Boutaniers always gave him six. This capital blunder of the artist was aggravated by the grand master of the ceremonies to the devil, with all the zeal of a man justly jealous of his master's rights, and of the sacred and immemorial custom of the kingdom of Boutan. He insisted that the sculptor should atone for his crime by the loss of his head. The sculptor replied that his five clutches were exactly equal in weight to six ordinary clutches; and the King of Boutan, who was a prince of great clemency, granted him a pardon. From that time the people of Boutan were undeceived with regard to the devil's six clutches.

The same day His Majesty needed to let blood. A surgeon from Gascony, who had come to his court in a ship belonging to our East India Company, was appointed to take from him five ounces of his precious blood. The astrologer of that quarter cried out that the King would be in danger of losing his life if he opened a vein while the heavens were in their present state. The Gascon might have told him that the only question was about the state of the King's health; but he prudently waited a few minutes; and then, taking an almanac in his hand, 'You were in the right, great man!' said he to the astrologer of the quarter, 'the king would have died had he been bled at the instant you mention: the heavens have since changed their aspect; and now is the favorable moment.' The astrologer assented to the truth of the surgeon's observation. The King was cured; and by degrees it became an established custom among the Boutaniers to bleed their kings whenever it was necessary.

A blustering Dominican at Rome said to an English philosopher, 'You are a dog; you say it is the earth that turns round, never reflecting that Joshua made the sun stand still.' 'Well! my reverend father,' replied the other, 'and since that time the sun has been immovable.' The dog and the Dominican embraced each other; and even the Italians were, at last, convinced that the earth turns round.

An augur and a senator, in the time of Caesar, lamented the declining state of the republic. 'The times, indeed, are very bad,' said the senator; 'we have reason to tremble for the liberty of Rome.' 'Ah!' said the augur, 'that is not the greatest evil; the people now begin to lose the respect which they formerly had for our order: we seem barely to be tolerated; we cease to be necessary. Some generals have the assurance to give battle without consulting us; and, to complete our misfortunes, those who sell us the sacred pullets begin to reason.' 'Well, and why don't you reason likewise?' replied the senator, 'and since the dealers in pullets in the time of Caesar are more knowing than they were in the time of Numa, should not you modern augurs be better philosophers than those who lived in former ages?'

CHAPTER 6

Account of the Illness, the Confession, the Death, and the Apparition of the Jesuit Berthier* ('*Relation de la maladie, de la confession, de la mort et de l'apparition du jésuite Berthier*')

First published in November 1759, this piece was augmented in 1760 with a third section, the 'Account of the Journey of Brother Garassise'. It was prompted by the suspension of the Encyclopédie *in February 1759, a matter which was in part the achievement of the Jesuits, especially through their periodical the* Journal de Trévoux, *which had been directed since 1745 by Guillaume-François Berthier (1704–82). Voltaire's mockery of Berthier is directly inspired by his reading of Swift. In 1756, he had added comments on Swift's* Tale of a Tub *to letter* XXII *of the* Letters Concerning the English nation, *and in a letter to Mme du Deffand, dated 13 October 1759,* he praises the* Tale *again for its freedom of expression – possible in the United Kingdom, though not in France. Yet Voltaire's witty adaptation of the* Tale of a Tub – *the tale of Pot-pourri – was not published until 1765. Meanwhile, in 1759, the 'Account . . . of the Jesuit Berthier' had appeared, inspired by Swift's* Bickerstaff Papers *(1708–9), and the 'Elegy on the supposed Death of Partridge the Almanack-maker' (1708). We should note, however, that although both Swift and Voltaire begin with the description of an imaginary death, Swift's 'Elegy' tells that Partridge's soul has been 'Install'd as good a Star / As any of the Caesars are', to become the thirteenth sign of the Zodiac – while Berthier is packed off to Purgatory.*

It was on 12 October 1759 that Brother Berthier went – unluckily for him – from Paris to Versailles with Brother Coutu, his customary companion. Berthier had put a few copies of the *Journal de Trévoux* into the conveyance, to present them to his several protectors; such as the chamber-maid to madame the wet-nurse, one of the palace cooks, one of the King's apprentice apothecaries, and to several other noblemen who encourage talent. On the way Berthier started to retch; his head grew heavy: he yawned again and again. 'I don't know what's the matter with me,' he said to Coutu, 'I've never yawned so much.' – Brother Coutu replied 'Reverend Father, it's only to be expected.' – 'What d'you mean, expected?' said Brother Berthier. – 'Well,' said Brother Coutu, 'I'm yawning too, and I don't know why, because I haven't read a thing all day, and you haven't said a word to me since we went out together.' As he said this, Brother Coutu yawned more than ever. Berthier then yawned and yawned and couldn't stop. The coachman turned round, and when he saw them, he began to yawn too; the sickness spread to all the passers-by: they yawned in all the neighbouring houses. The very presence of a learned man has sometimes such an influence on human beings!

Meanwhile Berthier came out in a cold sweat. 'I don't know what's wrong with me,' he said, 'I'm utterly chilled.' – 'I know just what you mean,' said his companion. – 'What's that, you know what I mean,' said Berthier, 'what makes you say that?' – 'Well, I'm frozen too,' said Coutu. – 'I'm almost alseep,' said Berthier. – 'I'm not surprised,' said the other. – 'Why's that?' said Berthier. – 'Well, I'm falling asleep too,' said his companion. And there they were, gripped by a soporific, lethargic sickness, and thus they drew up at the coach entry to Versailles. When the coachman opened the door of the coach, he tried to waken them from their profound slumber, but he was unable to: he called for help. At last the companion, more robust than Brother Berthier, gave some signs of life; but Berthier was colder than before. Some of the court doctors, who were returning from dinner, passed by the carriage; they were asked to cast an eye on the sick man: one of them, having taken his pulse, went off, saying that he wouldn't have anything more to do with medicine, not since he'd come to the court. Another, having looked at Berthier more carefully, stated that the sickness came from the gall-bladder, which was full to bursting; a third maintained that it was all related to the brain, which was utterly empty.

While they were discussing the case, the patient's condition worsened. His convulsions took on a fatal character, and the three fingers with which one holds a pen were already completely clenched, when a senior doctor, who had studied under Mead and Boerhaave,* and knew rather more than the others, forced open Berthier's mouth with a baby's bottle, and, having carefully considered the odour of his breath, declared that he had been poisoned.

At this, everyone cried out. 'Yes, gentlemen,' he went on, 'he's been poisoned; just feel his skin, one can tell that the exhalations of a chilly poison have passed through the pores; I would diagnose a poison worse even than a mixture of hemlock, black hellebore, opium, nightshade and henbane. Coachman, have you by chance brought some parcel for our apothecary in your coach?' – 'No, sir,' replied the coachman; 'the only package is the one the Reverend Father told me to bring.' And then he rummaged in the trunk, and pulled out two dozen copies of the *Journal de Trévoux*. 'Well, then, gentlemen, wasn't I right?' said the great doctor.

Everyone admired his prodigious sagacity, they all recognised the origin of the evil: at once the pernicious packet was burnt, under the nose of the patient. The action of the fire lessened the weight of the particles, and Berthier was slightly relieved; but as the harm was considerable, and his head was affected, he was still in great danger. The doctor proposed that he should be made to swallow a page of the *Encyclopédie*, taken in white wine, to reanimate the humours of his clotted bile; this produced a copious evacuation, but his head was still horribly weighed down, the vertigo continued, and the few words he could utter made no sense: he remained in this state for two hours, after which it was thought necessary for him to make his confession.

At that moment two priests were walking along the rue des Récollets: they were approached. The first refused: 'I will not' – he said – 'be responsible for the soul of a Jesuit, it's too difficult: I don't want anything to do with those people, neither for the affairs of this world, or the next. Whoever wishes to confess a Jesuit, it won't be me.' The second priest was not so difficult. 'I'll undertake this task,' he said; 'one can turn everything to account.'

He was led at once to the room where the sick man had been carried; and as Berthier could still not speak distinctly, the confessor resorted to questions. 'Reverend Father,' he began, 'do you believe in God?' – 'That's a strange question,' said Berthier. – 'Not so strange,' said the other; 'there's believing and believing: to be sure that you believe in the right way, one must love God and one's neighbour; do you love them sincerely?' – 'I would make some distinction,' said Berthier. 'No distinction, please,' replied the confessor; 'and no absolution, if you do not accept these two duties at the outset.' – 'Very well, then,' said Berthier, 'since you force me, yes, I love God, and my neighbour as best I can.'

'Have you not often read bad books?' asked the confessor. – 'What do you mean by bad books?' asked the confessed man. – 'I don't mean,' said the confessor, 'books which are simply tedious, like the *Roman History* by Fathers Carrou and Rouillé, and those college tragedies, and your volumes of "polite literature", and Lemoine's *Louisiade*, and Ducerceau's verses about piquant sauce, and his noble stanzas on the messenger from Le Mans, and his expression of thanks for pâtés to the Duc du Maine [...] But what I do mean is those fantasies by Father Bougeant, condemned by Parliament and by the Archbishop of Paris; I mean those sweet writings by Father Berruyer, who's changed the Old and the New Testament into a kind of gutter-romance in the style of *Clélie*, properly scorned both in Rome and in France* [...] I mean above all your Sanchez, in his book *De Matrimonio* [Of Marriage], where he has made a collection of all those things that Aretino,* and *The Carthusian Porter* would never have dared to say. Should you have read any works of this kind, your salvation is in danger.' [...]

'I would distinguish, sir,' said Berthier. – 'More distinctions!' said the confessor; 'Well! I make no distinction, and I shall not give you absolution.'

As he was speaking, up hurries Brother Coutu, running, breathless, sweating, panting, stinking; he had made enquiries about the man who had the honour to confess the reverend father. 'Stop, stop,' he cried, 'no sacrament, no sacrament, Reverend Father, I beg of you, my dear Reverend Father Berthier, die without the sacraments; this priest is the author of the *Nouvelles ecclésiastiques** [the Ecclesiastical News], you're the fox confessing to the wolf: if you've told the truth, you're lost.'

Amazement, shame, sorrow, anger, rage then enlivened, for a moment, the spirit of the sick man. 'You are the author of the *Nouvelles ecclésiastiques*!' he exlaimed; 'And you've caught a Jesuit!' – 'Yes, my friend,' replied the confessor with a twisted smile. – 'Give me my confession back, you scoundrel,' said

Berthier; 'give me my confession back at once! Oh, it's you, God's enemy, the enemy of kings, even of the Jesuits; it's you who's taken advantage of the state I'm in: you traitor – why haven't you had an apoplexy, and come to me for extreme unction! So you think you're less tedious, less of a fanatic than me? Yes, I've written silly things, I agree; I've made myself despicable, hateful, I allow; but you, aren't you the lowest, vilest of paper-scribblers to whom madness has ever granted a pen? Admit it, then: isn't your history of convulsions equal to our *Lettres édifiantes et curieuses?** We want to be in control everywhere, I admit; and you, you'd hope to cause discord everywhere. We would wish to seduce those in authority; you would rather raise sedition against them. The courts have had our books burnt, I agree; but have they not burnt yours as well? We've all been imprisoned in Portugal, that's true; but have you, and your accomplices, not been pursued by the police a hundred times? If I have been foolish enough to criticise enlightened men, who had until then disdained to attack me, have you not been just as impertinent? Are we not both, therefore, equally ridiculous? Should we not therefore admit, both of us, in this century, the sewer of all ages, that we are, the pair of us, the vilest of any of the insects hovering round the mud of the midden?' The force of truth tore these words from Berthier's mouth. He spoke like one inspired; his eyes, filled with a dusky flame, rolled in frenzy; his lips were twisted, covered in spittle, his body was tensed, his heart was quaking: soon these convulsions were followed by a general collapse; and in this weakness he tenderly clasped Brother Coutu's hand. 'I admit,' he said, 'that there are many inadequacies in my *Journal de Trévoux*; but you must excuse human weakness.' – 'Ah! my Reverend Father, you are a saint,' said Brother Coutu; 'you are the first author ever to admit that he was tedious; go now, die in peace; you may smile at the *Nouvelles ecclésiastiques*; die now, Reverend Father, and be sure that you will work miracles.'

So passed Brother Berthier from this life to the next, on 12 October, at half past five in the evening.

*Apparition of Brother Berthier to Brother Garassise,
the continuer of the* Journal de Trévoux.

'On 14 October, I, Brother Ignatius Garassise, grand-nephew of
Brother Garasse, at two hours past midnight, and being awake,
I had a vision, and here was the ghost of Brother Berthier
coming towards me, and this gave me the longest and the most
terrible yawning fit I have ever experienced. "Are you dead,
then, Reverend Father?" I asked. As he yawned at me, he
nodded to mean "yes". "That's good," I said to him, "since
Your Reverence must doubtless be among the saints; you must
have one of the most important places. What a pleasure to see
you in Heaven with all our brothers, past, present and future!
It's true, isn't it, that there are now some four millions of heads
with haloes, since the founding of our Society until today? I
don't think there are as many from the Fathers of the Oratory.
Speak to me, Reverend Father, stop yawning, and tell me of
your happiness."

'"Oh, my son!" said Brother Berthier in a mournful voice,
"How wrong you are! Alas! the *Paradise open to Philagie**
is closed to the Fathers!" – "Is it possible?" I exclaimed. – "Yes,"
he said, "shun the pernicious vices which have damned us; and
above all, when you work on the *Journal de Trévoux*, do not
imitate me; do not calumniate, nor reason falsely, and above all
do not be tedious, as I had the misfortune to be, and which is,
of all sins, the most unforgivable."

'I was gripped with holy horror at Brother Berthier's fearful
account. "So you're damned?" I exclaimed. – "No," he replied,
"Happily, I repented at the last moment, I'm in Purgatory for
three hundred and thirty-three thousand, three hundred and
thirty-three years, three months, three weeks and three days,
and I shall not be released unless one of our Brothers is found
who is humble, peaceful, who has no wish to live at Court, who
will not speak slanderously of others to princes, who will not
meddle in the affairs of the world; and who, when he writes
books, does not make people yawn, and who will pass all his
merits to me."

'"Ah, Brother," I said to him, "your Purgatory will last a long
while. Tell me then, if you will, what is your penitence in
Purgatory?" – "I am obliged," he replied, "to prepare the

chocolate for a Jansenist every morning; at dinner-time I have to read one of the *Provincial Letters** aloud, and for the rest of the time I am busied with mending the shifts of the nuns at Port-Royal."* – "You make me tremble!" I replied; "what's happened then to all our Fathers, for whom I had such veneration? Where is the Reverend Father Le Tellier,* the leader, the apostle of the Gallican Church?" – "He's damned without mercy," replied Brother Berthier, "and he deserved it fully: he deceived his King, he lit the flame of discord, forged letters from bishops, and in the most cowardly and hot-headed way he persecuted the most worthy Archbishop ever to have been appointed in the capital of France, he has been irrevocably condemned as a forger, calumniator, and disturber of the public peace: he's the one who has betrayed us all, it's he who has doubled our folly, which now sends us to Hell in hundreds and thousands. Since Brother Le Tellier was respected, we believed we should all be respected; we imagined, since he had deceived his penitent, that we should all deceive ours; we believed, since one of his books had been condemned in Rome, that we too should only write books which should likewise be condemned; and, to cap it all, we wrote the *Journal de Trévoux*."

'As he spoke to me, I turned on my left side, then on my right, then I sat up, and exclaimed: "Oh, dear creature in Purgatory, what must one do to avoid the state you are in? Which sin is most to be feared?"

'Berthier opened his mouth, and said: "As I passed by Hell to go into Purgatory, I was taken into the cavern of the seven capital sins, which is on the left-hand side of the entrance; first I considered Lust: she was a plump, jolly creature, fresh and appetising; she was lying on a bed of rose-leaves, with Sanchez' book at her feet and a young abbé at her side; I said to her: "Madame, it would seem, that you are not the one who damns us Jesuits?" – "No," she replied, "I do not have that honour; I have, it is true, a younger brother who took possession of Abbé Desfontaines and a few others of his kind, while they wore your habits; but for the most part I am not involved in your affairs; my pleasures are not for everyone."

'Avarice sat in a corner, weighing out grass from Paraguay against gold. "Is it you Madame, who has the most credit with us?" – "No, Reverend Father, I damn only a few of your procurators." – "Might it be you?" I said to Wrath. – "Talk to the others; I am transient, I enter all hearts, but I do not remain; my sisters soon take over." Then I turned to Gluttony, who was at table. "As for you, Madame, I'm well aware, thanks to our brother the cook, that it's not you who has lost us our souls." Her mouth was full, so she could not reply; but she made a sign, shaking her head, that we weren't worthy of her attention.

'Sloth was resting on a couch, half asleep; I did not wish to waken her: I could tell the aversion she would have for people like us who chase all over the world.

'In a corner I spotted Envy, who was gnawing at the hearts of three or four poets, a few preachers and a hundred pamphlet-eers. "You look just the one" – I said to her – "to have a hand in our sins." – "Ah, Reverend Father," she replied, "you are too kind; however could people who have such a high opinion of themselves depend on me? – I am just skin and bones. You should talk to my father."

'Indeed, her father was beside her, seated in an armchair, clothed in a coat trimmed with ermine, his head held high, with a scornful look, and red, full hanging cheeks; I knew he was Pride: I prostrated myself; he was the only being with whom I could perform this duty. "Forgive me, my Father," I said, "that I did not approach you first of all; I have always kept you in my heart: yes, it is you who rule us all. The most trivial of writers, even the author of the *Année littéraire** [the 'Literary Year'], is inspired by you. Oh splendid devil! you reign over mandarin and pedlar, grand lama and capucin, sultana and city wife; but our Fathers are your chiefest favourites: your divinity shines out in us, through all the veils of policy; I have always been the most arrogant of your disciples, and I feel, that I love you still." He replied to my hymn of praise with a protective smile, and I was led at once to Purgatory.'

Here ends the vision of Brother Garassise; he resigned from the *Journal de Trévoux*, and moved to Lisbon, where he was in long conference with brother Malagrida,* and at last he went to Paraguay.

CHAPTER SEVEN

Memoirs Related to the Life of M. de Voltaire, Written by Himself

(Mémoires pour servir à la vie de M. de Voltaire, écrits par lui-même)

Completed end 1759 – early 1760, but not published until after Voltaire's death; clandestine editions circulated around 1784, – before Frederick's death in 1786. Officially published in 1789.*

Voltaire never wrote an autobiography. This is well known, often stated. We may scan or scour his thousands of letters, and from them find countless details of who saw him when, and said what about this or that. But there is little indeed about Voltaire himself.

The Memoirs are as near to an autobiography as anything he wrote, spanning the period 1733 to early 1760, beginning with his long association with Mme du Châtelet, their years of literary and scientific study together, and the correspondence (from 1736) between Voltaire and Frederick, Crown Prince of Prussia. But Voltaire quickly concentrates on Frederick's affairs, as Crown Prince and then, from 1740, as King – and warrior. When Mme du Châtelet died in 1749, Voltaire travelled to Berlin and Potsdam, staying until 1753, and his descriptions are again of Frederick's way of life, his wars, his companions (or rather, intellectual satellites), his love of music, his skill as a flautist – all fascinating, but with little about Voltaire himself.

What does emerge about Voltaire is his irrepressible, sometimes cruel, often tactless, mockery of other people's follies and weaknesses. Macaulay, who published a long essay on Frederick, draws copiously on Voltaire's Memoirs for details of Frederick's life in Berlin and Potsdam, and carefully distinguishes the directions, for good or evil, in which Voltaire's mockery might be aimed: 'In truth, of all the intellectual weapons which have ever been wielded by man, the most terrible was the mockery of Voltaire ... How often that rare talent was exercised against rivals worthy of esteem; how often it was used to crush and

*torture enemies worthy only of silent disdain; how often it was
perverted . . . to destroying the last solace of earthly misery . . .
how often it was used to vindicate justice, humanity and
toleration . . .'*

Certainly Voltaire used this talent while he was Frederick's
guest. No doubt, he had a lot to put up with – the envy of the
other guests, and the egotism of his royal host. But often he was
unwise, given the delicate nature of his position.

The delicacy of the situation comes out with a terrible clarity
in the matter of the orange-skin, and Voltaire's riposte. Voltaire
wrote about these matters to his niece, Mme Denis. First, on 2
September 1751, he describes how La Mettrie, another guest,
had told him of a conversation with Frederick:

> He talks to me in confidence; he's sworn to me that in talking
> with the King, in the last few days, about my favoured position
> here, and the jealousy which this has aroused, the King had replied
> to him: *I'll need him here for one more year, at the longest; when
> you've squeezed the orange, you throw the skin away.*
>
> I made him repeat these charming words to me; I asked him
> about them again and again; he swore again that it was true.
> Would you believe it? Should I believe it? Is it possible? . . .*

*True it probably was; and Voltaire replied in kind a few months
later, again telling Mme Denis of the event. This time the
spreader of bad news was Maupertuis, who had experienced
enough of Voltaire's sarcasms.*

> Maupertuis has discreetly spread the rumour, that I find the
> King's poetic compositions extremely poor . . . and he has been
> telling people privately that when the King last sent me some verse
> to correct, I exclaimed: 'Won't he ever be tired of sending me his
> dirty linen to clean?' He's whispered this extraordinary thing in
> the ear of ten or a dozen people, urging them to keep it absolutely
> secret. I have a feeling that the King has now heard it . . .*

*And so, in 1753, Voltaire 'escaped' from Frederick – only to be
humiliated at Frankfurt. By the end of 1754, reaching Geneva,
he had resolved to buy himself a security which could never be
his, were he to depend on royal favour. With the purchase of
Les Délices, in February 1755, and of Ferney in 1758, he had*

*acquired his own little territory, where he stayed until the last
months of his life.*

The Memoirs, *written in 1758–9, finished in 1760, are a
record of peaceful existence away from kings – at Cirey, at Les
Délices – and of the follies and fury of kings and war.*

I was weary of the idle, turbulent life of Paris, of the crowd of
coxcombs, of bad books, printed with royal consent and
approval, of the intrigues of men of letters, of the pettiness and
knavery of the wretches who were a disgrace to literature. In
1733, I encountered a young gentlewoman whose ideas were
much the same as mine, and who formed the resolution to go
into the country for several years, to cultivate her mind there far
from the tumult of the world: this was Mme the Marquise du
Châtelet, who, of all the women of France, had a mind most
capable of the different branches of science.*

Her father, the Baron de Breteuil, had taught her Latin, which
she understood as perfectly as Madame Dacier.* She could
repeat the most beautiful passages in Horace, Virgil and Lucretius, and all the philosophical works of Cicero were familiar to
her. Her inclination bent more strongly towards mathematics
and metaphysics than any other studies; and seldom have there
been united in the same person such justness of discernment,
elegance of taste, and such an ardent wish for information; yet
she took an equal delight in the world, and in the amusements
fitted to her age and sex. None the less she gave these up in
order to bury herself in a shabby château* on the borders of the
Champagne and Lorraine, on a mean and unfruitful estate. She
beautified the château, and adorned it with pleasing gardens.
There, I constructed a gallery; and in this I formed a very fine
laboratory. Several men of learning came to this retreat to join
in our philosophy. For two whole years we had the famous
Kœnig, who died at the Hague, as professor and librarian to
Mme the Princess of Orange, Maupertuis came with Jean
Bernouilli;* and from that time Maupertuis, who was from
birth the most jealous of men, picked me as the object of his
envy – a passion which he has always cherished.

I taught Mme du Châtelet English, and after three months she
understood it as well as myself, and could read Locke, Newton,
and Pope with equal ease. She learnt Italian just as rapidly;

together, we read all Tasso, all Ariosto. So it was, that when Algarotti* came to Cirey, where he completed his *Newtonianismo per le dame*, he found her well enough acquainted with his language to give him advice – from which he profited. Algarotti was a Venetian, a most amiable man, son of a very rich tradesman; he had travelled all over Europe, knew a little of everything, and gave to everything a grace. In this delightful retreat we wished only to study, without following what took place elsewhere in the world. For a long time our attention was directed towards Leibnitz and Newton. Mme du Châtelet attached herself first to Leibnitz, and explained one part of his system in a book, excellently written, entitled *Institutions de physique*.* She did not seek to adorn philosophy with the ornaments to which it is a stranger; such affectation formed no part of her character, which was masculine and just. Clearness, precision, and elegance were the properties of her style; and if it were possible to give the semblance of truth to the ideas of Leibnitz, it will be found in this book. But today what Leibnitz thought begins to concern us less and less.

Born with a love of truth, she soon gave up systems, and applied herself to the discoveries of the great Newton; she translated the whole of his *Principles of Mathematics* into French; and, when she had increased her knowledge, added an algebraical commentary* [. . .]

At Cirey we cultivated all the arts. There I composed *Alzire, Mérope, L'Enfant prodigue, Mahomet*. For her sake, I worked on an *Essay on History from Charlemagne until the Present Day*:* I chose the epoch of Charlemagne for my commencement, because it was the period at which Bossuet* had stopped, as I durst not attempt the same subject which he had so well treated. Yet Mme du Châtelet was far from admiring the *Universal History* of this great master; she thought the prelate Bossuet was eloquent *only*, and had wasted too much labour on the Jewish nation.

Having spent six years in this retreat, devoted to the arts and sciences, it was necessary for us to go to Brussels, where the du Châtelet family had for many years been in litigation with the family of Honsbrouk. There I was happy to meet a grandson of the illustrious and ill-fated grand almoner de Witt,* who was first president of the chamber of accounts. He possessed one of the finest libraries in Europe, which greatly helped me with the *Essay on History*; but in Brussels I enjoyed a yet more uncommon delight, and which meant more to me: I brought to a close the lawsuit whose costs had been ruining the two families for the last sixty years. I had M. the Marquis du Châtelet paid 220,000 livres in cash, by which the matter was concluded.

When I was still in Brussels, in 1740, the great King of Prussia, Frederick-William,* the least tolerant of kings, without question the most thrifty and the one with the most ready cash, died in Berlin. His son, who has made himself so exceptional a reputation, had been in regular correspondence with me for more than four years.* Nowhere in the world, maybe, have there been a father and son less alike than these two monarchs. The father was truly a vandal, thinking only – and throughout his reign – of accumulating money, and of maintaining, as cheaply as he could, the finest soldiers in Europe. Never were subjects poorer than his, never was a king so rich. He had acquired the major part of his nobles' estates at the lowest price – and they had quickly devoured the little money they had received, while half of this had come back to the royal treasury through taxes on food and drink. All the royal estates were farmed out to agents who were, at one and the same time, extortioners and judges. In this way, when a tenant had not paid his rent by the agreed date, the agent put on his judge's robe, and condemned the delinquent to pay a double rent. One might note that should this same judge not pay the king at the end of the month, he too was taxed at the double rate on the first of the following month.

Should a man kill a hare; should he prune a tree near to the King's domain or commit some other fault, he must pay a fine. Should a girl become pregnant, then the mother, or father, or the parents must give money to the king for the pregnancy.

Mme the Baroness de Kniphausen, the richest widow in Berlin – that is to say, she had an income of seven to eight thousand livres – was accused of bringing a subject of the King into the world in the second year of her widowhood; the King wrote to her personally that, to save her honour, she should send thirty thousand livres to his treasury: she was forced to borrow this sum, and was ruined.

At the Hague, he had a minister named Luiscius: he was, assuredly, the worst paid of all the ministers of the crowned heads [of Europe]; to keep himself warm, this wretched man cut down a few trees in the garden of Hons-Lardik, which then belonged to the Prussian crown; soon after, he received a note from the King his master, cancelling a year's salary. In despair Luiscius cut his throat with the only razor he possessed: an old servant came to help him, and, alas! saved his life. Since then I have come across his Excellency at the Hague, and have given him alms at the gate of the palace called *The Old Court*, a palace belonging to the King of Prussia, and where this wretched ambassador had lived for twelve years.

One must allow that Turkey is a republic, beside the despotic rule of Frederick-William. By means like this, during the twenty-eight years of his reign, he succeeded in amassing some twenty million crowns, safely stored in iron-ringed barrels in the cellars of his palace in Berlin. It pleased him to furnish this entire grand apartment of the palace with bulky items in solid silver, where art was inferior to the material. To the Queen, his wife, he also gave – on account – a cabinet furnished entirely in gold, down to the very handles of the pokers, tongs and coffee-pots.

The monarch would leave this palace on foot, wearing a threadbare coat of blue cloth, with copper buttons, which came half-way down his thighs; and when he bought a new coat, he made use of the old buttons. Dressed like this, His Majesty, armed with a clumsy sergeant's cane, would undertake the daily review of his regiment of giants.* This regiment was his particular delight, and his greatest expense. The front line of his company was formed of men of whom the smallest was seven foot tall: he would buy them from the furthest ends of Europe and Asia. I saw some of them after his death. The King, his son, who liked men who were handsome, rather than tall, had installed these with his wife, the Queen, as guards. I recall that they accompanied an antique ceremonial coach which was set in front of the Marquis de Beauvau, when he arrived to congratulate the new King in November 1740. The late King Frederick-William, who had earlier sold all his father's magnificent furniture, had not been able to get rid of this huge tattered gilt coach. The guards, who were positioned on either side to hold it steady, shook hands over the roof.

When Frederick-William had completed his review, he would then walk on into the city; all fled at once: should he meet a woman, he asked her, why she was wasting her time in the street: 'Get you home, you hussy; any honest woman would be at home.' And he would join this reproach with a cuff on the ear, or a kick, or several blows with his cane. He dealt with ministers of the Gospel in the same way, when they thought to watch the review.

You may wonder whether this vandal was surprised, or grieved, that he had a son who was witty, elegant, polite, and eager to please, who wished to learn, and who played music and wrote verse. When he saw the Crown Prince holding a book, he threw it in the fire; and should the Prince be playing the flute, his father broke the flute, and sometimes treated His Royal Highness as he did the ladies and the clergymen at the review.

The Prince, wearied by his father's cares and concerns, decided one fine day in 1730 to run away, not knowing yet whether he would go to England or to France.* The paternal economy did not leave him free to travel as the son of a tax-farmer, or of an English merchant. He borrowed a few hundred ducats.

Two charming young men, Katt and Keith,* agreed to accompany him. Katt was the only son of a courageous officer. Keith was the son-in-law of the identical Baroness de Kniphausen who had been fined ten thousand crowns for bearing children. The day and the time were settled; the father had been told it all: the prince and his two travelling companions were arrested together. To begin with, the King believed that Princess Wilhelmina* his daughter (who later married the Markgraf of Bayreuth), was involved in the affair; and since he favoured prompt settlement in matters of justice, he propelled her, using his feet, through a window which burst open to the floor. The queen mother, who was present at the very moment Wilhelmina was falling out, held her back by her skirt. From all this the princess received a contusion below her left breast, which she kept all her life as a token of paternal sentiment, and which, to my honour, she has shown me.

The Prince had a kind of mistress, the daughter of a schoolmaster in the town of Brandenburg, who was settled in Potsdam. She played the harpsichord after a fashion; the crown prince accompanied her on the flute. He believed he was in love with her, but he was mistaken, his vocation was not for the fair sex.

Nonetheless, as he had made it appear that he loved her, his father obliged this young lady to go right round the square at Potsdam, led by the public hangman, who whipped her before the eyes of his son.

Having entertained him with this spectacle, he had him transferred to the fortress of Custrin, sited in the middle of a marsh. Here he was shut up for six months, with no servants, in a kind of dungeon; and after six months he was given a soldier to serve him.* This soldier – young, handsome, well-made, and who played the flute – was able in more than one way to amuse the prisoner. So many fine qualities have since made his fortune. I have seen him, at one and the same time, as valet and prime minister, with all the insolence which can accompany these two posts.

The Prince had been for some weeks in his castle at Custrin, when an old officer, followed by four grenadiers, came into his room, dissolved in tears. Frederick had no doubt that they had come to slit his throat. But the officer – still weeping – had him seized by the four grenadiers, who placed him at the window and held his head steady, while the head of his friend Katt was cut off, on a scaffold erected directly outside the window-frame. He stretched out his hand to Katt, and fainted. His father was present at this spectacle, as he had been at that of the girl who was whipped.

As for Keith, the prince's other confidant, he escaped to Holland. The King despatched soldiers to seize him: they only missed him by a minute, and he took ship for Portugal, where he remained until the death of the merciful Frederick-William.

This was not all the King wished to do. His intention was to have his son's head cut off. He reflected that he had three other boys, none of whom wrote poetry, and that this was sufficient for the dignity of Prussia. Measures had already been taken to have the crown prince condemned to death, as the Czarevitch had been – the oldest son of Czar Peter I.

It does not seem too certain in the laws of heaven and earth that a young man should have his head cut off for having wished to travel. But the King would have found judges in Berlin as skilful as those in Russia. And in any case, his paternal authority would have sufficed. The Emperor Charles VI, who held that the crown prince, as a prince of the Empire, could not be condemned

to death except by an [Imperial] Diet, sent Count von Seckendorf* to his father to remonstrate with him most seriously.
Count von Seckendorf, whom I have since seen in his retirement
in Saxony, swore to me that he had had great difficulty in
obtaining an assurance that the prince would not be decapitated.
This is the same Seckendorf who commanded the Bavarian
forces, and of whom the prince – when he became King of
Prussia – draws a frightful portrait in the history of his father,
which he inserted into thirty or so copies of the *Brandenburg
Memoirs*.[1] After that, serve princes if you will, and prevent their
decapitation.

After eighteen months, the Emperor's repeated requests and
the tears of the Queen of Prussia obtained the liberty of the
hereditary prince, who turned to writing poetry and making
music more than ever. He read Leibnitz, and even Wolff, whom
he termed a collector of balderdash, and he dabbled as much as
he could in all the sciences at once.

As his father allowed him hardly any part in affairs, and as
indeed there were no affairs in the country, where parades were
all that happened, he spent his moments of leisure writing to
those men of letters in France who were known to the world at
large. The heaviest burden fell on me.* He sent letters in verse;
he sent treatises, on metaphysics, on history, on politics. He
termed me a godly being; I termed him a Solomon. Such epithets
cost us nothing. Some of this silly stuff has been printed in my
collected works; happily not even a thirtieth part has reached
print. I ventured to send him a beautiful inkstand, made by
Martin; he had the kindness to make me a present of a few
trifles in amber. Meanwhile the wits in the cafés in Paris
imagined – with horror – that my fortune was made.

A young Courlander, named Keyserling, who was a rhymer,
and a favourite with Prince Frederick, was despatched from the
frontiers of Pomerania to us at Cirey. We prepared a fête for
him, with fine illuminations; the cypher and the name of the
Prince Royal were composed of lamps, as were also these words:
The hope of the human race. For my part, had I wished to build
up hopes for myself, I would have been fully entitled to: since I

[1] I have given the copy which the King of Prussia presented to me to the
Elector Palatine.

was written to as *My dear friend*, and much was said to me, in missives, of the solid tokens of friendship which were destined for me, once he was upon the throne. He came to the throne at last* when I was in Brussels; and his first act was to send to France, as his ambassador extraordinary, a one-armed man named Camas,* formerly a French refugee, and at that time an officer in the Prussian army. The King said that there was an ambassador at Berlin from the court of France who had but one hand, and that to acquit himself of all obligation to the King of France, he had despatched a one-armed ambassador to Paris.

Camas was no sooner arrived safe at his hotel than he despatched a messenger, a lad whom he had created his page, to inform me that being too much fatigued to come to my house, he entreated me to repair instantly to him, as he had the most valuable and most magnificent gift for me, from the King his master, that ever was presented. 'Fly! fly!' said Mme du Châtelet, 'His Majesty has certainly sent you the finest diamonds of the crown.' Away I flew, and found the ambassador; he showed me a small keg of wine tied behind his chaise; this part of his baggage was the magnificent present which the reigning monarch of Prussia had sent me from the cellar of the late king, with a royal command for me to drink. Full of my high-raised expectations, I emptied myself by expressions of astonishment and protestations of gratitude for this *liquid* mark of His Majesty's bounty, instead of the more *solid* one I had been taught to expect, and shared the contents of my keg with Camas.

My Solomon was then at Strasbourg. While visiting his long and narrow land, which extends from the Guelders to the Baltic ocean, he had taken a whim to come *incognito* and view the frontiers and troops of France. He gave himself this pleasure at Strasbourg, where he assumed the title of Count du Four, a Bohemian nobleman; his brother, the Prince Royal, who accompanied him, took also a travelling title: Algarotti, who had already attached himself to His Majesty, was the only one of the party who travelled undisguised [. . .]

From Strasbourg he went to visit his territories in Lower Germany, and sent me word that he would come *incognito* to see me at Brussels. We accordingly prepared elegant apartments for him; but, having fallen ill in the little Château de Meuse,* some two leagues from Clèves, he informed me that he expected

I should make the first advances; I went therefore to pay him my most profound respects. Maupertuis, having the mania of becoming president of an academy, had already formed his plan, and presented himself. He lodged in one of the garrets of the palace, with Algarotti and Keyserling. I found no guard except one soldier. Rambonet, the privy counsellor and minister of state, was walking in the courtyard, blowing his fingers, over which hung deep, coarse, and dirty ruffles; a hat, full of holes, partially shaded by an old judge's wig, one side of which hung into his pocket, and the other scarcely touched his shoulder. I was credibly informed that Rambonet was at that moment charged with a state affair of great importance.

I was conducted to His Majesty's apartment, in which I saw nothing but four bare walls, until, by the light of a taper, I perceived in a closet a small camp bed, two and a half feet wide, on which, wrapped in a morning gown of blue cloth, partially covered with a mean looking quilt, lay a little man, shaking in a violent fit of ague. It was the King. I made my bow, and commenced my acquaintance as if I had been appointed his first physician, by feeling his pulse. The fit soon abated. His Majesty then arose, dressed himself and sat down to supper with Algarotti, Keyserling, Maupertuis, and the ambassador of the States General, and myself. Our conversation at table treated of Plato's androgynes, liberty, and the immortality of the soul.

While we were philosophising at our ease, the privy counsellor Rambonet was travelling all night, mounted on a post-horse, to Liège, at the gates of which he ordered a trumpet to sound, and proclaimed the name of the King his master, and the contribution he laid on that city; which was enforced by the appearance of two thousand soldiers from Wesel. It was to me His Majesty committed the task of drawing up the manifesto to prove his rights, which I performed as well as the nature of the case would permit, not in the least suspecting that a king, with whom I supped, and who called me his friend, could possibly be in the wrong. The affair was soon concluded by the payment of a million livres in good hard ducats, which served to defray the expenses of his tour to Strasbourg.

I could not but feel attached to him, for he had wit, agreeable manners, and was a sovereign; which in itself is a circumstance of seduction scarcely to be vanquished by human weakness. In general it is the occupation of men of letters to flatter kings, but I had the honour of being praised by a monarch from the crown of my head to the sole of my feet, at the very time I was being libelled at least once a week by the Abbé Desfontaines* and other insignificant poets of Paris.

Some while before the death of his father, the King of Prussia had thought proper to refute the principles of Machiavelli; and if Machiavelli had been tutor to the prince, he would have advised him to have done so politically; the royal Frederick however was not then master of so much finesse; he wrote as he really thought; he was not at that time a king, and his father disgusted him with despotic power; therefore, in the ardour of his enthusiasm, he praised moderation and justice with all the energy of his soul, and regarded all usurpation as an absolute crime. He had sent his manuscript to me in Brussels, to correct it and to have it printed; and I had already handed it over to a bookseller in Holland, named Van Duren,* the most notorious swindler of his kind. But then I felt remorse at printing the *Anti-Machiavel*,* while the King of Prussia, with a hundred millions in his treasury, was taking a million from the citizens of Liège through the hands of counsellor Rambonet. I concluded that my Solomon would not stop at that. His father had left him excellent troops – 66,400 men; he was adding to these, and appeared to wish to make use of them at the first opportunity.

I pointed out to him that it was not exactly fitting to print his book at the very moment when he might be reproached for violating its precepts. He gave me permission to halt the publication. I travelled to Holland solely to propose this little service on his behalf; but the bookseller asked for so much money that the king – who was in any case not genuinely grieved to appear in print – preferred to be printed for nothing, rather than to pay not to be. While I was in Holland, busy with this task, the emperor Charles VI died, in October 1740, after indigestion from mushrooms, which led to apoplexy; this dish of mushrooms changed the destiny of Europe. It soon appeared that Frederick II, King of Prussia, was not such an enemy of Machiavelli as the crown prince had seemed to be. Although he was already meditating the invasion of Silesia, he invited me nonetheless to attend his court.

I had already indicated to him that I was not able to stay at his court, that I was bound to prefer friendship to ambition, that I was attached to Mme du Châtelet, and that, philosopher for philosopher, I'd rather a lady than a king.

He approved this liberty, though he did not like women. I left to pay court to him in October. Cardinal de Fleury wrote a long letter to me with praise of the *Anti-Machiavel* and its author; and of course I showed it to him. He was already mobilising his troops, though none of his generals or his ministers had fathomed his intention. The Marquis de Beauvau, despatched to Frederick to compliment him, believed that he intended to declare himself opposed to France, and in favour of Maria Theresa, the Queen of Hungary and Bohemia, and the daughter of Charles VI; that he wished to support the election to the Empire of Francis of Lorraine, the Grand Duke of Tuscany, the husband of this queen; and that he would find this highly advantageous.

I, more than anyone else, would have thought that the new King of Prussia would adopt this policy, as he had sent me three months earlier a political text of his composition, in which he considered France to be the natural enemy and ravager of Germany. But it was in his nature always to do the very opposite of what he said and wrote, not through dissimulation, but because he wrote and spoke with one kind of enthusiasm, and then acted with another.

He set out on 15 December, suffering from the ague, to conquer Silesia, leading 30,000 well-equipped and well-disciplined troops; as he mounted his horse he said to the Marquis de Beauvau: 'I shall play the same game as yourself; if I get the aces, we shall share the winnings.'

Since when he has written the history of this conquest; and has shown me the entire text. Here is one of the curious sections from the beginning of these annals; I was particularly careful to transcribe it, as a unique statement: 'Add to these considerations the complete readiness of my troops, my well-stocked treasury, and the liveliness of my character: these were my reasons for making war on Maria Theresa, Queen of Bohemia and Hungary.' A few lines further on came these very words: 'Ambition, self-interest, the wish to make a name for myself carried the day; and the war was decided.'

Ever since there have been conquerors, or ardent spirits who have wanted to be conquerors, he is I think the first to have justified himself like this. Never perhaps has a man been so aware of reason, yet responded so fully to his passions. His character has always contained such philosophical explanations and such imaginative fantasies. It is a pity that I persuaded him to cut this passage when I edited his works later on: so rare an avowal should go down to posterity, to help to show how almost all wars are begun. Men of letters like us, poets, historians, academic orators, we celebrate these fine exploits: here is a king who both performs them, and condemns them.

The Prussian troops had entered Silesia: then the minister at Vienna, Baron de Gotter, proposed to Maria Theresa, Queen of Hungary and Bohemia, the ceding of three-fourths of Silesia to the Elector and King his master, for which His Prussian Majesty would lend her three million crowns, and make her husband emperor.

Maria Theresa, although at that time she had neither troops, money, nor credit, was inflexible. Rather would she lose everything, than yield them to a prince whom she considered merely as the vassal of her ancestors, and whose life had been saved by the emperor her father. Her generals could scarcely muster 20,000 men; yet Marshal Neipperg, who commanded them, forced the King of Prussia to give battle under the walls of Neisse, at Molwitz.* At the first onset the Prussian cavalry was put to the rout by the Austrians, and the King, not *then* accustomed to stand fire, fled at the first shock as far as Oppeln, twelve leagues from the field of battle. Maupertuis, who was anxious to make his fortune in a hurry, had the honour of being in the royal suite at this campaign; but finding that it was not the monarch's custom to provide horses for his followers. Maupertuis on the day of battle was reduced to the necessity of buying an ass, which he did for two ducats, and set off after His Majesty on ass-back as best he could. His noble steed however was soon distanced; poor Maupertuis was taken prisoner and stripped by the Austrian hussars.

Frederick passed the night on a truckle bed in a village alehouse near Ratibor, on the confines of Poland. He was in despair, and imagined that he would have to traverse half of Poland in order to enter the northern part of his dominions, when one of his horsemen arrived from the camp at Molwitz, and informed His Majesty that he had obtained the victory. The news was presently confirmed by an aide-de-camp. It was true. If the Prussian cavalry was no good, the infantry was the best in Europe; it had been above thirty years under the discipline of the old Prince of Anhalt. Marshal Schwerin, who commanded, was a pupil of Charles XII; he turned the fate of the day as soon as the King of Prussia had fled. The monarch returned on the morrow, and the victorious general was, as makes no difference, disgraced.

I returned to philosophy in my haven at Cirey. I spent my winters in Paris where I had a host of enemies: this was because, long before, I had thought fit to write the *History of Charles XII*,* to produce several works for the stage, and even to write an epic poem; it was reasonable, then, that my persecutors should include any – and everyone who dabbled in verse or prose. And then, as I had even had the impertinence to write on philosophy, it was wholly proper for these people who are termed *devout* to call me an atheist, as was the fashion in the past.

I had been the first to have dared to expound Newton's discoveries to my nation in intelligible terms. Cartesian prejudices, which followed on the prejudices of the peripatetics in France, were so firmly rooted at the time that Chancellor d'Aguesseau considered anyone who should recommend discoveries made in England as an enemy of reason and of the State. He would never consent to authorising the printing of the *Elements of Newton's Philosophy.**

I was a great admirer of Locke: I considered him to be the only reasonable metaphysician; above all I recommended the restraint – new, and at the same time wise and audacious – with which he stated that on its own our reason will never be adequate to maintain that God is unable to endow *matter* with feeling and thought.

You cannot conceive the savagery, the fearless ignorance with which they hounded me after this article appeared. Locke's thought had previously received no attention in France, since the theologians were still reading Saint Thomas and Quesnel,* and ordinary people read romances. Once I had praised Locke, they condemned both him and myself. No doubt, the poor creatures who fulminated in this dispute knew neither what was *matter* nor what was *spirit*. The fact remains that by ourselves we know nothing, that we experience movement, life, feeling and thought, without knowing how; that the elements of matter are as unknown to us as anything else; that we are blind creatures, walking and reasoning in the dark; and that Locke was wise indeed to admit that it is not for us to decide what the Almighty can or cannot do.

The success of my dramatic pieces and of my other works drew upon me a whole library of pamphlets, in which the writers endeavoured to prove that I was the son of a peasant, a very bad poet, and an atheist.*

All this was asserted in a history of my life. A German with great industry collected all the tales which had been crammed into the libels my enemies had published against me. They invented adventures for me with persons I never knew, and with others who had never existed.

While writing this I have found a letter from the Marshal de Richelieu, which informed me of a ridiculous lampoon, proving that his wife had given me an elegant carriage, and granted me favours still *more* valuable. The marshal had *no wife* when this was printed. At first I took a pleasure in making a collection of these calumnies, but they multiplied so fast that I was compelled to leave off.

This was the sole reward which came to me from my labours. I found consolation quickly enough, sometimes in the haven of Cirey, sometimes in good company in Paris.

While the excrement of literature made war on me like this, France did likewise to the Queen of Hungary: and one must allow that this was equally unfair; for – having solemnly stipulated, guaranteed and sworn to the pragmatic sanction of the Emperor Charles VI, and the succession of Maria Theresa to her father's inheritance; having received Lorraine in payment for these promises – it did not seem at all consonant with public law to betray such an agreement. Cardinal de Fleury was involved beyond the extent of his power. He could not claim, like the King of Prussia, that his lively character had driven him to arms. This fortunate priest was still in control at the age of eighty-six, holding the affairs of state in a most feeble hand. An alliance had been made with the King of Prussia at the time when he was taking Silesia; two armies had been sent into

Germany, while Maria Theresa did not even have one. One of the French armies had advanced to within five leagues of Vienna without encountering any enemy: Bohemia had been apportioned to the Elector of Bavaria, who was elected Emperor, after he had been named lieutenant-general to the armies of the King of France. But it was not long before enough errors were made to lose all that had been gained.

The King of Prussia, having matured his courage, gained several victories, concluded the peace with the Austrians, and obliged the Queen of Hungary, much against her will, to relinquish him Glatz, with Silesia. Having broken abruptly with France, once this was achieved, in June 1742, he wrote to me that he had taken the necessary medicine, and that he would advise others who were ill to try to recover.

He had arrived at the height of his power; he commanded 130,000 warriors, besides the cavalry which he himself had formed. He drew from Silesia twice as much as it had produced for the house of Austria, saw himself firmly seated in his new conquest, and was happy; while all the other contending powers were suffering the miseries of depredation. Princes in our times ruin themselves by war – he enriched himself.

He then turned his attention to the embellishment of Berlin, to which city he invited artists of all denominations, and built there one of the finest opera-houses in Europe; he wished to acquire glory of every kind in the most economical manner.

The *late* King had resided in a frightful old house at Potsdam; the *present* transformed it into a palace. Potsdam became a pleasant town, Berlin grew daily more extensive, and the Prussians began to enjoy the comforts of life, which the former sovereign had totally neglected. Many people had decent furniture in their houses, and even wore shirts, sleeves and fronts tied on with packthread having been thought quite sufficient, until the reigning monarch improved the uncouth fashions in which he had been brought up. He changed the scene as if by magic; Lacedemon became Athens, deserts were peopled, and a hundred and three villages arose on marshy land which had been cleared and drained. Nor were poetry and music neglected by his majesty, whom I had not been wrong in calling the Solomon of the North. It was I who coined this name for him, in my letters, and it stayed with him for many years [. . .]

Cardinal de Fleury died 29 February 1743, aged ninety. Never was there a man made prime minister so late in life, and never did one preserve that exalted station so long. His good fortune to be ruler of France began in the seventy-third year of his age, continuing his reign indisputably until his death. He modestly contented himself with power divested of pomp, nor was he anxious to amass riches. He has left a reputation of being an artful and amiable person, rather than a man of genius, and to have been better acquainted with the intrigues of court than with the political affairs of Europe [. . .]

Several academicians wished me to be given his place in the Académie Française. At the King's supper, the question was raised as to who should deliver the Cardinal's funeral oration at the Académie. The King replied that it should be me. This was the wish of his mistress, the Duchess de Châteauroux; but Count de Maurepas,* the secretary of state, did not want this at all. It was his frequent whim to quarrel with his master's mistresses, and it brought him into difficulty.

An aged imbecile named Boyer* – the tutor to the dauphin – who had previously been a Theatine monk, and then became Bishop of Mirepoix, took it upon himself to second M. de Maurepas in his caprice [. . .]

Finally, the priest triumphed over the mistress. So that I was not granted an appointment, about which I hardly cared. It is amusing for me to recall this episode, which demonstrates the pettiness of those who are called *the great*, and at the same time reveals how *trifles* are sometimes all-important for them.

Meanwhile, since the death of the cardinal, public matters had fared no better than in his last two years of office. The house of Austria was arising from its ashes into new life; France was hardly pressed by *her* and England; we had no resource but in the King of Prussia, who had led us into war and forsaken us in our necessity.

France conceived the design of sending me secretly to learn the intentions of the Prussian monarch, whether he was not inclined to prevent the storm which seemed to be gathering at Vienna, and must fall upon him after visiting us; and to try whether he would lend us a thousand men on this occasion, and by so doing fix himself more firmly in his Silesian conquest. The Duke de Richelieu and Mme de Châteauroux suggested this scheme, and the King adopted it; I was fixed on to be the negotiator, and M. Amelot, the minister for foreign affairs, was solely charged to hasten my departure.

A pretext for my visit was wanting, and I seized that of my dispute with the old Bishop of Mirepoix, which met with the King's approbation. I wrote to the King of Prussia, that not being able to endure any longer the persecutions of that Theatine monk, I must take refuge with a king who was a philosopher far from the snares of a bishop who was a bigot. As this prelate always signed his letters with the abbreviated phrase *l'anc. évêq. de Mirepoix* ['previously bishop of Mirepoix'], and since his handwriting was somewhat unclear, this was read instead as *L'âne de Mirepoix* ['the ass Mirepoix']: it was a matter for pleasantry; rarely can negotiations have been more lively.

The King of Prussia, who struck with an iron fist when it involved monks and abbés, replied with a deluge of sarcasms on the ass of Mirepoix, and an earnest invitation. I took care that my letters and the answers were made public, and the bishop complained to His Majesty of being ridiculed in a foreign court. The King answered, that it was a matter agreed on, and that he must let it pass without notice.

This answer has so little of the character of Louis xv that it appeared extraordinary to me. Thus had I at once the pleasure of avenging myself upon the bishop who excluded me from the Academy, and of taking a very agreeable journey, and of having an opportunity to exert myself in the service of the King and state [. . .]

Whatever money I required for my expenses was given, upon *my* receipt merely, by M. de Monmartel, which power I took care not to abuse. While His Majesty of Prussia was galloping from one end of his territories to the other, in order to be present at the reviews, I stayed in Holland. I had apartments in the palace of the Vieille Cour, which at that time belonged to the King of Prussia in participation with the House of Orange. My stay at the Hague did not prove useless; the Prussian envoy, the young Count de Podewils,* had an intrigue with a lady, from whom he obtained copies of all the secret resolutions of their High Mightinesses, which at that period were very preju-dicial to the interest of France. The count gave me those copies, and I sent them to the French court, which found my service very acceptable.

When I arrived at Berlin,* His Majesty lodged me in his palace, as he had done on my earlier visits. At Potsdam he led the same life which he has led consistently since he came to the throne. This life deserves some detailed description.

His Majesty arose at five in the summer and at six in the winter. The functions of high almoner, the great chamberlain, lords of the bedchamber, and gentleman ushers, were all comprised in *one* lackey, who lighted his fire, shaved him, and finished his dressing, for he required very little assistance in that business. His chamber was in appearance very elegant; a rich balustrade of silver, ornamented with little cupids exceedingly well sculpted, seemed to form the alcove of the state bed, the curtains of which were seen, but behind those curtains, instead of a bed, there was a library, and the royal couch, a common camp bedstead, without sacking, only cross-corded under a thin mattress, was concealed behind a screen. Marcus Aurelius and Julian, the two greatest men among the Romans, and the apostles of the Stoics, lay not on a harder couch.

When His Majesty was dressed and booted, the stoic yielded for a few moments to the sect of Epicurus: he sent for two or three of his favourites – either lieutenants from the regiment, or pages, or foot-soldiers, or young cadets. Coffee was brought. The one who received the handkerchief would stay for ten or twelve minutes intimacy. None of this went to an extreme, since the prince (in his father's lifetime) had been vilely treated in his passing fancies, and had only poorly recovered. He could not take the leading part; he could only be a subordinate.

Once these student pleasures were done, matters of state took over. His senior minister entered through a private staircase, with a great bundle of papers under his arm. This senior minister was a clerk, who lived on the second floor in Fredersdorf's mansion – this was the soldier who had become the King's valet de chambre and his favourite, and who had previously served the King when he was a prisoner in the fortress of Custrin. The secretaries of state sent all their despatches to the senior minister, who brought extracts of these to the King; and the King wrote his answers on the margins in a few words. Thus were the national affairs expedited in an hour. Rarely did the secretaries of state, or the principal ministers, speak to him directly: there were some, to whom he never spoke at all. The King his father had put the finances under such exact regulations, all was executed in such a military manner, and obedience was so blind, that four hundred leagues of territory were governed as easily as an abbey.

About eleven the King booted, and reviewed his regiment of guards in his garden, while his colonels did the same throughout the provinces. In the interval of parade and dinner time, the princes his brothers, the general officers, and one or two of his chamberlains, dined with His Majesty, whose table was as well furnished as could be expected in a country which afforded neither game, poultry, nor fine meat, and where they were obliged to get all their wheat from Magdeburg.

When his dinner was over, the King retired to his cabinet, and amused himself with writing until five or six; when a young man named Darget, formerly secretary to M. de Valori, the French envoy, read to him. At seven he had a little concert, at which he played the flute as well as any of the best performers. His own compositions were frequently played among other pieces, for there was no art he did not cultivate; and had he lived among the Greeks he would not have had the mortification to confess, like Epaminondas, that he did not understand music.

Dinner took place in a little hall whose most remarkable ornament was a painting which he had commissioned from Pesne,* his artist, and one of our best colourists. It was a gorgeous priapic scene – young fellows embracing women, nymphs with satyrs, cupids in all sorts of positions; and spectators delighted with these encounters, turtle doves which billed and cooed, bucks leaping on hinds, and rams on sheep.

Our meals were hardly less philosophical. Had some passer-by chanced to hear us, and seen this painting, he might have thought us the seven wise men of Greece – in a brothel. Never, in any corner of the world, had one spoken with such freedom about human superstitions; never were these discussed with such humour and such scorn. God was respected, but not one of those who had deceived mankind in his name was spared.

Neither women nor priests ever entered this palace. In short, Frederick lived here without court, counsellors or Church.

Certain provincial judges wished to have an obscure and

wretched peasant burnt, who had been accused by a priest of amorous affairs with a donkey: no one could be executed until the King had confirmed the judgment – a most humane law, practised in England and other countries; Frederick wrote, below the judgment, that in his dominions he allowed 'freedom of conscience and of c—' [. . .]

Frederick governed the Church as despotically as he did the State. It was he who announced divorces when a man and a woman wished to re-marry elsewhere. A clergyman once referred him to the Old Testament concerning one of these divorces; 'Moses' – replied Frederick – 'directed his Jews as he wished to, while I govern my Prussians as I think best.'

This exceptional way of government, these private ways of an even rarer kind, this contrast of Stoic and Epicurean attitudes, of strictness in military discipline and indulgence within the palace, of pages who provide delight in one's private room, and of soldiers who are flogged thirty-six times below the King's windows while he watches them; of moral exhortations and unrestricted freedom: seen together, this comprised a bizarre picture, which few at that time knew, and which has since spread through Europe.

The greatest economy was observed at Potsdam in every particular: the King's own table, and those appointed for his officers and domestics, were regulated at thirty-three crowns a day, exclusive of wine. Instead of the officers of the crown taking charge of that expense, as at other courts, it devolved solely on His Majesty's valet de chambre, Fredersdorf, who was at once his high steward, great cup bearer, and first pantler.

Whether it was for thrift, or for political reasons, he never allowed the slightest of favours to his earlier favourites, least of all to those who had risked their life for him when he was crown prince. He did not repay the money he had borrowed at that time; just as Louis XII failed to make good the wrongs done by the Duke of Orleans, so the King of Prussia ignored the debts he had incurred as crown prince.

That wretched mistress of his, who had been whipped for his sake by the public hangman, had by this time been married to the clerk in charge of the city cabs: for there were eighteen in Berlin; and her erstwhile lover granted her a pension of seventy crowns, which has always been most scrupulously paid. Her name was Mme Shommers; she was tall, thin, and like one of the Sybils – in no way resembling someone who should be whipped for a prince.

Meanwhile, at Berlin, on public days, the King displayed great magnificence. *Then* it was a superb spectacle to see him at table, surrounded by twenty princes of the empire, attended by thirty-two pages, and an equal number of young heiduques all spendidly clothed, and bearing salvers of massy gold; the complete table service being of that metal, and the richest in Europe. The officers of state had their respective employments on these occasions – but at no other time.

After dinner, there was the opera, in that great room, three hundred feet in length, built – without an architect – by Knobelsdorff, one of his chamberlains. He paid willingly for the best singers and dancers. La Barberina* then danced on his stage: she is the one who later married his chancellor's son. The King had captured this dancer in Venice, and his soldiers carried her, via Vienna, all the way to Berlin. He was somewhat attached to her, since she had masculine legs. What no one could understand, is that he paid her a salary of thirty-two thousand livres.

In contrast, his Italian poet received only twelve hundred livres. For this, he had to versify all the operas which had been devised by the King; but one should reflect that he was extremely ugly, and that he did not dance. In short Barberina received on her own more than the ministers of state. As for the Italian poet, he eventually repaid himself with his own hands. In a chapel adorned by the first King of Prussia, he detached and abstracted the gold lace with which it was decorated. The King – who never visited this chapel – said that he had not lost anything. In any case, he had only just written a Dissertation approving of thieves, which had been printed in the records of his Academy; and on this occasion he did not think it appropriate to contradict his writings by deeds.

This indulgence did not extend to military matters. In the prison at Spandau there was an aged nobleman from Franche-Comté, six feet tall, whom the late king had acquired on account of his stature; he had been promised a post as chamberlain, but he was made a soldier. This wretched man soon deserted with several of his comrades; he was captured and brought before the late king, to whom he had the naivety to say that his sole regret was not to have killed such a tyrant as the King. In response, his nose and ears were cut off; he had to run the gauntlet in front of the regiment thirty-six times; after which he was sent to wheel a barrow at Spandau prison. He was still behind a barrow when M. de Valori, our envoy, urged me to ask for his pardon from the most clement son of that most hard-hearted Frederick-William [. . .] At length I wrote to him, in verse [. . .]

If it is in verse, one has the privilege of saying what one wants. The King promised to amend the matter; and a few months later he even had the grace to lodge the gentleman in question in an alms-house, granting him sixpence a day.* He had refused this kindness to the Queen, his mother – who had, it seems, made the request in prose.

In the midst of feasts, operas, and suppers, my secret nego-tiation proceeded; the King encouraged me to speak on every-thing, and I contrived to intermingle questions concerning France and Austria with the *Aeneid* and Livy's *Roman History*. The conversation was sometimes animated; the King would tell me warmly, that while France was knocking on every door to obtain peace, he would not think it advisable to declare war in her defence. I sent my reflections to His Majesty upon a paper with a blank margin. To this question, 'Can it be doubted that the house of Austria will seize the very first opportunity to re-demand Silesia?' the monarch wrote in the margin this answer:

Ils seront reçus, biribiri,	Just let them come, tra la, tra la,
À la façon de Barbari,	We'll thump them dumb,
Mon ami.	Ha ha, ha ha.

This new kind of negotiation ended by the Prussian monarch saying to me in one of his lively conversations, criticising the King of England – his dear uncle: 'George of England was the uncle of *Frederick*, but not of the *King of Prussia*. Let France declare war on Great Britain, and I will march.'

This was all I wanted. I returned instantly to France, and gave an account of my journey. I conveyed such hopes to the French ministry as had been given to me at Berlin; nor were they false, for in the following spring the King of Prussia concluded a new treaty with France, and advanced into Bohemia with 100,000 men, while the Austrians were in Alsace [. . .]

[Mme de Châteauroux, the mistress of Louis xv, died in 1744.]

A new mistress was necessary. The choice fell on a young lady by the name of Poisson,* daughter of a kept woman and a peasant from La Ferté-sous-Jouarre, who had made money selling corn to food merchants. This poor man was at the time in hiding, having been convicted of some malpractice. His daughter had been married to the deputy tax-farmer Le Normand, lord of the manor of Étiole, nephew of the senior tax-farmer Le Normand de Tournehem, who kept the mother. The daughter was well-educated, sensible, pleasing, indeed charming and accomplished, and born with good sense and kindness. I knew her well – in fact she confided in me, telling me of her love. She admitted to me that she had always had a secret feeling that the King would love her, and that she had experienced a violent attraction towards him, though she had not fully comprehended what it meant.

This idea, which might have seemed fanciful in her position, was based on her having often attended the hunts which the King held in the forest of Sénart. Tournehem, her mother's lover, owned a country residence nearby. Mme d'Étiole would be driven in an attractive open carriage. The King would notice her, and often sent a present of venison. Her mother repeatedly said to her that she was prettier by far than Mme de Châteauroux, and Tournehem would then exclaim: 'One must admit that Mme Poisson's daughter is fit for a king.' Later, when she had held the King in her arms, she told me that she believed most firmly in destiny; and she was right. I spent some months at Étiole with her, while the King was campaigning in 1746.

This brought rewards which had never been accorded to my writings, nor to my services. I was judged worthy to be one of the forty useless members of the Académie.* I was appointed Historiographer* of France; and the King awarded me the post of gentleman-in-ordinary* to his chamber. I concluded from these matters that, to make even the tiniest fortune, it was more profitable to say four words to a king's mistress than to write a hundred volumes.

No sooner did I appear to be a happy man than all my colleagues and fellow-wits in Paris turned on me, with all the savagery and hatred they could express against a person who had been given the rewards which they believed were due to them.

Meanwhile I remained bound to the Marquise du Châtelet by an unchanging friendship, and by a common love of study. We stayed together, both in Paris and in the country. Cirey is on the frontier of Lorraine: King Stanislas* then kept his small and charming court at Lunéville. Old and pious as he was, he had a mistress: this was Mme the Marquise de Boufflers. He allowed his soul to be divided between her, and a Jesuit named Menou, the most scheming and audacious priest I have ever known. This man had extorted nearly a million livres from King Stanislas by means of the Queen's importunities (Menou had governed this lady). A part of this sum was employed to erect a magnificent mansion for himself and for other Jesuits in the city of Nancy. This mansion was endowed with rents of twenty-four thousand livres – twelve thousand for Menou's table, and twelve thousand for him to distribute as he wished.

The mistress was not so well treated by any means. At that time she hardly received enough from the King of Poland to pay for her clothing; yet even so the Jesuit envied what she received, and was frantically jealous of the Marquise. They were publicly at odds. The King, poor man, had constant difficulties at the end of mass to reconcile his mistress and his confessor.

In the end the Jesuit, who had heard of Mme du Châtelet, who was extremely handsome and still very beautiful, fancied that he might substitute her for Mme de Boufflers. Stanislas occasionally spent time writing little works of a mediocre kind: Menou imagined that a woman who wrote might succeed with him better than a woman who did not. So he came to Cirey to execute this cunning plot: he flattered Mme du Châtelet, saying that King Stanislas would be enchanted to see us: then back he went to the King, saying that we were hoping most eagerly to pay him our respects; Stanislas proposed to Mme de Boufflers that she should arrange for us to come.

So in fact we went to Lunéville, where we spent the whole of 1749. What happened was exactly the opposite of what the Reverend Father wished. We became attached to Mme de Boufflers, and the Jesuit had to fight two women, not one.

Life at the court of Lorraine was pleasant enough, though – as elsewhere – there were intrigues and machinations. Towards the end of the year Poncet, Bishop of Troyes,* who had great debts and little reputation, wished to join our court and join in the machinations: when I say that he had little reputation, understand that this includes the quality of his funeral orations and his sermons. With the help of our two ladies, he obtained the post of grand almoner to the King – who was gratified to have a bishop among his employees, and for a very low wage.

The bishop only arrived in 1750. He began by falling in love with Mme de Boufflers, and was expelled. His anger fell on Louis xv, Stanislas's son-in-law: for when he returned to Troyes, he wished to take part in the ridiculous matter of the 'confessional notes', invented by Beaumont, the Archbishop of Paris, and resisted parliament and defied the King. It was not the best way to repay his debts; but it served to get him locked up. The King of France sent him to Alsace, imprisoned in a convent of coarse German monks. But I must return to my real concern.

Mme du Châtelet died in Stanislas's palace, after two days' illness.* We were all so distressed that none of us thought to send for a priest, a Jesuit or the sacrament. She knew none of the horrors of death; these were felt only by ourselves. I was prey to the most sorrowful affliction. Kindly King Stanislas came to my room to comfort and weep with me. Few of his equals would do as much on these occasions. He wished to keep me with him: but I could no longer endure Lunéville, and I returned to Paris.

It was my fate to hurry from king to king, despite my idolatrous love of freedom. The King of Prussia – to whom I had often indicated that I would never leave Mme du Châtelet for him – wished to capture me by any means that he could, once he was rid of his rival. At that moment he was enjoying a period of peace, achieved through victories, and all his leisure hours were employed in writing verses, or the history of his country and his campaigns. To be sure, he was in himself fully convinced that his verse and his prose were far superior to my verse and my prose; but he calculated that, for form's sake, I might, as an academician, add some slight touch of elegance to his writings; there was no limit to the flattery, the enticements he held out, to persuade me to come.

Who could resist a hero, a poet, a musician, and a philosopher, who seemed to love me, and whom I thought I loved in return? I set out once more for Potsdam in June 1750. Astolphus did not meet a kinder reception in the palace of Alcina* than I did of His Prussian Majesty. I was lodged in apartments which had been occupied by Marshal Saxe, had the royal cooks at my command when I chose to dine alone, and the royal coachmen when I was inclined to take the air. But these were trifling favours compared to the honours conferred on me by the King. Our suppers were very agreeable, and, so I thought, most witty occasions. The King was witty, and excited the wit of others. I worked two hours each day with His Majesty, corrected all his compositions, praised what was most deserving of praise, and rejected all that was unworthy of him. I explained to him in writing all that I thought necessary concerning rhetoric and criticism. He profited by my advice, but his own genius assisted him more effectually than my lessons. I never felt myself more at ease. I had no court to make, no visits to pay, no duty to fulfil. I led the life of liberty, and felt myself perfectly happy in my situation.

Alcina-Frederick, who saw that I was already half persuaded, doubled his enchanted draughts to bewitch me entirely. The final seduction came with a letter written in his apartment and sent to mine. A mistress could not declare her feelings more tenderly; in his letter, he endeavoured to dispel any fears which I might have, on account of his rank and character; it contained these remarkable phrases:

> How could I ever desire to render the man whom I esteem and love unhappy? the man who gives up for my sake his country – all that is reckoned dear among men? . . . I respect you as my master in learning and eloquence, I love you as a virtuous friend. What change, what slavery, what unhappiness, or inconstancy of fortune have you to fear in a country where you are as highly valued as you are in your own, and with a friend whose heart is grateful? I respected the friendship which attached you to Mme du Châtelet; but *now* I am one of your oldest friends. I promise you, that you will be happy here, so long as I shall live.*

Few majesties have written such a letter. It was the final glass which intoxicated me. And his spoken assurances were far greater than what he had written. He was used to remarkable demonstrations of emotion with favourites far younger than myself; and, forgetting for a moment that I was no longer their age, and that my hand was no longer beautiful, he seized and kissed it. I kissed his hand, and became his slave. Permission was needed from the King of France that I might belong to two masters. The King of Prussia undertook all this negotiation.

He wrote to France, to the King my master, asking to have me. It had not crossed my mind that Versailles would be shocked, that a gentleman in waiting – the most useless of courtiers – should become a useless chamberlain in Berlin. Full permission was granted. But much offence was taken; and I was not forgiven. I had greatly displeased the King of France, without giving any corresponding pleasure to the King of Prussia, who sneered at me in his private thought.

So I was rewarded with a silver-gilt key, hung on my coat, a cross round my neck, and an allowance of twenty thousand francs. It made Maupertuis fall ill, but I was not aware of this. There was at this time a doctor in Berlin, by the name of La Mettrie,* the most outspoken atheist in any faculty of medicine in Europe: at the same time he was cheerful, humorous, careless, as well-versed in theory as any of his colleagues, and without argument the world's worst doctor in practical matters; there-fore, thank God, he did not practise at all. He had mocked the entire Faculty at Paris, and had even written a great deal against their doctors in personal terms – which they by no means forgave; they obtained a warrant for his arrest. La Mettrie therefore withdrew to Berlin, where his cheerful manner gave much entertainment; meanwhile he continued to write, and printed the most outrageous matters concerning morality. His books delighted the King, who made him, not his physician, but his reader.

One day, after a reading, La Mettrie – who could say to the King whatever came into his head – told him that there was much envy of me, for my favour and for my fortune. 'Let us talk,' replied the King. 'An orange is for squeezing; when you've drunk the juice, you throw it away.'* La Mettrie did not fail to transmit to me this pithy remark – a saying worthy of Dionysius of Syracuse.

From that moment I determined to find a safe place for the skin of the orange. I had some three hundred thousand crowns to protect. I took care not to deposit this sum in my Alcina's territory; I invested it, to my advantage, in the lands in France owned by the Duke of Wurtemberg.* The King – he opened all my letters – saw clearly that I was not expecting to stay with him. But a frenzy of poetry-writing had seized him, as it did Dionysius. So I was needed, endlessly trimming, and tidying, and re-editing his *History of Brandenburg*, and everything else that he wrote.

La Mettrie died after eating an entire truffle pâté, at the end of a very large dinner at Lord Tyrconnel's, the French ambassador. It was claimed that he had confessed before he died; the King was horrified: he made exhaustive enquiries, to see if it was true; he was assured that it was the vilest slander, and that La Mettrie had died as he had lived, denying both God and all doctors. Satisfied, His Majesty promptly composed his funeral oration, which was read aloud in his name by Darget, his secretary, in the public assembly of the Academy, and he gave an allowance of six hundred crowns for a lady of fortune whom La Mettrie had brought to Paris after he had abandoned his wife and children.

Maupertuis, who had heard the story of the orange skin, chose this moment to spread the rumour that I had said the post of Atheist to the King* was vacant. This calumny came to nothing; but he added, later, that I thought poorly of the King's poetry, and that found its mark.

I was aware from that moment that the King's suppers were not so joyous; I was not given so many verses to correct; my disgrace was complete.

Algarotti, Darget and another Frenchman named Chasot,* who was one of his best officers, all left him at the same time. I was preparing to do the same. But I wished first to make fun of a book Maupertuis had just published.* It was the moment to do so – never had such ridiculous, stupid stuff been written. This good fellow was seriously proposing that a voyage should be made directly to the north and south poles; that giants' heads should be dissected, to know, via their brains, the nature of the soul; to build a city, where only Latin should be spoken; to dig out a hole, right down to the centre of the earth; to cure illnesses by covering the sick in pine-resin; and finally to predict the future by becoming delirious.

The King laughed at this book, I laughed, everyone laughed.

But a more serious matter then arose, to do with some mathematical matter which Maupertuis wished to class as a 'discovery'. A far more learned geometrician, named Kœnig, librarian to the Princess of Orange at the Hague, proved to him that he was wrong, and that Leibnitz (who had earlier examined this concept) had demonstrated the error of this idea in several of his letters, which Kœnig had shown to him.

Maupertuis – president of the Berlin Academy – was indignant that an associate from another country should reveal his errors, and instantly persuaded the King that Kœnig (insofar as he was established in Holland) was his enemy, and had spoken most unkindly of His Majesty's prose and verse to the Princess of Orange.

Having taken this essential precaution, he suborned a few hangers-on of the Academy, who were dependent on him, and had Kœnig condemned (as a forger of documents) to be struck off the register of academicians. The Dutch geometrician had already taken action sending back his certificate of appointment to the Academy of Berlin. Throughout Europe, men of letters were as indignant at Maupertuis' scheming as they were bored with his book. He brought on himself the hatred and scorn of those who took an interest in philosophy, and of those who couldn't understand it at all. In Berlin, we were content to shrug our shoulders, since the King had taken sides in this wretched affair, and no one dared to say a word; I was the only one who spoke up.* Kœnig was my friend; it was my pleasure to defend both the liberty of men of letters, and a friend's cause, and at the same time to strike out at any enemy who was as much an enemy of modesty as he was of myself. I had no intention of staying in Berlin; I had always preferred freedom above all else. Few men of letters can do this. Most are poor; and poverty saps one's courage; and any philosopher who lives at court becomes just as much a slave as a first officer of the crown. I was aware how much my freedom must displease a monarch who was more absolute than the Grand Turk. Within his residence, one must admit, he was a king with a singular sense of humour. He would protect Maupertuis, yet mocked him more than any other. He began to write a piece against him, and sent his manuscript to my room, carried by Marwitz, one of the agents of his private pleasures; he had demonstrated the absurdity of the hole dug to the centre of the earth, of his method of curing complaints with a smearing of pine-resin, of the journey to the south pole, of the Latin-speaking city, and of the pusillanimous behaviour of his Academy which had condoned the tyrannous treatment of poor Kœnig. But since his motto was *No noise – unless I make it*, he had everything about this affair burnt, except his own piece.

I returned to him the decoration of his order, his chamberlain's key, his allowances; then he did all that he could to keep me, and I did my best to leave. He sent me back his cross and key, and desired me to take supper with him; so I partook of another Damocles' supper; after which I left, promising to return, and firmly resolved never to see him again.

There were therefore four of us who got away, in a short space of time, Chasot, Darget, Algarotti and myself. The situation had in fact become unbearable. One knows, that one must suffer as a king's companion; but Frederick took too much advantage of his prerogative. There are rules in society – unless it is the society of the lion and the goat. Frederick regularly broke society's first law – never to speak discourteously to anyone. He would often ask his chamberlain, Pöllnitz,* if he would be willing to change his religion for the fourth time, and offered to pay him a hundred crowns, cash down, if he would agree to be converted. 'God help me, Pöllnitz' – he would say – 'I've forgotten his name again, the name of that man you robbed at the Hague, when you sold him impure silver as the real thing; remind me who he was, would you?' He behaved in much the same way with poor d'Argens.* And yet these two victims stayed there. Pöllnitz had spent all he possessed, and was constrained to swallow these serpents for his living; he had no other resource; while d'Argens' only worldly goods were his *Lettres juives* and his wife, whose name was Cochois. She was a poor provincial actress, so ugly that she could not earn any money in any trade, though she attempted several. As for Maupertuis, who had foolishly invested his capital in Berlin, never dreaming that it would be better to have a hundred pistoles in a free country than a thousand in one ruled by a tyrant, he had no choice but to stay in the chains which he had made for himself.

On leaving Alcina's palace, I went for a month to stay with Mme the Duchess of Saxe-Gotha, the best princess in the world, the sweetest, wisest and calmest, and who, thank goodness, wrote no poetry. From her, I travelled on to spend a few days with the Landgravine of Hesse-Kassel, in her country residence – and she was even less inclined to poetry than the Princess of Gotha. I could breathe again. Soon after, I continued on my way to Frankfurt. There the oddest fate was awaiting me.

At Frankfurt I fell ill; one of my nieces,* the widow of a captain in the regiment of Champagne, a most likeable and talented lady (and who was also considered in Paris as excellent company) had the courage to leave Paris in order to meet me on the banks of the Main; but she arrived to find a prisoner of war. Let me explain how this choice adventure had come to pass. There was then at Frankfurt a fellow by the name of Freytag. He had been banished from Dresden, after being condemned to the pillory and hard labour. Later, he had become the Frankfurt agent of the King of Prussia, who was happy to use such servants, since their wages were no more than what they could extract from passing travellers.

This ambassador, and a merchant by the name of Schmid, who had earlier been found guilty and fined for counterfeiting, signified to me – on behalf of His Majesty the King of Prussia – that I would not be allowed to leave Frankfurt until I had returned the valuable effects which I had abstracted from His Majesty. 'Alas, gentlemen! I've taken nothing away from that country, I swear to you – not even the slightest regrets. So what are the jewels from the crown of Brandenburg which you wish to recover?' – 'Vell thir,' replied Freytag, 'itth the poetic verk of the King my graciouth mathter.' – 'Ah, I'll return his prose and his verse with all my heart,' I answered, 'even though I've more than sufficient right to the work. He gave me a fine copy of it, printed at his own expense. Unfortunately, that copy is at Leipzig, with the rest of my belongings.' Whereupon Freytag proposed that I stay in Frankfurt until this treasure which was in Leipzig arrived; and he inscribed this charming note:

Sir, as soon as the big package from Leipzig has arrived, which contains the Work of Poetry of the King my master, which His Majesty requires, and this Work of Poetry has been handed to me, you may go wherever you please. Frankfurt, 1 June 1753, (signed) Freytag, resident of the King my master.

I wrote at the bottom of the note: *This bond for the Work of Poetry of the King your master*; with which the resident was very satisfied.

On 17 June the big package of *poetic verks* arrived. In good faith I handed over this second trust, imagining that I might now go, without disrespect to any crowned head whatsoever; but at the moment I was leaving, I was arrested – myself, my secretary, and my servants; my niece was arrested; four soldiers dragged her through the muddy streets to this merchant, Schmid, who boasted some kind of title as the privy counsellor to the King of Prussia. This Frankfurt merchant now saw himself as a Prussian general: in this momentous matter he had charge of a dozen municipal soldiers, which he exercised with all appropriate pomposity. My niece had a passport from the King of France; and, more important, she had never corrected the King of Prussia's poetry. It is customary to respect ladies during the horrors of war; but counsellor Schmid and resident Freytag, acting on Frederick's behalf, believed that they were following his desire as they dragged this poor lady through the mud. We were both crammed into a kind of hostelry, with a dozen soldiers posted at the door: four others were put in my room, four in the attic (where my niece had been lodged), four in a hovel open to the winds, where my secretary had to sleep on the straw. To be truthful, my niece did have a little bed; but her four soldiers, each with a bayonet on his gun, took the place of curtains and a lady's maid.

In vain did we say that we were appealing to Caesar, that the Emperor had been elected in Frankfurt, that my secretary was a Florentine and a subject of His Imperial Majesty, that my niece and I were subjects of the Most Christian King, and that we had no quarrel with the Markgraf of Brandenburg: we were answered that the Markgraf had better credit in Frankfurt than the Emperor. We were prisoners of war for twelve days, and we had to pay for it – one hundred and forty crowns a day.

The merchant, Schmid, had seized all my belongings, which were returned to me lighter by half. I could not have paid more dearly for the *poetic verk of the King of Prussia*. I lost, more or less, the sum he had laid out to bring me to Berlin and have lessons from me. At the end, therefore, we came out quits.

To complete this adventure, a certain Van Duren,* a bookseller at the Hague, a professional rogue and habitual bankrupt, had come to live in Frankfurt. This was the same person to whom, thirteen years before, I had entrusted the manuscript of Frederick's *Anti-Machiavel*. He claimed that His Majesty still owed him some twenty ducats, and that this was my responsibility. He calculated the interest, and the interest due upon the interest. A certain M. Fichard, burgomaster of Frankfurt, who was at that moment the senior burgomaster, as it is called, declared – in his capacity as burgomaster – that this reckoning was indeed correct, and in his senior capacity, he made me hand over thirty ducats, took twenty-six for himself, and gave four to this rogue of a bookseller.

Once this matter of Ostrogoths and Vandals was over, I shook hands with my hosts, and thanked them for their kindly care.

Soon after, I went to take the waters at Plombières, but I really drank the waters of Lethe, for I knew that misfortunes, of whatever kind, should only be forgotten. My niece, Mme Denis, who consoled me in my difficulties, and who had become attached to me through love of letters, and through most tender friendship, accompanied me from Plombières to Lyons [. . .]

I had been advised to take the waters at Aix-en-Savoie; even though these were controlled by a king, I directed my course towards them. Thus I had to travel through Geneva: the celebrated Dr Tronchin, only recently established in Geneva, declared to me that the waters at Aix would kill me, and that he would keep me alive.

I accepted his wager. Catholics are not allowed to live in Geneva, no more than they are in the Protestant cantons. It seemed an amusing thing, that I should acquire land in the one part of the world where I was not allowed to do so.

Following an extraordinary and unprecedented agreement, I bought a modest property of some ninety acres,* which was sold me for twice what it would have cost near Paris; but pleasure never costs us too much; the house is attractive and convenient; its setting is charming; on arrival, one is surprised, but never bored. On one side, you have lake Geneva; on the other, the city. The river Rhône comes foaming out of the lake, to form a canal at the bottom of my garden; the river Arve, coming down from Savoy, pours into the Rhône; and further on, you see yet another river. A hundred country houses, a hundred happy gardens adorn the shores of the lake and the river banks; the Alps rise up in the distance, and through their precipices you can glimpse twenty leagues of mountains, covered in perpetual snow. At Lausanne, I have an even finer house,* with an even wider prospect; but my house near Geneva is much more pleasant. In these two dwellings I possess what kings will never give you – or rather, what they will take away: tranquillity and freedom; and I still have what they sometimes give, but which I have not received from them; I have put into practice what I described in 'The Man of the World' [Le Mondain]: 'How good it is, this iron age!'

All the amenities of life – furnishings, carriages, the pleasures of the table – are present in my two houses; the company of amiable and intelligent people occupies those moments which remain to me after my studies and the care of my health. There is enough in all this to make more than one of my dear colleagues in the fraternity of letters burst with envy: yet I was not born to riches – far from it. People ask me, what is the secret which has enabled me to live like a wealthy tax-farmer; it is proper to reveal it, so that my example may be of use. I have seen so many men of letters despised for their poverty that I determined long ago not to become one of their number.

In France, one is either the hammer or the anvil: I was born as an anvil. A modest inheritance becomes even more modest as the days go by, since prices are bound to rise, and the government often tampers with pensions and with funds. One must pay attention to all the manipulations which the administration (always in debt, and always illogical) makes in the State's finances. There is always some point where a private person can benefit, without obligation to anyone; and there is nothing so gratifying as making one's fortune for oneself: the first stage may be laborious; the rest is easy. When young, one must be thrifty; in old age, one discovers that one has surprising resources. This is the time when a fortune is most necessary; I am now enjoying it; and, having lived as the guest of kings, I have made myself a king in my own property, in spite of immense losses.

Since I have lived in this peaceful state of opulence, enjoying the greatest kind of independence, the King of Prussia has come back to me;* in 1755 he sent me an opera which he had made from my tragedy *Mérope*. It was, without argument, the very worst piece he has ever written. Since then he has continued to write to me; I have always maintained a correspondence with his sister, the Margravine of Bayreuth, who has invariably shown me great kindness.

Meanwhile, as I was enjoying in my retreat the sweetest life one could imagine, I had the modest philosophical pleasure to observe that the kings of Europe were not in fact savouring such happy tranquillity, and to conclude that the situation of a private person is often preferable to that of the greatest kings – as you shall see.

England waged a war of piracy on France, all for a few acres of snow, in 1756;* at the same time the Empress, the Queen of Hungary, appeared to have some desire to recover – if she could – her cherished Silesia, torn from her by the King of Prussia. Having this plan, she was negotiating with the Empress of Russia and with the King of Poland – but only in his quality as Elector of Saxony: for one never negotiates with the Poles. The King of France, for his part, wanted revenge on the territory of Hanover, for the harm which the Elector of Hanover (the King of England) was doing him on the high seas. Frederick, who was at that moment allied with France, and who had a profound contempt for our government, preferred an alliance with England to the one he had with France, and linked himself with the Hanoverians, calculating that, on the one hand, this would prevent the Russians from advancing into Prussia, and, on the other, it would stop the French from entering Germany; in these two ideas he was mistaken; but there was a third in which he was not in the least mistaken: to invade Saxony under the pretext of friendship, and to make war on the Empress, the Queen of Hungary, with the money he had pillaged from the Saxons.

Through this exceptional manoeuvre the Marquis of Brandenburg [*i.e.,* Frederick] was able on his own to change the entire policy of Europe. The King of France, who wished to keep him as an ally, had sent him the Duc de Nivernais – a witty man, who wrote delightful verse. An ambassador who was both duke, peer and poet would have flattered Frederick's vanity and his taste; but he laughed at the King of France, and signed his treaty with England on the very day that the ambassador arrived in Berlin – receiving the duke and peer most civilly, and writing an epigram against the poet [. . .]

[At this time] Mademoiselle Poisson, Madame Le Normand, Marquise de Pompadour, was effectively the Prime Minister. Certain outrageous phrases uttered against her by Frederick – who spared neither women nor poets – had struck the Marquise's heart, and had no slight part in the revolution in affairs which instantly united the houses of France and Austria, after more than two centuries of a supposedly undying hatred. The court of France, which had thought to have crushed Austria in 1741, supported Austria in 1756, and shortly one saw France, Russia, Sweden, Hungary, half Germany and the paying part of the Empire declared against the Marquis of Brandenburg alone.

This prince, whose ancestor was barely able to maintain 20,000 men, had an army of 100,000 infantry and 40,000 cavalry, well-organised, better-trained, and fully equipped; but against this, there were over 400,000 men in arms opposed to Brandenburg.

In this war, to begin with, it fell out that each party took what it was in a position to take. Frederick took Saxony, France took Frederick's territories from the town of Guelders as far as Minden, on the Wesel, and took possession for a while of the entire Electorate of Hanover, and of Hesse, one of Frederick's allies; the Empress of Russia took the whole of Prussia: while its King, defeated at first by the Russians, then defeated the Austrians, was afterwards beaten by them in Bohemia on 18 June 1757.*

The loss of a battle should have destroyed this monarch – or so one might think. Harried on every side by the Russians, the Austrians and by France, he himself thought he was lost. At Stade, Marshal de Richelieu had just signed a treaty with Hanover and Hesse, which resembled that of the Romans at the Caudine Forks.* Their army was no longer to be in service; the Marshal was poised to enter Saxony with 60,000 men; the Prince de Soubise was about to invade from another point with more than 30,000, and was supported by the army of the Imperial allies; from there, they would proceed to Berlin. The Austrians had been victors in a second engagement, and had already reached Breslau; indeed, one of their generals had pressed on to Berlin, and had exacted tribute; the King of Prussia's treasury was virtually empty, and there would soon be not even a single village remaining to him; he would soon be banished from the Empire; the matter was in the courts; he was declared a rebel; and had he been captured, it seems that he would have been condemned to lose his head.

Being in such desperate straights, he wondered if he should kill himself. He wrote to his sister, Mme the Margravine of Bayreuth, that he was going to put an end to his life: he would conclude the matter with some lines of poetry; his passion for verse was stronger than the hatred of life. So he wrote a long epistle in verse* to the Marquis d'Argens, in which he explained his resolution, and bade him farewell [. . .]

Frederick sent me a copy of this epistle, written in his own hand. Several lines are stolen in part from the Abbé de Chaulieu or myself. The ideas are incoherent, most of the lines are poorly turned, but some are good; and it is indeed something for a king to have composed two hundred lines of bad verse, given the state he was in. He wished it to be said that he had kept his presence of mind, his freedom of thought, at a moment when most men are bereft.

The letter he wrote to me displayed the same feelings; but there were fewer myrtles and roses, *Ixions*, and deepest grief. Replying in prose, I opposed the decision, which he said he had taken, to die, and I had no trouble in persuading him to live. I advised him to undertake negotiations with the Marshal de Richelieu, and imitate the Duke of Cumberland; in fact I took all the liberties one may take with a poet in despair, who is quite prepared to be a king no longer. He did in fact write to the Marshal de Richelieu; but, when he received no reply, he determined to defeat us. He sent me word that he would do battle with the Prince de Soubise; his letter ended with lines more worthy of his situation, his dignity, his courage and his mind:

> And should my verses now be wrecked,
> Then grant that in the tempest's teeth
> I think, and live, and die a king.*

As he advanced towards the French and Imperial forces, he wrote to Mme the Margravine of Bayreuth, his sister, that he would kill himself; but he was happier than either his words or his expectations. On 5 November 1757, he awaited the French and Imperial army in a somewhat advantageous position, at Rosbach, on the border of Saxony; and as he had regularly spoken of getting himself killed, he determined that his brother, Prince Heinrich, should fulfil his promise at the head of four Prussian battalions, which were to withstand the first assault of the hostile armies, while they were battered by his artillery and while his cavalry attacked theirs.

In the event Prince Heinrich was slightly wounded in the breast by a musket shot; and he was, I believe, the only Prussian to be wounded on that day. The French and the Austrians fled at the first volley. It was the most unprecedented, the completest rout in the whole of recorded history. The battle of Rosbach will long be famous: 30,000 French and 20,000 Imperial troops fled headlong and shamefully from five battalions and a few squadrons of horse. The defeats of Agincourt, Crécy, and Poitiers were not so humiliating.

The discipline and military drill established by his father, and perfected by his son, were the true cause of this memorable victory. The Prussian exercise had been coming nearer and nearer to perfection for fifty years. France and other countries had endeavoured to imitate them, but without effect, particularly the French, who had a natural aversion to discipline, and could not possibly accomplish in four years what it had cost the Prussians fifty to complete. In France they changed their manoeuvres at each review, by which means neither officers nor soldiers were perfect in their evolutions, and they took the field ignorant and undisciplined. The mere prospect of the regular conduct of the Prussians threw them into disorder, and within fifteen minutes Fortune snatched Frederick from despair to place him on a pinnacle of glory.

Yet he feared that this happiness might quickly pass; he feared he would have to resist the combined and weighty power of France, Russia and Austria, and he would gladly have separated Louis xv from Maria Theresa.

The fatal day of Rosbach made all France ill-pleased with the Abbé de Bernis' treaty with the court of Vienna [. . .]

Yet there was a kind of greatness in the French ministry, to refuse to make peace with the King of Prussia, after he had beaten and humiliated them; there was good faith and much good will to continue suffering for the house of Austria: and for long enough these virtues had but little recompense.

Those from Hanover, Brunswick and Hesse were less loyal to their treaties, and did better for themselves. They had agreed with the Marshal de Richelieu that they would not take up arms against us; that they would re-cross the Elbe, beyond which they had been expelled; they went back on their agreement of the Caudine Forks, the moment they learnt that we had been beaten at Rosbach. Poor discipline, desertions, illness destroyed our army, and by the spring of 1758 the result of all our labours was that we had lost 300,000,000 crowns, and 50,000 men in Germany for Maria Theresa, just as we had done in the war of 1741 – when we fought against her.

Having beaten our army at Rosbach, in Thuringia, the King of Prussia left to fight the Austrian army some sixty leagues away. The French could still have entered Saxony, their victors were marching elswhere; there was nothing to stop the French; but they had thrown away their arms, lost their cannon, ammunition, provisions – and their head. They scattered. With difficulty, their equipment was gathered together. Meanwhile Frederick, a month later to the day, gains another victory,* more noted and more difficult, over the Austrian army near Breslau; he recaptures Breslau, takes 15,000 prisoners; the rest of Silesia returns to his rule: Gustavus Adolphus never achieved as much. After this one must indeed forgive him his poetry, his little jokes, his spitefulness, and even his faults as regards the feminine sex. All the defects of the man are effaced, before the glory of a hero.

At *Les Délices*, 6 November 1759
I had left off my *Memoirs* there, thinking they were as futile as Bayle's *Letters* to his beloved mother, as the *Life of Saint-Évremond* written by Des Maiseaux, and as that of the Abbé de Montgon which he wrote for himself; but a flood of things which seem new or amusing bring me back to the foolishness of talking of myself – to myself.

From my windows I can see the city where Jean Chauvin, called Calvin, from Picardy, was ruler, and the square where he had Servet burnt – for the good of his soul. Almost all the priests in this country think today as did Servet, and would indeed go further. Not for a moment do they believe in Jesus Christ as God; and these gentlemen, who have in the past rejected purgatory, have even become so human as to pardon those souls who are in hell. They maintain that their punishments are in no way eternal, that Theseus will not sit for ever in his chair, that Sisyphus will not always push his rock uphill: and so, from hell, in which they no longer believe, they have created purgatory, in which they used not to believe. It's an amusing revolution in the history of the human mind. There was enough in all this for throats to be cut, people to be burnt at the stake, St Bartholomew's massacres; but they haven't even abused each other, so much have manners changed. I am the only one any of these preachers has reproached, because I dared to suggest* that Calvin – the one from Picardy – was wrong and intolerant, and that he was mistaken to have Servet burnt. Do note, I beg you, this world's illogicalities. Here are people who are almost openly followers of Servet, and who abuse me for having thought it bad that Calvin had him burnt over a slow fire with green wood.

They wished to prove to me in due form that Calvin was a man of good will; they asked the council in Geneva to send them the documents concerning Servet's trial: the council, wiser than these people, refused; and they were not allowed to write against me in Geneva. I consider this little triumph as the noblest example of the progress of reason in our age.

Philosophy has achieved another, even greater, victory over its enemies at Lausanne. Certain ministers had thought, in that province, to compile a kind of volume against me – for the honour, as they said, of the Christian religion. I had no trouble to have these pamphlets seized, and to have them suppressed by magistrate's order; this is perhaps the first time theologians have been compelled to be silent, and respect a philosopher. Tell me, should I not love this country most passionately? To you, thinking beings, I say that it is a joy to live in a republic, and say to its leaders 'Come and dine with me tomorrow.' Yet I had still not found sufficient liberty; and – to my mind, a matter worth notice – to achieve this most fully I bought properties in France.* I found two that were suitable, a league distant from Geneva, which had in the past enjoyed all the rights and privileges of the city. It has been my fortune to receive from the King a warrant whereby I have retained these privileges. In short, I have so arranged my life that I am now independent, in Switzerland, in Geneva, and in France.

I've heard a lot of talk about liberty, but I don't think there has ever been any private person in the whole of Europe who has made himself a liberty like mine. Let who wishes, or who is able to, follow my example.

I could not have spent my time better, than in seeking such liberty and tranquillity away from Paris. At this time, they were as mad and embroiled in childish feuds as in the time of the Fronde; all they needed was a civil war; but since Paris neither had a popular leader, like the Duke of Beaufort, nor a coadjudicator giving his blessing with a dagger, there were only civil squabbles: they had begun with the banker's notes for the world to come, invented, as I've said already, by the Archbishop of Paris (Beaumont, a bigoted man, doing evil to the utmost of his ability by excess of zeal, seriously mad, a true saint in the line of Thomas à Becket). The dispute became more poisonous over an appointment which the Parliament of Paris thought was in its power, and which the Archbishop thought was a sacred post, dependent on the Church alone. All Paris joined in, the wretched Jansenists and Molinists plunged into the affray; the King wished to deal with them as one might with people fighting in the street; you throw buckets of water over them to separate them. Properly enough, he declared both sides were in the wrong; but they only became more vicious: he exiled the Archbishop, he exiled the Parliament; but a master should not dismiss his servants unless he knows he has others to replace them [. . .]

Indignation was voiced, and there were some who spoke openly in the Palace of Justice against the King. The fire in peoples' words spread, alas! to the brain of a servant named Damiens,* who had often to go to the great hall of the Palace. When, later, this fanatic was tried, it was proved that he had not thought to kill the King, but merely to inflict a little chastisement. There's no limit to what people will imagine. This miserable fellow had been a servant in the Jesuit college – a college where I have sometimes seen the students strike out with penknives, and the servants strike them back. Damiens went therefore to Versailles with this intention, and there, in the midst of the guards and the courtiers, he wounded the King with one of those little penknives used for trimming a quill.

In the first horror of this affray, the blame was, of course, laid on the Jesuits, who were – it was said – past masters in such matters [. . .]

The King mistakenly awarded large pensions to those of his councillors who conducted Damiens' trial, as if they had rendered some noted and difficult service. This had the result of inspiring the gentlemen of the court with fresh confidence; they saw themselves as people of importance, and their fantasies of representing the nation and acting as the mentors of the King were revived: once the trial was over, and they had nothing further to do, they amused themselves by persecuting the philosophers.

In front of the assembly, Omer Joly de Fleury, the advocate-general of the Parliament of Paris, gained the greatest triumph which ignorance, bad faith and hypocrisy have ever achieved. Various men of letters, admirable for their knowledge and their deeds, had joined together to compile an immense dictionary,* containing everything which can inform the human mind: it was a great undertaking for the French book trade: the chancellor and the ministers gave encouragement to this fine project. Seven volumes had already appeared; they were being translated into Italian, English, German and Dutch; and this treasure, offered to all nations by the French, could be considered as the noblest thing our nation was doing [. . .]

And then, on 23 February 1759, Omer Joly de Fleury accuses these wretched people of being atheists, deists, corrupters of youth, rebels against the King, etc. To prove such accusations, Omer quotes Saint Paul, Theophilus, and Abraham Chaumeix.[1] The only thing he hadn't done was to read the book he was attacking – or if he *had* read it, Omer was strangely mad. He appeals to the court for justice against the article *Soul*, which – according to him – is the purest materialism. You should note

---

[1] Abraham Chaumeix (1730–90), who had once been a vinegar merchant, had become a Jansenist and a convulsionary, and was at this time the oracle of the parliament of Paris. Omer Fleury referred to him as if he was one of the Fathers of the Church. Since then, Chaumeix has become a school teacher in Moscow.

that this article, *Soul*, is the work of a miserable doctor from the Sorbonne who cripples himself in condemning materialism through thick and thin. Omer Joly de Fleury's entire speech was composed of similar blunders. So he submits to justice a book which he has not read, or which he has not understood; and the entire parliament, accepting Omer's motion, condemns the work, not just without examining it, but without reading a single page [. . .]

The publishers had been granted royal authority. Parliament certainly lacks the right to annul privileges granted by His Majesty; it has no business to judge either decisions of the council, or matters appointed to the chancellery: yet it assumed the right to condemn what the chancellor had approved; and it named councillors to make decisions concerning the questions of geometry and metaphysics contained in the *Encyclopaedia* [. . .]

You must admit that, in such circumstances, Paris is no fit place for a philosopher, and that Aristotle was indeed right to withdraw to Chalcis while fanaticism was reigning in Athens. Besides, the status of a man of letters in Paris comes just above that of a tightrope-walker: the position of a gentleman-in-waiting to His Majesty, which the King had given me, is nothing very much. Men are foolish creatures, and I must conclude that it is far more worthwhile to build a fine mansion, as I have done, to produce plays there and live well, than to be harassed in Paris, as was Helvétius,* by those who ran the stables in the Sorbonne. As, most assuredly, I could neither make men more reasonable, nor make parliament less pedantic, nor logicians less ridiculous, I continued to be happy at a distance from them all.

I am mildly ashamed to be happy, looking out from my harbour at all these storms: I see Germany drenched in blood, France utterly in ruins – our armies and our fleets defeated, our ministers dismissed one after another, without our affairs in any way improving; the King of Portugal assassinated, not by a servant, but by the nobles of the land – and this time the Jesuits cannot say: *It is not our fault.** It was their prerogative, and it has been fully proved since then that the good fathers had piously slipped the knife into the hands of the murderers. They say in justification that they are sovereign rulers in Paraguay, and that they dealt with the King of Portugal as one crowned head to another.

Let me tell you a little adventure as extraordinary as any which has occurred since kings and poets have walked the earth: having spent long enough guarding the frontiers of Silesia, in an impregnable fortress, Frederick became restless, and so, to pass his time, he composed an ode against France and against the King. At the beginning of May 1759, he sent me his ode, signed Frederick, together with a huge packet of verse and prose. I opened the packet, and saw at once that I was not the first to have opened it: it was apparent that the seals had been broken on the way. I was petrified, when I read the following lines:

> Oh vain and foolish nation,
> Where are your warriors now,
> Who lived for glory once,
> Defying danger and death?
> Oh, now I see them clustered round,
> Bravest in pillage and theft,
> In combat, cowards all.
>
> I see your feeble king,
> Plaything of Pompadour,
> His features scarred with signs
> Of shameful, guilty lechery [. . .]

I trembled therefore as I read this ode, in which some lines are very good, or will at least be thought so. I have, unfortunately, earned the reputation of correcting the King of Prussia's verses – until now. The packet had been opened en route, the verses will have been seen by the public, the King of France will believe they are mine, and so I am guilty of high treason, and – which is far worse – guilty towards Mme de Pompadour.

Wholly perplexed, I requested the French resident in Geneva to come and see me; I showed him the packet; he agreed that its seals had been broken before it reached me. It was his opinion that, in a matter where my head was in danger, there was no other course but to send the packet to the Duke de Choiseul, the minister in France: in any other circumstances, I would never have taken such a step; but I was obliged to prevent my ruin: I wrote to the court, explaining the full nature of Frederick's character. I was confident that the Duke de Choiseul would not abuse this confidence, and that he would do no more than persuade the King of France that the King of Prussia was an implacable enemy who should be crushed, if this was possible. The Duke de Choiseul did not in fact stop there; he is a highly intelligent man, he writes verse, he has friends who do so; he replied to the King of Prussia in kind, and sent me an ode against Frederick which was fully as mordant, as ferocious as was Frederick's against us [. . .]

When he conveyed this reply to me, the Duke de Choiseul assured me that he would have it printed, should the King of Prussia publish *his* work, and that they would defeat Frederick with the pen, just as they expected to beat him with the sword [. . .]

To round off this pantomime, I imagined that one might base the beginnings of European peace on these two compositions, which could prolong the war until Frederick was crushed. The idea sprang from my correspondence with the Duke de Choiseul; it seemed so ridiculous to me, so appropriate to all that was happening at the time, that I seized on it; and I had the pleasure of proving on my own how the destiny of whole kingdoms may turn on such slight and puny matters. M. de Choiseul wrote me several letters which were ostensibly designed to allow the King of Prussia to suggest certain proposals for peace, without making Austria suspicious of the French ministry; and Frederick wrote similar letters to me in which he carefully avoided offending the court at London. These delicate exchanges continue; they are like the gestures of a pair of cats, who offer a velvet paw on one side, claws on the other. The King of Prussia, beaten by the Russians, and having lost Dresden, needs peace for a while; France, beaten on land by Hanover, and on the sea by the English, and having lost its money in the most foolish way, is forced to end this ruinous war.

And so, fair Emilie, you find us now.*

At *Les Délices*, 27 November 1759
Let me continue – these matters are still extraordinary. On 17 December the King of Prussia wrote to me: 'I'll tell you more of this from Dresden, where I shall be within three days';* and on the third day he was beaten by Marshal Daun, and lost 18,000

men. To me, it seems that all this is like the fable of *Perrette and the milk jug*.* Our great sailor, Berryer – recently lieutenant-general of police in Paris, and who moved from this post to that of secretary of state and minister for the marine, without ever having seen more of a fleet than the Saint-Cloud ferry and the coach from Auxerre; our friend Berryer, as I was saying, took it into his head to raise a great naval force, in order to invade England: hardly had our fleet ventured out of Brest than it was defeated by the English, holed on the rocks, crippled by the wind, or swallowed up in the sea.

Our general supervisor of finance is someone called Silhouette,* known only for translating a few lines of Pope's verse into prose: they thought he was an eagle; but in less than four months the eagle had changed into a chicken. He has discovered the secret of annihilating credit, to such a point that the State suddenly lacks money to pay its soldiers. The King has been obliged to send his silver plate to the Mint; and a fair part of the kingdom has followed his example.

12 February 1760

At last, after several of the King of Prussia's perfidies, such as sending to London letters which I had despatched to him in confidence, and trying to promote discord between our allies – admittedly perfidies which may be allowed to a great king, above all in time of war – I received proposals for peace, written by the King of Prussia – accompanied by lines of verse; he can't help writing them. I've sent them to Versailles; I doubt if they will be accepted: he's not prepared to give up anything, and he proposes, to compensate the Elector of Saxony, that he should be given Erfurt, which belongs to the Elector of Mainz: he always takes something from someone else; it's his way. We'll see what comes from these ideas, especially after the next campaign.

As this huge, horrible tragedy is continualy tinged with comedy, they have just printed in Paris the *Poetic verks of the King my master*, as Freytag called them; there is an epistle to Marshal Keith, in which he makes great fun of the immortality of the soul, and of Christians. The Catholic church-goers aren't pleased, and the Calvinist priests are grumbling; these dull divines used to think he was the bulwark of the faithful, they applauded when he put the magistrates of Leipzig in jail, and sold their bedding to get their money. But since he's turned to translating a few passages from Seneca, Lucretius and Cicero, they think he's a monster. Had that bandit Cartouche* gone to church, the priests would have made him a saint.

CHAPTER 8

A Prophecy
(*Prophétie*)

First published in 1761 several times, translated into English the same year, and reproduced in the Gentleman's Magazine *(September 1761), the* London Magazine *(October 1761) and the* Annual Register *for 1761. A bilingual edition –* Prophétie – A Prophecy – *appeared in 1761 in Geneva.*

This short piece is mainly to do with the novel Julie ou La Nouvelle Héloïse *by Jean-Jacques Rousseau (1712–78), which was published in 1760–61 (first in London, then Paris). Voltaire was never on friendly terms with Rousseau, although Rousseau had contributed items to the* Encyclopédie, *concerning music. Again and again Rousseau's publications had expressed views wholly contrary to Voltaire's. In 1750, he had written a* Discourse on the Arts and Sciences, *stating that human beings were better off in the 'state of nature' than in modern society, and in 1755 he published his* Discourse on Inequality, *which prompted Voltaire to write to him on 30 August 1755*

I have received, monsieur, your new book against the human race. I thank you for it. You will please men, to whom you tell truths which concern them, but you will not correct them. One could not paint in stronger colours the horrors of human society, from which our ignorance and our weakness expect so many consolations. No one has ever employed so much intellect in the attempt to prove us beasts. A desire seizes us to walk on all four paws when we read your work. Nevertheless, as it is more than sixty years since I lost the habit, I feel, unfortunately, that it is impossible for me to resume it, and I leave that natural mode of walking to those who are more worthy of it than you and I . . .*

Voltaire's desire to 'walk on all four paws' when reading Rousseau was taken up most vividly in 1759, when a minor dramatist, Palissot, produced his play Les Philosophes *('The*

Philosophers'). * *In this, many of the contemporary philosophers appeared in ridiculous ways (but not Voltaire), while Rousseau, alas! came on to the stage on all fours, eating a lettuce-leaf.*

Earlier, Rousseau had written and composed for the opera, notably his Devin du village – 'The Village Soothsayer' – *in 1752,* * *and in 1758 he had written against the French theatre in his* Lettre sur les spectacles ('Letter on the Theatre'). *By this time, Rousseau had decided that Voltaire was not his friend. On 17 June 1760 he wrote to him, disapproving Voltaire's having allowed the publication of a much earlier letter which he, Rousseau had written to Voltaire. After several paragraphs, he bursts out 'I do not like you, Sir, at all; you have done me the most painful of injuries [. . .] So, I hate you, it's what you wished: but I hate you as a man who is even more worthy to love you, had this been your wish* * [. . .]*

In late 1760 his novel Julie ou la Nouvelle Héloïse (Julie or the New Eloise) *was published in London, and in early 1761 in Paris. This novel unleashed Voltaire's scorn, as appears in the following* Prophecy. *Voltaire wrote a sheaf of articles and essays against Rousseau in the following years.*

Geneva, 1761

In those days there will appear in France a very extraordinary person, come from the banks of a lake. He will say unto the people, I am possessed by the daemon of enthusiasm;* I have received from heaven the gift of inconsistency;* and the multitude shall run after him, and many shall believe in him; and he shall say unto them, Ye are all villains and rascals; your women are all prostitutes; and I am come to live amongst you: and he will take advantage of the natural lenity of this country to abuse the people: And he will add, all the men are virtuous in the country where I was born,* and I will not stay in the country where I was born; and he will maintain, that the sciences and the arts* must necessarily corrupt our morals, and he will treat of all sorts of sciences and arts; and he will maintain, that the theatre is a source of prostitution and corruption, and he will compose operas and plays.* He will publish, that there is no virtue but among the savages, though he never was among them; he will advise mankind to go stark naked, and he will wear laced clothes when given him. He will employ his time in copying French music, and he will tell you there is no French music.* He will tell you, that it is impossible to preserve your morals, if you read romances; and he will compose a romance,* and in this romance shall be seen vice in deeds and virtue in words, and the actors in it shall be mad with love and with philosophy; and in this romance we shall learn how to seduce a young girl philosophically; and the disciple shall lose all shame and all modesty: and she shall practise folly, and raise maxims with her master, and she shall be the first to give him a kiss on the lips, and she shall invite him to lie with her, and he shall actually lie with her, and she shall become pregnant with metaphysics; and his love letters shall be philosophical homilies. And he shall get drunk with an English nobleman,* who shall insult him, and he shall challenge him to fight; and his mistress, who has lost the honour of her own sex, shall decide with regard to that of men; and she shall teach her master, who taught her everything, that he ought not to fight. And he shall go to Paris,* where he shall be introduced to some ladies of pleasure; and he shall get drunk like a fool, and shall lie with these women of the town; and he shall write an account of his adventures to his mistress, and she shall thank him for it. The man* who shall marry his mistress, shall know that she is loved to distraction by another, and this good man, notwithstanding shall be an Atheist, and immediately after the marriage, his wife shall find herself happy, and she shall write to her lover, that if she were again at liberty, she would wed her husband rather than him. And the philosopher shall have a mind to kill himself, and shall compose a long dissertation to prove that a lover ought always to kill himself when he has lost his mistress: and her husband shall prove to him, that it is not worth his while; and he shall not kill himself. Then he shall set out to make the tour of the world,* in order to allow time for the children of his mistress to grow up, and that he may get to Switzerland time enough to be their preceptor, and to teach them virtue, as he had done their mother. And he shall see nothing in the tour of the world, and he shall return to Europe, and when he shall be arrived there, they shall still love one another with transport, and they shall squeeze each other's hands, and weep. And this fine lover being in a boat alone with his mistress, shall have a mind to throw her into the water, and himself along with her; and all this they shall call philosophy and virtue, and they shall talk so much of philosophy and virtue, that nobody shall know what philosophy and virtue is. And the mistress of the philosopher shall have a few trees, and a rivulet in her garden, and she shall call that her elysium:* and nobody shall be able to comprehend what that elysium is; and every day he shall feed sparrows in her garden; and she shall watch her domestics, both males and females, to prevent their playing the same foolish prank that she herself had played; and she shall sup in the midst of her harvest people; and she shall cut hemp with them, having her lover at her side; and the philosopher shall be desirous of cutting hemp the day after, and the day after that, and all the days of his life; and she shall be a pedant in every word she says, and all the rest of her sex shall be contemptible in her eyes; and she shall die, and before she dies, she shall preach according to custom; and she shall talk incessantly, till her strength fail her, and she shall dress herself out like a coquette, and die like a saint.

The author of this book, like those empiricks, who make wounds on purpose, in order to show the virtue of their balsams, poisons our souls for the glory of curing them; and this poison will act violently on the understanding, and on the heart, and the antidote will operate only on the understanding, and the poison will triumph, and he will boast of having opened a gulph, and he will think he saves himself from all blame, by crying, woe be to the young girls who shall fall into it; I have warned them against it in my preface; and young girls never read a preface; and he will say, by way of excuse for his having written a book which inspires vice, that he lives in an age, wherein it is impossible to be good; and to justify himself, he will slander the whole world, and threaten with his contempt all those who do not like his book; and everybody shall wonder how, with a soul so pure and virtuous, he could compose a book which is so much the reverse; and many who believed in him shall believe in him no more.

CHAPTER 9

A Short Account of the Death of John Calas*
(Histoire abrégée de la mort de Jean Calas)

The Short Account *is Chapter 1 of the Treatise on Religious
Toleration, published in French in 1763 and in English the following
year. The terrible events described in the first chapter began in 1761,
and were to lead Voltaire into writing a flood of letters and pamphlets,
including this treatise, and were to be followed by many others in
defence of different people – Sirven, La Barre and others – who were
victims of intolerance and injustice.*

In October 1761 a young man, Marc Antoine Calas, hanged
himself in a fit of depression. This was in Toulouse, a town in
southern France where the majority of the inhabitants were
passionately opposed to the Protestants – the Huguenots – in
the district. Young Calas, and most of his family, were Huguenots, and a rumour quickly circulated that his death, far from
being suicide, was the work of his parents, who killed him rather
than let him convert to Roman Catholicism.

Quickly, his family was arrested, imprisoned, tried; and on 9
March 1762, his father, Jean Calas, was executed for the murder
of his son.

At first Voltaire thought that the father was guilty. On 22
March 1762 he wrote to Antoine Le Bault:

> You may have heard of a good Huguenot who has been broken
> on the wheel of the Parlement of Toulouse for having strangled
> his son. Yet this saintly Protestant thought his action was good,
> since his son wanted to become a Catholic, and this averted an
> apostasy. He had sacrificed his son to the Lord, and thought
> himself far superior to Abraham, for Abraham had done no more
> than obey, while our Calvinist hanged his son of his own accord,
> to keep his conscience clear. We are not worth very much, but the
> Huguenots are worse than us . . .*

*Within days Voltaire's attitude changed. Where was the truth?
On 25 March 1762 he wrote to Claude de La Marche:*

> It interests me as a man, a little even as a philosopher. I want to
> know on which side the horror of fanaticism lies. The Intendant
> for Languedoc is in Paris. I beg you, speak to him or get him to
> speak. He knows the facts of this fearsome affair. Be so kind, I
> pray you, to let me know what I should think of it all. What an
> abominable age it is: Calas, Malagrida, Damiens, the loss of all
> our colonies, notes of confession, and the comic opera.*

*Quickly the 'comic opera' faded from Voltaire's sight, as he
learnt more of the details. He met Calas' widow, and was
convinced that her husband was wrongly executed; and he
began to write, to protect the widow and her family, and to
campaign for the 'rehabilitation' of the executed man. His
efforts achieved support – in the highest quarters, as from Mme
de Pompadour (see the Introduction, p. xxiii) – and his letters
to other sympathisers continued, to Damilaville for example, on
24 January 1763:*

> True, one cannot undo the cruel execution of John Calas; but his
> judges can be rendered execrable, and I desire this to be done. I
> took it upon myself to write down all the reasons which might
> justify these judges; I cudgelled my brains to find excuses for them,
> and found only reasons to shred them . . .*

*What he 'wrote down' in this matter was expressed most clearly
in the following* Short Account of the Death of John Calas.

The murder of Calas, perpetrated, with the sword of justice, at
Toulouse, on 9 March 1762, is an event of the most affecting
and interesting nature, both to ourselves and to posterity. We
soon forget those numerous victims to human passions, who
perish fighting in the field; not only because they risk the chance,
and share the inevitable fate, of war; but because those who fall
in battle, are at liberty to defend themselves, and offend their
enemies. In war, where the dangers and advantages of the
combatants are equal, we cease to admire, and almost even to
pity, the fate of the vanquished: but, if an innocent father of a
family is delivered up into the hands of ignorance, prejudice or
fanaticism; if when accused, he hath no other means of defence

than his own innocence; if his judges run no other risk, in taking away his life, than that of merely making a simple mistake; if they can kill him with impunity by the forms of law; in such a case, the public takes the alarm, the general cry is up, and every one justly fears for hisself. It is obvious to all, that the life of no one is secured by the judgment of such a tribunal, though erected immediately for their personal security; hence, with united voices, they call out unanimously for vengeance.

The particulars of this strange affair involve at once religion, suicide and parricide: it is to be considered, whether a father and mother have strangled their own son, with a view to please God Almighty; whether a brother hath strangled his brother; a friend his friend; or whether, lastly, the judges ought to reproach themselves for having condemned an innocent father to be broken alive on the wheel, or for having acquitted a mother, brother, and friend, equally guilty?

Jean Calas, this unfortunate father, who had attained the sixty-eighth year of his age, had been a merchant at Toulouse for above forty years, and was allowed, by all those who had lived with him, to be a kind and indulgent parent. By religion, he was a protestant, as were also his wife and children, except one who had abjured that persuasion, and to whom the father gave a little annuity. The unhappy Calas, indeed, appeared to be so far from harbouring any thing of that absurd fanaticism, which breaks asunder all the bonds of society, that he even approved of the conversion of his son Louis, and had kept, in his house, for more than thirty years, a woman servant, who was a zealous Catholic, and had nursed all his children.

One of the sons, named Marc Antony, was a man of letters, and had long passed for a person of a restless, gloomy, and violent disposition: having no prospect of succeeding in trade, for which he was totally unfit, and incapable of being called to the bar, through want of the necessary certificates of his being a Catholic, he became so disgusted with his situation, that he formed a resolution to destroy himself, and even went so far as to give some intimation of his design to one of his friends. In this desperate resolution, it appears he was confirmed by the perusal of every tract that had been written on the subject of suicide.

At length, having one day lost all his money at play, he

determined on the immediate execution of his design. It happened, that a common friend of the family, one Lavaisse, the son of a celebrated advocate of Toulouse, a young man of nineteen, remarkable for the ingenuousness of his disposition and behaviour, and who was just arrived from Bordeaux, supped that evening at their house;[1] the father, the mother, Marc Antony, their eldest son, and Peter their second son, supping together. As they retired after supper into an adjacent saloon, Marc Antony left the company; nothing being seen or heard of him, till young Lavaisse desirous of going home, Peter Calas attended him downstairs, where they found Marc Antony, stript to his shirt, and hanging on the door of the warehouse; his clothes being laid, folded up, on the counter; his hair smoothly combed out, and his shirt quite unrumpled: on his body also there was not the least mark of violence.[2]

We shall pass over a detail of the particular circumstances attending this affair, of all which the lawyers have given sufficient account; nor shall we pretend to describe the grief and horror of the unhappy parents; to these their neighbours were witnesses; as also that Lavaisse and Peter Calas, terrified out of their wits, ran immediately for a surgeon, and to the magistrate. In the mean time, the people of Toulouse assembled about the house; a people the most extravagantly superstitious and fanatical, who would look upon their own brothers as monsters, if of a different religion. It is at Toulouse that a solemn thanksgiving is made to God, on account of the death of Henry the Third, and that an oath is taken to cut the throat of the first man who should speak in favour of Henry the Fourth. In this city is annually solemnised, by public procession and bonfires, the massacre of four thousand heretical citizens about two centuries ago. It hath been to no purpose that six arrêts of council have been issued against this abominable practice; the people of Toulouse still celebrate this horrid festival.

Among such a people it is not to be wondered at, that a fanatic in the mob should cry out, *John Calas had murdered his*

---

[1] 12 October 1761.
[2] After the body was carried to the town hall, there appeared only a scratch on the end of the nose, and a slight bruise on the chest, occasioned by some accident in the removal.

own son: nor that such a cry should become general; as was really the case; some persons adding that the deceased was to have abjured protestantism the next day, and that the young Lavaisse with the rest of the family had made away with him, out of their hatred to the Romish religion. This was hardly repeated before it was universally believed: the whole town was persuaded, that it was a religious tenet among the protestants, for a father and mother to assassinate their children, if they were about to change their religion.

When the spirits of a people are once excited, they know not where to stop. It was reported, that the protestants of Languedoc had assembled on the preceding day, and had chosen for this purpose an executioner out of their own sect; that the choice had fallen on the young Lavaisse, who, within the space of four and twenty hours, had both received the news of his election and come to Bordeaux, to assist John Calas, his wife, and their son Peter, to murder a friend, a son, a brother.

The Sieur David, capitoul, or first magistrate, of Toulouse, influenced by these absurd reports, and willing to make a merit of his assiduity in office, began a prosecution directly contrary to law and custom. The family of Calas, Lavaisse, and even the Catholic maid-servant, were put in irons. A monitory warning respecting the affair was published, no less illegal than the prosecution. Matters were carried still farther: Marc Antony Calas died a Calvinist, and if he had really made away with himself, his body should have been dragged through the streets: on the contrary, however, he was buried in great pomp, in the church of St Etienne, notwithstanding the curate himself protested against such profanation.

There are in Languedoc four fraternities of penitents, *viz* the white, the blue, the grey and the black. The brothers of these orders wear a long capuche, or cowl, with a woollen mask, through which are two holes for them to see through: they are numerous, and of such importance that they wanted to engage the duke Fitz-James, commandant of the province, to become one of their order: this honour, however, he refused them. The white brothers celebrated a solemn service to Marc Antony Calas, as to a martyr; and that with greater pomp than ever was known at the like celebration for a real martyr. This pomp was nevertheless extremely terrible. On a magnificent bier was placed a kind of moving skeleton, to represent Marc Antony Calas, holding in one hand a bough of the palm-tree, and in the other the pen with which he should have signed his abjuration, and which wrote in effect the sentence of death afterwards passed on the father.

Nothing farther was now wanting than to canonise this unhappy suicide: the people all looked upon him as a saint; some invoked him in their prayers; others went to pray at his tomb; some requested miracles of him, and others related those he had actually done. A certain monk wrenched out some of his teeth, in order to possess the durable relics of so great a martyr. A pious woman, who was a little deaf, declared she could now hear the sound of bells; and an apoplectic priest was cured, after having taken a proper emetic. Formal accounts were drawn up of these miracles, and the author of this relation is also possessed of an attestation on oath, that a young man of Toulouse actually went distracted, on account of his having prayed for several nights at the tomb of this new saint, without being able to obtain of him the miracle he solicited.

Now several of the magistrates being of the fraternity of white penitents, the condemnation and death of John Calas appeared, from this time, infallible. The circumstance, however, which more particularly accelerated his sentence, was the approach of the above-mentioned extraordinary festival, which the people of Toulouse annually celebrate, in memory of the massacre of four thousand Huguenots, in the year 1562. This being the jubilee or secular year, therefore, it was intended to be celebrated with unusual pomp; accordingly the preparations which were making for this end throughout the city, inflamed anew the glowing imaginations of the people. It was publicly said, the scaffold on which John Calas ought to be broke on the wheel, would be one of the greatest embellishments to the splendour of the festival; that Providence had evidently furnished such delinquents to be sacrificed as victims to our holy religion. These, and even more violent expressions than these, were heard by more than twenty persons. And this is in our day! in times when philosophy hath made such considerable progress, and while so many academies are constantly employed in cultivating humanity and gentleness of manners! It appears to me that *fanaticism*, enraged at the success of *reason*, vents its spleen with redoubled fury on itself.

In the prosecution carried on against the prisoners, thirteen judges assembled daily to enquire into the circumstances of the affair. They had not, nor could have, any evidence against the family; but their mistaken notions of religion supplied the place of proof. Six of the judges persisted a long time in condemning John Calas, his son, and Lavaisse, to the wheel, and the mother to the stake. Seven others, more moderate, were, at least, for a further examination. The debates were reiterated and long; in the mean time, one of the judges, convinced of the innocence of the accused, and of the impossibility of the crime, spoke warmly in their favour; opposing the zeal of humanity to that of religious severity. He became, indeed, the public advocate for the Calas family, all over Toulouse, where the continued cries of mistaken religion demanded the blood of the unfortunate prisoners. Another judge, well known for the violence of his temper and disposition, exerted himself, on the other hand, as strenuously against them as the former did in their favour. At length their opposition made so much noise, that they were both obliged to except themselves as judges, and retire into the country.

By a strange fatality, however, the judge, whose opinion was favourable to Calas, had the delicacy to persist in his exception; while the other returned, to give his judgment against those whom, in such circumstances, he ought not to have judged. It was by virtue of this single voice that the poor old man was condemned to the wheel; one of the six opposing judges having been, after much altercation, brought over to the severer side.

It seems reasonable to me that, in cases of parricide, where it is debated whether the father of a family shall be sentenced to the most cruel death, the judges should be unanimous; as the proofs of such a singular[3] crime ought to be evident to the whole world.

---

[3] I know but of two examples in history, of fathers having been accused of assassinating their children on account of religion; the first is of the father of St Barbara, or as we usually call her St Barbe. The old man, it seems, had made but *two* windows in the bagnio-room; Barbe in his absence had a *third* constructed, in honour of the holy Trinity; after this she made the sign of the cross, with her finger, on the marble columns, which sign remained deeply engraven on the stone. At this her father, being put into a violent passion, pursued her sword in hand to a mountain, that good naturedly gave way and opened to let her through, to save her the trouble of going up hill. The father, however, running round the foot of it, caught his daughter on the other side, and gave her a sound whipping on the bare backside. To prevent the continua-

The least doubt or probability of the party's guilt, in such a case, ought to make a judge tremble when he is going to sign the sentence of death. We are every day made sensible of the fallibility of the human judgment, and the imperfection of our laws: but on no occasion whatever are they more conspicuous than when the majority of a single voice is sufficient to condemn a citizen to be broke on the wheel. Sentence of death could not be pronounced at Athens, by less than a majority of fifty voices. But what do we deduce from that? nothing but the useless reflection that the Greeks were more wise and humane than we are.

It appeared evidently impossible that John Calas, a feeble old man, upwards of sixty-eight years of age, and afflicted with swelled legs, could have, alone, strangled and hung up his son, a young man of twenty-eight, and remarkably robust: he must then have been assisted in the execution of this horrid act by his wife, his son Peter, young Lavaisse and the servant: all of them having been in company together, nor quitted each other a moment, during the whole evening of this fatal adventure. This latter supposition, however, was as absurd as the former; for how could it be imagined that a woman, who was a zealous Roman Catholic, and had brought up this unhappy young man from a child, should suffer a parcel of Huguenots to assassinate him because he had a regard to her own religion? How could it be imagined that Lavaisse should come express from Bordeaux to murder his friend, of whose pretended conversion he was totally ignorant? How can it be conceived that a tender mother should lay hands on her own son? Indeed how could they, even all together, thus murder a man, who was himself as strong as them all, without long and violent struggles, without his cries alarming the neighbourhood, without giving reiterated blows, bruising him, or tearing his clothes?

It was clear that, if this parricide was really committed, the accused were all equally guilty, because it appeared evidently

---

tion of this indecency, an angel was sent post-haste to cover her with a white sheet or cloud; which provoking her father still more, he fairly cut off her head. This is told in the *Lives of the Saints*.

The second example is of prince Hermenegildus, who revolted against the king his father, gave him battle in the year 584, was defeated, and killed by an officer. He was deemed a martyr, because truly his father was an Arian.

they were all the while in company together. Nothing could be more evident than that the father could not be alone guilty: and yet the father alone was condemned to be broken alive on the wheel.

The motive for passing this cruel sentence was also as inconceivable as all the rest. The judges who gave their voice for the execution of John Calas persuaded the others that, as such a feeble old man could not support the torture of the execution, he would confess his guilt and impeach his accomplices before he expired. They were confounded however, when they heard him, in the midst of his torture, call upon God to witness his innocence, and with his last breath entreat him to forgive his deluded judges.

They were now, therefore, obliged to pass a second sentence directly contradictory to the first, by which the mother, her son Peter, young Lavaisse and the servant-maid were to be set at liberty. One of the counsellors, however, soon pointed out the absurdity of this proceeding, by which they condemned themselves: for, as the accused were all in company at the time of the supposed parricide, the release of the survivors was a proof of the innocence of the father, whom they had executed. On this, they took upon them to banish Peter Calas, the son: which sentence of banishment was also equally absurd; for Peter either was innocent or guilty; if guilty, he should have been executed as well as his father; if innocent, they ought not to have banished him. But the judges, shocked at the cruel execution of the father, and the affecting piety of his last moments, thought to save their credit by seeming to favour the son, as if this very favour was not a new instance of their prevarication; they probably imagined also that the banishment of this poor friendless young man would be attended with no momentous consequences, and was after all, not an act of such very great injustice after what they had already been so unhappy as to commit.

They began with urging him, while in prison, to turn Roman Catholic, threatening that, if he did not, he must expect to suffer the same fate as his father. This the young man hath solemnly affirmed upon oath.[4]

---

[4] A Jacobin came into my dungeon, and threatened me with the same death, if I did not abjure my religion. This I solemnly avow in the presence of Almighty God. 23 July 1762. Peter Calas.

When he was actually sent out of the town, he had not gone far before he met with a converting Abbé, who obliged him to return back to Toulouse; where he was shut up immediately in the convent of the Dominicans, and compelled to perform all the external ceremonies of the Popish religion. This was indeed in part their design, it was the price of his father's blood, and the religion, whose cause they intended to avenge, seemed by these means satisfied.

The daughters of this unfortunate family were also taken from the mother, and shut up in a convent: while the unhappy woman, witness of the shocking suicide of her eldest son, besprinkled, as it were, with the blood of her husband, seeing her other son banished and her daughters torn from her, remained alone in the world, without bread, without hope, to perish with excess of misery. At this time there were some persons, who, having maturely considered all the circumstances of this horrible affair, were so struck with the cruelty and injustice of it, that they pressed the widow Calas to throw herself at the foot of the throne. The poor woman was then, indeed, in too dejected a state to take such a step; add to this, that being born in England, and coming into a French province very young, she was terrified at the thought of going to Paris. She imagined that the metropolis of the kingdom must be still more barbarous than Toulouse. At length, however, her duty and regard to the memory of her husband, got the better of her weakness. She arrived, almost dead with grief and fatigue, at Paris, where she was astonished to find a welcome, and help, and compassion.

Good sense prevails in Paris over fanaticism, whereas in the provinces fanaticism generally prevails over common sense.

Mr de Beaumont, a celebrated advocate of the parliament of Paris, immediately undertook her defence, and drew up a consultation, which he got signed by no less than fifteen gentlemen of the same profession. Mr Loiseau, an orator of no less abilities, composed a memoir also in behalf of this unfortunate family. At the same time Mr Mariette, advocate of the council, drew up a judicial tract on the subject, which carried with it irresistible conviction.

These three liberal advocates for justice and innocence, generously gave the widow the profit arising from the publication of their several pieces written on this subject.[5] Not only Paris, but all Europe sympathised with the sufferer, and shuddered at the fact; demanding, with the unhappy widow, that justice which crowned heads and the supreme magistrate owe to their injured subjects. The public judgment anticipated the arrêt long before it was signed by the council.

The ministry were affected by a like compassion, even amidst that multiplicity of business which often drowns the cries of the oppressed, and in spite of the habit of frequently seeing the miserable, which steels the heart still more. The daughters were now ordered to be restored to their mother. This unhappy family, however, had still some enemies; their sufferings being owing to religion. Many of those persons who are called in France *dévots*,[6] scrupled not publicly to affirm it much better that an old Calvinist should be broke alive on the wheel, though innocent, than that the characters of eight counsellors of Languedoc should be exposed to the censure of the public, by their confessing themselves mistaken. They even made use of the following expression, 'There are more magistrates than Calas'; whence they inferred, that this unfortunate family should be sacrificed to the honour of the magistracy. They did not reflect that the true honour of a judge consists, like that of other men, in repairing his faults. It is not believed in France that the Pope himself, assisted by all his cardinals, is infallible: Why then might it not be allowed that eight judges of Toulouse are not infallible? All sensible and disinterested persons, indeed, declared that the sentence passed at Toulouse, would be reversed in any country in Europe; whatever particular considerations might prevent its being annulled in Council.

Such was the state of this astonishing case, when several impartial and sensible persons projected the design of offering to the public some reflections on toleration, religious indulgence, and on that compassion for the deluded, which the Abbé Houtteville calls a monstrous tenet; but which reason calls the inseparable appendage of humanity.

Either the judges of Toulouse, misled by the fanaticism of the

[5] Surreptitious copies, however, were printed in various parts of the kingdom, and the widow Calas was thus deprived of the fruits of their generosity.
[6] This term is derived from the Latin *devotus*. But the *devoti* of ancient Rome were persons devoted to the service of the republic.

populace, condemned the father of an innocent family to be broken on the wheel, a proceeding without example, or that the father and his wife actually hanged up their eldest son, with the assistance of another son and his friend; a fact that appears impossible in nature. In either case, it is certain that the abuse of our most holy religion has been productive of a most horrid crime. It is, therefore, in the interest of mankind, to examine whether religion should be persecuting or charitable.

CHAPTER 10

Discourse Addressed to the Welsh*
(*Discours aux Welches*)

*First published in 1764, this piece seems almost a variation on the
Letters Concerning the English Nation. There, Voltaire tells the French
what England can offer them; here, thirty years later, he tells the
French how foolish they have been – and remain – in ignoring or
rejecting the useful and excellent qualities of other countries. It is a
light-hearted, yet disturbing composition, of which the first half is
printed here. The remainder goes on to compare French and Latin
writings, usually to the advantage of Latin.*

Oh Welsh!* my countrymen, if you surpass the ancient Greeks
and Romans, never bite the bosom of your nurses, never insult
your masters, be modest in your triumphs; consider who you
are, and from whom you descend.

It is true you had the honour to be subdued by Julius Caesar,
who caused all the members of your Parliament of Vannes to be
hanged, sold the remainder of the inhabitants, ordered the hands
of the inhabitants of Quercy to be cut off, and then governed
you with great mildness. You remained for more than five
hundred years subject to the laws of the Roman Empire: your
Druids, who treated you as slaves and animals, who piously
burned you in osier baskets, no longer retained their influence
when you became a province of the Roman Empire. But honestly
confess that you were always somewhat barbarous.

In the fifth age of your vulgar era, Vandals, to whom you
gave the sonorous appellation of Bourgonsions, or Bourguig-
nons, people of great genius, and extremely cleanly, who rubbed
their hair with strong butter, to use the phrase of Sidonius
Apollinaris, *infundens acido comam butyro;** these people, I
say, made you all slaves, from the territory of your town of
Vienne to the source of your river Seine; and it is one of the
remaining customs of that illustrious age, for monks and canons
to have vassals in this country. This fine prerogative of the

human species subsists among you as a testimony of your wisdom.

One part of your remaining provinces, which you so long called the provinces of Oc, and which you so nobly distinguished from the provinces of Oui, were invaded by the Visigoths: and as to your provinces of Oui, they were taken from you by a Sicambrian named Hildovic (otherwise Clovis), whose ancestors had been condemned to be devoured by wild beasts at Trier, by the Emperor Constantine. This Sicambrian, dignified with the title of the Roman Patrician, reduced you to slavery with a handful of Franks, who came out of the marshes of the Rhine, the Main, and the Meuse. The noble exploits of this great man were the assassinations of three petty kings, his friends and relations, one near the town of Boulogne upon the sea, the other near the village of Cambray, and the third near the village of Mans, which your chronicles call cities: it was at that time that the Welsh country had the melodious name of Frankreich, the ancient name of France, in commemoration of its conquerors; and you were the first nation of the world, for you had the standard of St Denis.

Northern pirates came some time after to pillage you, and took from you the province which has been since called Normandy. You were afterward divided into many different nations under different masters, and each nation had its peculiar laws, as well as its peculiar jargon.

One-half of your country soon belonged to the inhabitants of the island called Britain, or England, in their idiom, which was then as harmonious as yours. Normandy, Brittany, Anjou, Maine, Saintonge, Guienne, Gascony, Angoumois, Périgord, Rouergue, and Auvergne were a long time in the hands of this people, the Angles; while you had neither Lyons, nor Marseilles, nor Dauphiny, nor Provence, nor Languedoc.

Notwithstanding this your miserable situation, your compilers, whom you take for historians, often call you 'the first people of the earth', and your kingdom 'the first kingdom'. This is treating other nations somewhat impolitely. You are a brilliant and amiable people; and if you add modesty to your graces, the rest of Europe will be highly pleased with you.

Return your hearty thanks to God for delivering you from the Angles, by the factions of the red and white roses; and above all, return thanks that the civil wars of Germany prevented Charles V from swallowing up your country, and making it a province of the Empire.

You had a brilliant moment under Louis XIV, but don't for that reason think yourselves superior in everything to the ancient Romans and Greeks.

Consider that during the space of six hundred years scarcely anybody among you, except a few of your new Druids, could either read or write. Your excessive ignorance gave you up to the Flamen of Rome and his associates, like children, whom pedagogues govern and correct as they think proper. Your contracts of marriage, when you made contracts, which was but seldom, were written in bad Latin, by clerks; you did not know what you had stipulated: and when you had children, there came a shaven monk from Rome, who proved to you, that your wife was not your wife, that she was your cousin in the last degree, that your marriage was sacrilegious, that your children were bastards, and that you were damned if you did not, without delay, make over one-half of your property to the chamber called Apostolical.

Your *basiloi* – kings – were not better treated than yourselves: you had nine excommunicated – if I am not mistaken – by the servant of the servants of God. Excommunication implied, of course, the confiscation of goods; so that your *basiloi* lost all right to their crown, which the Roman pontiff presented to whichever of his friends he thought proper.

You will tell me, my dear Welsh, that the people of Britain, or England, and even the Teutonic emperors, have been worse used than you, and that they were fully as ignorant. That is true, but that does not justify you: and if the British nation was so stupid as to be a long time a feudatory province to a Druid beyond the Alps, you will acknowledge that it contrived to revenge the affront; endeavour to follow the example if you can.

You had formerly a king* who, though unfortunate in all his designs and expeditions, deserves some praise for having taught you to read and write; he even sent to Italy for persons who taught you the Greek language, and for others who taught you to paint and make statues: but there passed more than a hundred years before you had a tolerable painter or sculptor; and as for those who learned the Greek, and even the Hebrew, they were almost all burned alive, having incurred the suspicion of reading certain Judaical books; a thing highly dangerous.

I am willing to allow you, my dear Welshmen, that your country is the first country in the world; and yet you do not possess the largest domain in the smallest of the four quarters of the earth. Consider that Spain is of somewhat greater extent, that Germany is still more so, that Poland and Sweden are bigger, and that there are provinces in Russia of which the country of the Welsh would not make a fourth part.

I wish your country may prove the first in the world for the fertility of its soil; but, for God's sake, think of your forty leagues of lands toward Bordeaux, of that part of your Champagne to which you have given the noble appellation 'flea-bitten', of whole provinces where the inhabitants live entirely upon chestnuts, and of others, where there is no bread to be had but rye bread: take notice of the prohibition you lie under to export corn out of your country; a prohibition founded upon your want, and perhaps, too, upon your character, which would excite you to sell all you have as fast as possible, in order to purchase it again at a very high price three months after; in this you resemble certain Americans, who sell their beds in the morning, forgetting that they will want them at night.

Add to this, that the expense which the fashionable part of the nation is at, in flour to powder themselves, whether you have your hair dressed in the royal bird fashion, or whether you wear it loose, like King Clodio and the privy councillors, is an expense so universal that it is very reasonable to prevent the exportation of a commodity of which you make so good a use.

First people of the earth, consider that you have in your kingdom of Frankreich about two millions of inhabitants who walk in wooden shoes for six months of the year, and who go barefooted during the remaining six.

Are you the first people of the earth for commerce and maritime glory? Alas!

I have heard it said, but I cannot believe that yours is the only nation in the world that buys the right of judging men, and even of leading them to be killed in battle. I have been assured that you make the public treasure pass through fifty hands before it arrives at the royal treasury; and when it has gone through all these strainers, it is at last reduced to the fifth part of its value at most.

In answer to this you will allege that you are extremely successful in comic operas: but can you deny that you are indebted to Italy for your comic as well as your serious operas? I will own that you have invented some modes, though you now adopt almost all those of the people of Britain. But was it not a Genoese who discovered the fourth part of the world, where you possess only two or three little islands? Was it not a native of Portugal who opened to you a passage to the East Indies, where you lately lost your little factories?*

Perhaps you may be the first people in the world for the invention of arts: yet, was not the compass invented by John Goya, of Melphi? Was it not the German, Schwartz, who discovered the secret of inflammable powder? Was not printing, of which you make so much use, the fruit of a German's ingenious labour?

When you are disposed to read the new pamphlets, which represent you as so learned a people, you sometimes make use of spectacles: thank Francis Spina for this; for without him you would never have been able to read small print. You have telescopes; for them thank James Metius, the Dutchman, and Galileo, the Florentine.

If you sometimes amuse yourselves with barometers and thermometers, to whom are you indebted for them? To Torricelli.

Many of you study the true system of the planetary world: it was a man born in Polish Prussia who discovered this secret of the Creator. You are aided in your calculations by logarithms; it is to the immense labour of Lord Napier and his associates that you are obliged for them: it is Guericke of Magdeburg that you should thank for the air-pump.

It was this same Galileo, whom I have just mentioned, who first discovered the satellites of Jupiter, the spots in the sun, and its rotation upon its axis. The Dutchman, Huyghens, could see the ring of Saturn; an Italian, Cassini, could see its satellites when you could perceive nothing at all.

In fine, it was the great Newton* who demonstrated to you the nature of light, and who discovered the great law which causes the stars to move, and which directs heavy bodies toward the centre of the earth.

First people of the world, you love to adorn your closets, you hang up fine prints in them; but reflect, that the Florentine Finiguerra is the father of this art, which immortalises what the pencil cannot preserve. You have also fine clocks; this likewise is an invention of the Dutchman, Huyghens.

You sometimes wear brilliants upon your fingers; reflect that it was the people of Venice that first began to cut them, and to imitate pearls.

You sometimes contemplate yourselves in a looking-glass; it is to Venice likewise that you are indebted for this invention.

I should therefore be glad if you would show in your books a little more respect for your neighbours. You don't indeed do like Rome, where all those who discover any truth are brought before the Inquisition, let that truth be of what nature it will; and where Galileo was obliged to fast upon bread and water, for having taught them that the planets move round the sun. But what do you do? As soon as a useful discovery renders another nation illustrious, you combat it, and that for a long time. Newton shows the astonished world the seven primitive and unchangeable rays of light; you, for twenty years, deny what has been proven by experiments, instead of making those experiments yourselves. He demonstrated gravitation to you: and during forty years, you, in opposition to him, maintain the impertinent romance of the Cartesian vortices. In a word, you never yield, till all Europe has laughed at your obstinacy.

In other countries, inoculation* saves the lives of thousands; you exert yourselves for above forty years in endeavours to decry this salutary practice. If sometimes, carrying your wives or your children to the grave, dead of a natural Small-Pox, you feel a moment's remorse – should you happen to have a moment of grief and regret – if you then repent not having adopted the practice of nations more wise and more resolute than you; if you sometimes venture to do that which is so common among them, this inclination will not last, prejudice and irresponsibility will soon resume their ancient empire over you.

You are either ignorant, or pretend to be ignorant, that in the London hospitals set apart for the natural and artificial Small-Pox, one-fourth of the patients who have common Small-Pox die, while scarcely one out of four hundred of those that have been inoculated dies.

Thus you let one-fourth of your fellow-citizens perish; and when you are shocked at this calculation, which shows you to be so imprudent and so blameworthy, what do you do? You consult licentiates, either those of the foundation of Robert Sorbon,* or others: you present requisitions! In this way you maintained theses against Harvey, when he had discovered the circulation of the blood: in this manner were decrees issued by the Parliament of Paris, which condemned to the galleys those who wrote against the 'Categories' of Aristotle.

Oh, first people of the earth, when will you become reasonable? You are under the necessity of acknowledging the truth of all I have said to you. You make answer, that all your follies do not prevent Mademoiselle Duchapt* from selling female habits and ornaments all over the North, no more than it prevents your language from being spoken in Copenhagen, Stockholm, and Moscow. I shall not take into consideration the importance of the first of these articles; the second is alone the subject of my discourse. You make it your boast that your language is almost as universal as the Greek and Latin were formerly. To whom are you indebted for this? To about a score of authors of genius; all of whom you neglected, persecuted, and tormented, during their lives. You chiefly owe this triumph of your language in foreign countries, to the multitudes of natives who were obliged to quit their country about 1685: Bayle, Leclerc, Basnage, Bernard, Rapin de Thoyras, Beausobre, Lenfant, and many more, departed to make Holland and Germany illustrious: literary commerce was one of the greatest advantages of the United Provinces, and was entirely lost to you. The misfortunes of your countrymen contributed greatly to make your language known to so many nations: the Racines, the Corneilles, the Molières, the Boileaus, the Quinaults, the La Fontaines, and your good writers in prose, have doubtless greatly contributed to spread abroad your language and your reputation; it is a great advantage, but it does not justify you in thinking that you surpass the Greeks and Romans in everything.

In the first place, be so good as to consider that you have no art or science for the knowledge of which you are not indebted to the Greeks; the very names of those arts and sciences sufficiently prove this; poetry, logic, dialectics, geometry, meta-physics, geography, even theology, if it be a science, all declare to you the source from which you derive them.

There is not a single woman that does not speak Greek without being aware of it; for if she says that she has seen a tragedy or a comedy; that an ode has been read to her; that one of her relations has had a fit of apoplexy, or is paralytic; that he has quinsy, or that a surgeon has bled him in the cephalic vein; that she has been to church, where a deacon has sung the litany; if she speaks of bishops, priests, archdeacons, pope, liturgy, anthem, eucharist, baptism, mysteries, decalogue, evangelists, hierarchy, etc., it is very certain that she has pronounced scarcely a word that is not Greek [. . .]

The Portable Philosophical Dictionary*
(Dictionnaire philosophique portatif)

*First published in 1764, this volume of articles was first in Voltaire's
mind as early as 1752, and had been well-nigh inevitable since 1759. It
was to be steadily enlarged – and altered – over the next decade,
ending up as the Questions sur l'Encyclopédie – 'Questions concerning
the Encyclopaedia' – with several hundred articles.*

*Two points urged Voltaire to produce such a book: first, the
weightiness of the great Encyclopédie, which had begun to appear in
1751, and which had reached Volume VII in 1757. Worthy and
wonderful though it was, the impecunious thinking man could not
afford it, and its trenchant, society-changing articles risked suffocation
among the heavier (though still worthy) pieces describing trades,
manufactures and industrial processes. As Voltaire wrote on 5 April
1762, 'Twenty folio volumes will never achieve a revolution. If the
Gospel had cost twelve hundred sesterces, the Christian religion could
never have been established.'**

*Second, the Encyclopédie itself had been suspended in 1759, as a
result, above all, of Jesuit opposition. Voltaire, though keenly
supporting d'Alembert and Diderot, was not a prolific contributor –
some twelve or so articles, no more – but he saw nonetheless that the
suspension was a serious blow to the progress of enlightened thought.
His 'portable' dictionary could present the keen edge of the movement
to a wide and eager public.*

*The following articles have widely different forms – verging even in
'God', on a 'philosophic dialogue', a kind of dramatic argument which
could be imagined on the stage. The mood and direction of the articles
is also varied – mocking, with 'Vampires', serious and approving with
'Julian' and 'Quakers'.*

Abbé

*For Voltaire, as for most eighteenth-century thinkers, the category of
Abbé was one of the least logical elements of the Roman Catholic*

hierarchy, since the people involved were for the most part able – if they wished – to live in society as ordinary people, while receiving financial support from the Church. True, they were bound to be celibate, but this in Voltaire's view was a denial of an essential human obligation – to beget children; and many abbés lived worldly, even profligate lives.

The word *abbé*, let it be remembered, signifies father. If you become one, you render a service to the state; you doubtless perform the best work that a man can perform; you give birth to a thinking being; in this action there is something divine.

But if you are only *Monsieur l'abbé*, because you have had your head shaved, wear a small collar, and a short cloak, and are waiting for a fat benefice, you do not deserve the name of *abbé*.

The ancient monks gave this name to the superior whom they elected; the *abbé* was their spiritual father. What different things do the same words signify at different times; the spiritual *abbé* was once a poor man at the head of others equally poor; but the poor spiritual fathers have since had incomes of two hundred or four hundred thousand livres, and there are poor spiritual fathers in Germany who have a regiment of guards.

A poor man, making a vow of poverty, and in consequence becoming a sovereign! Truly, this is intolerable. The laws exclaim against such an abuse; Religion is indignant at it; and the really poor, who want food and clothing, appeal to heaven against *Monsieur l'abbé*.

But I hear the *abbés* of Italy, Germany, Flanders, Burgundy, ask, 'Why are not we to accumulate wealth and honours? Why are we not to become princes? The bishops are, who were originally poor like us; they have enriched and elevated themselves; one of them has become superior even to kings; let us imitate them as far as we are able.'

Gentlemen, you are right. Invade the land; it belongs to him whose strength or skill obtains possession of it. You have made ample use of the times of ignorance, superstition, and infatuation, to strip us of our inheritances and trample us under your feet, that you might fatten on the substance of the unfortunate. Tremble, for fear that the day of reason will arrive!

Cannibals (Anthropophages)

These quotations from a longer sequence of articles are – for the first and main part – from 1764; for the second, 1772, and for the third, 1774. Voltaire's account of meeting a cannibal from the Mississippi is curiously similar to that in Montaigne's essay 'Des Cannibales' – 'Of Cannibals' (Essays, 1, xxxi), which Voltaire refers to in another section of this item.

We have spoken of love. It is hard to pass from people *kissing* to people *eating* one another. It is, however, but too true, that there have been cannibals. We have found them in America; they are, perhaps, still to be found; and the Cyclops were not the only individuals in antiquity who sometimes fed on human flesh. Juvenal relates* that among the Egyptians – that wise people, so renowned for their laws – those pious worshippers of crocodiles and onions – the Tentyrites ate one of their enemies, who had fallen into their hands. He does not tell this tale on hearsay; the crime was committed almost before his eyes; he was then in Egypt, and not far from Tentyra. On this occasion he quotes the Gascons and the Saguntines, who formerly fed on the flesh of their countrymen.

In 1725, four savages were brought from the Mississippi to Fontainebleau, with whom I had the honour of conversing.* There was among them a lady of the country, whom I asked if she had eaten men; she answered, with great simplicity, that she had. I appeared somewhat scandalized; on which she excused herself by saying, that it was better to eat one's dead enemy than to leave him to be devoured by wild beasts, and that the conquerors deserved to have the preference. We kill our neighbours in battles, or skirmishes; and, for the meanest consideration, provide meals for the crows and the worms. There is the horror; there is the crime. What matters it, when a man is dead, whether he is eaten by a soldier, or by a dog and a crow?

We have more respect for the dead than for the living. It would be better to respect both the one and the other. The nations called polished have done right in not putting their vanquished enemies on the spit; for if we were allowed to eat our neighbours, we should soon eat our countrymen, which would be rather unfortunate for the social virtues. But polished nations have not always been so: they were all for a long time savage; and, in the infinite number of revolutions which this globe has undergone, mankind has been sometimes numerous, and sometimes very scarce. It has been with human beings as it now is with elephants, lions, or tigers, the race of which has very much decreased. In times, when a country was but thinly inhabited by men, they had few arts; they were hunters. The custom of eating what they had killed, easily led them to treat their enemies like their stags and their boars. It was superstition that caused human victims to be immolated; it was necessity that caused them to be eaten.

Which is the greater crime? – to assemble piously together to plunge a knife into the heart of a girl adorned with fillets, or to eat a worthless man who has been killed in our own defence.

Yet we have many more instances of girls and boys sacrificed, than of girls and boys eaten. Almost every nation of which we know anything has sacrificed boys and girls. The Jews immolated them. This was called *the Anathema:* it was a real sacrifice; and in Leviticus, it is ordained that the living souls which shall be devoted shall not be spared: but it is not in any manner prescribed that they shall be eaten; this is only threatened [. . .]

Well, two Englishmen have sailed round the world. They have discovered that New Holland is an island larger than Europe, and that men still eat one another there, as in New Zealand. Whence come this race? supposing that they exist. Are they descended from the ancient Egyptians, from the ancient people of Ethiopia, from the Africans, from the Indians? – or from the vultures, or the wolves? What a contrast, between Marcus Aurelius or Epictetus and the cannibals of New Zealand! Yet they have the same organs, they are alike human beings* [. . .]

One word more on cannibalism. In a book which has had considerable success among the well-disposed, we find the following, or words to the same effect –

'In Cromwell's time, a woman who kept a tallow-chandler's shop in Dublin, sold excellent candles, made of the fat of Englishmen. After some time, one of her customers complained that the candles were not so good. "Sir", said the woman, "it is because we are short of Englishmen."'

I ask which were the most guilty – those who assassinated the English, or the poor woman who made candles of their fat? And further, I ask, which was the greatest crime – to have Englishmen cooked for dinner, or to use their tallow to give light at supper? It appears to me that the great evil is, the being killed; it matters little to us whether, after death, we are roasted on the spit, or are made into candles. Indeed, no well-disposed man can be unwilling to be useful when he is dead.*

Convulsionaries

First published in 1764. The events referred to occurred not in 1724 but in 1727 and afterwards, on and beside the grave of the deacon Pâris, a Jansenist priest. Miracles were supposed to have occurred. The cemetery was closed in 1732. In an early draft (1757) of his tale Candide, *Voltaire had included a scene of convulsionary hysteria at St Médard as a part of Candide's experiences in Paris, but he left it out in the final version, probably because the events were – by 1759 – well in the past. See also 'On Fanaticism', below.*

About the year 1724, the cemetery of St Médard abounded in amusement, and many miracles were performed there. The following epigram by the Duchess of Maine gives a tolerable account of the character of most of them:-

> Un décrotteur à la Royale,
> Du talon gauche estropié,
> Obtint pour grâce spéciale,
> D'être boiteux de l'autre pied.

> A Port-Royal shoe-black, who had *one* lame leg,
> To make both alike the Lord's favour did beg;
> Heav'n listen'd, and straightway a miracle came,
> For quickly he rose up, with *both* his legs lame.

The miracles continued, as is well known, until a guard was stationed at the cemetery.

> De par le roi, défense à Dieu
> De faire miracle en ce lieu.

> Louis to God: – To keep the peace,
> Here miracles must henceforth cease.

It is also well known that the Jesuits being no longer able to perform similar miracles, in consequence of Xavier having exhausted their stock of grace and miraculous power, by resuscitating nine dead persons at one time, resolved, in order to counteract the credit of the Jansenists, to engrave a print of Jesus Christ dressed as a Jesuit. The Jansenists, on the other hand, in order to give a satisfactory proof that Jesus Christ had not assumed the habit of a Jesuit, filled Paris with convulsions, and attracted great crowds of people to witness them. The counsellor of parliament, Carré de Montgeron, went to present to the king a quarto collection of all these miracles, attested by a thousand witnesses. He was very properly shut up in a château, where attempts were made to restore his senses by regimen; but truth always prevails over persecution, and the miracles lasted for thirty years together, without interruption. Sister Rose, sister Illuminée, and the sisters Promise and Confite, were scourged with great energy, without, however, exhibiting any appearance of the whipping next day. They were bastinadoed on their stomachs without injury, and placed before a large fire, but being defended by certain pomades and preparations, were not burnt. At length, as every art is constantly advancing towards perfection, their persecutors concluded with actually thrusting swords through their chairs, and with crucifying them. A famous schoolmaster had also the benefit of crucifixion; all which was done to convince the world that a certain papal bull was ridiculous, a fact that might have been easily proved without so much trouble. However, Jesuits and Jansenists, all united against Montesquieu's *Spirit of Laws*, and against ... and against ... and against ... and ... And after all this, we dare to ridicule Laplanders, Samoiedes, and Negroes!

On Fanaticism

First published in 1742. We do not know whether Voltaire learnt of this episode some while after he left England, or whether he considered it too far in the past to include in the Letters Concerning the English Nation. *The 'noted Protestant' was a Swiss Huguenot, Nicolas Fatio de Duillier (1664–1753), who was eminent enough as a mathematician to be elected an F.R.S. He was also deeply involved with a millenarian group of Huguenot refugees living in London in the early eighteenth* *century. Their activities did indeed include the prediction of resurrection, notably of one of their number, Dr Thomas Emes, who had died in December 1707, and who they said would arise from the dead in the following year.* The 'demonstration' was at the cemetery at Bunhill Fields, not at St Paul's Cathedral. Otherwise, Voltaire's account is tolerably accurate.**

Geometry does not always produce a logical mind. What pitfalls there are still on the fringes of reason! A noted protestant, who was counted one of the foremost mathematicians of our time, following in the steps of Newton, Leibnitz and Bernouilli took it into his head some years ago to draw some extraordinary conclusions. It is said that with faith as a grain of mustard seed, one may move a mountain; and he said to himself, with a wholly geometrical conclusion: 'I have many grains of faith, so I shall do more than move mountains.' He was the one who was seen in London in 1707, in the company of several men of learning – some of them highly intelligent – who announced publicly that they would resurrect a dead man in whichever cemetery it was thought fit. Their reasoning always followed a logical course. They would say 'True disciples should work miracles; we are true disciples, and so we shall achieve all that we are pleased to do. Simple saints in the Roman church, who were in no way geometricians, have resuscitated many good people; it stands to reason, therefore, that we, who have reformed yet further, shall resurrect whomsoever we wish.'

To such arguments, there is nothing one can reply; their form is irreproachable. In this way, antiquity was overrun with marvels; in this way the temples of Aesculapius at Epidaurus and in other cities were filled with *ex voto* offerings; the roofs were hung with models of mended thighs, of arms set straight again, and little children in silver; all was miracle.

In the end, this famous protestant geometrician I have mentioned spoke so earnestly, asserted so firmly that he would resuscitate the dead, and made so great an impression on the populace with this plausible proposal, that Queen Anne was constrained to allow him a day, an hour and a cemetery of his choosing in which to perform his miracle in an honest way, and with appointed witnesses.* The saintly geometrician chose the cathedral Church of St Paul for his demonstration: the people stood in rows round about; soldiers were posted to maintain respect among the living and the dead; the magistrates took their place; the clerk of the court wrote down everything in the public register; one cannot record new miracles too carefully. At the saint's direction a corpse was exhumed; he prayed, fell on his knees, he fell into most pious contortions; his companions imitated him; the dead man gave no sign of life; he was put back into the grave, and the resuscitator and his followers were mildly punished. Since then, I have spoken with one of these wretched persons; he confessed to me that one of them was in a state of venial sin, and that the dead man had suffered as a result – otherwise the resurrection had been certain.

If one was allowed to reveal the baseness of people to whom one owes the most sincere respect, I would add here that *Newton*, the great *Newton*, found in the account of the Apocalypse that the pope was Antichrist, and many other things of this kind; I would add that he was a convinced Arian. I concede that this error of *Newton*'s, set beside that of my other geometrician, is like unity set beside infinity: one cannot make any comparison. But what sad creatures must we humans be, if the great *Newton* could imagine that he had found the history of modern Europe in the Apocalypse!

Superstition might seem to be an epidemic sickness, from which even the strongest natures are not always exempt. There are in Turkey men of great intelligence who would have themselves impaled for the sake of *Aboubeker*'s opinions. Once these principles have been accepted, their reasoning proceeds with fine logic: in their turn the Navaricians, the Radarists, the Jabarists damn themselves reciprocally with the most subtle arguments; all of them draw the most convincing conclusions; but they never dare question the first principle.

Let someone spread the news that there exists a giant seventy feet tall; it will not be long before the learned doctors are discussing what colour its hair should be, how big its thumb, the size of its nails: their voices rise, they scheme, they fight each other; those who maintain that the giant's little finger is only an inch and a half across will burn at the stake all those who insist that the little finger has a width of a foot. 'But, gentlemen, does your giant exist?' enquires a passer-by. 'What a fearful thing to doubt!' exclaim these quarrelling doctors. 'What blasphemy!

What monstrous absurdity!' And then, briefly, they hold a truce, that they may stone the passer-by, and when they have assassinated him with full ceremony, in the most edifying manner, they turn to fighting each other in the usual way – about the little finger and nails.

God* (Dieu)

Voltaire produced no less than six sections discussing 'God', of which the sixth is given here. It was first published in 1764.

In the reign of Arcadius,* Logomachos, a theologian from Constantinople, went into Scythia and stopped at the foot of Mount Caucasus in the fruitful plains of Zephirim, on the borders of Colchis. The good old man Dondindac was in his great hall, between his large sheepfold and his extensive barn; he was on his knees with his wife, his five sons and five daughters, his kinsmen and servants; and all were singing the praises of God, after a light repast. – 'What art thou doing, idolater,' said Logomachos to him. 'I am not an idolater,' said Dondindac. 'Thou must be an idolater,' said Logomachos, 'for thou art not a Greek. Come, tell me what thou wast singing in thy barbarous Scythian jargon?' – 'All tongues are alike to the ears of God,' answered the Scythian; 'we were singing his praises.' – 'Very extraordinary!' returned the theologue; 'a Scythian family praying to God without having been instructed by us!' He soon entered into conversation with the Scythian Dondindac; for the theologian knew a little Scythian, and the other a little Greek. This conversation has been found in a manuscript preserved in the library of Constantinople.

LOGOMACHOS

Let us see if thou knowest thy catechism. Why dost thou pray to God?

DONDINDAC

Because it is just to adore the Supreme Being, from whom we have everything.

LOGOMACHOS

Very fair for a barbarian. And what dost thou ask of him?

DONDINDAC

I thank him for the blessings I enjoy, and even for the trials which he sends me; but I am careful to ask nothing of him; for he knows our wants better than we do; besides, I should be afraid of asking for fair weather while my neighbour was asking for rain.

LOGOMACHOS

Ah! I thought he would say some nonsense or other. Let us begin further back. Barbarian, who told thee that there is a God?

DONDINDAC

All nature tells me.

LOGOMACHOS

That is not enough. What idea has thou of God?

DONDINDAC

The idea of my Creator; my master, who will reward me if I do good, and punish me if I do evil.

LOGOMACHOS

Trifles! trash! Let us come to some essentials. Is God infinite *secundum quid*, or according to essence?

DONDINDAC

I don't understand you.

LOGOMACHOS

Brute beast! Is God in one place, or in every place?

DONDINDAC

I know not . . . just as you please.

LOGOMACHOS

Ignoramus! . . . Can he cause that which has not been to have been, or that a stick shall not have two ends? Does he see the future as future, or as present? How does he draw being from nothing, and how reduce being to nothing?

DONDINDAC

I have never examined these things.

LOGOMACHOS

What a stupid fellow! Well, I must come nearer to thy level . . . Tell me, friend, dost thou think that matter can be eternal?

DONDINDAC

What matters it to me whether it exists from all eternity or not? I do not exist from all eternity. God must still be my master. He has given me the nature of justice; it is my duty to follow it: I seek not to be a philosopher; I wish to be a man.

LOGOMACHOS

One has a great deal of trouble with these blockheads. Let us proceed step by step. What is God?

DONDINDAC

My sovereign, my judge, my father.

LOGOMACHOS

That is not what I ask. What is his nature?

DONDINDAC

To be mighty and good.

LOGOMACHOS

But is he corporeal or spiritual?

DONDINDAC

How should I know that?

LOGOMACHOS

What; dost thou not know what a spirit is?

DONDINDAC

Not in the least. Of what service would that knowledge be to me? Should I be more just? Should I be a better husband, a better father, a better master, or a better citizen?

LOGOMACHOS

Thou must absolutely be taught what a spirit is. It is ... it is ... it is ... I will say what another time.

DONDINDAC

I much fear that you will tell me rather what it is not than what it is. Permit me, in turn, to ask you one question. Some time ago, I saw one of your temples: why do you paint God with a long beard?

LOGOMACHOS

That is a very difficult question, and requires preliminary instruction.

DONDINDAC

Before I receive your instruction, I must relate to you a thing which one day happened to me. I had just built a closet at the end of my garden, when I heard a mole arguing thus with an ant:- 'Here is a fine fabric,' said the mole; 'it must have been a very powerful mole that performed this work.' – 'You jest,' returned the ant; 'the architect of this edifice is an ant of mighty genius.' From that time I resolved never to dispute.

Julian* (Julien)

This section – one of several on Julian in the Philosophical Dictionary *– first appeared in 1756. It is one of Voltaire's strongly positive pieces in the* Philosophical Dictionary *– cf. 'Theist'. Voltaire had read sections of Julians's writings in La Bléterie's* Histoire de l'empereur Jovien et traductions de … l'empereur Julien *(2 volumes, 1748), including Julian's letter describing the little farm which was to be the inspiration for Candide's garden in 1758–9.* *

Let any one suppose for a moment, that Julian had abandoned false gods for Christianity; then examine him as a man, a philosopher, and an emperor; and let the examiner then point out the man whom he will venture to prefer to him. If he had lived only ten years longer, there is a great probability that he would have given a different form to Europe from that which it bears at present.

The Christian religion depended upon his life: the efforts which he made for its destruction rendered his name execrable to the nations who have embraced it. The Christian priests, who were his contemporaries, accused him of almost every crime, because he had committed what in their eyes was the greatest of all – he had lowered and humiliated them. It is not long since his name was never quoted without the epithet of apostate attached to it; and it is perhaps one of the greatest achievements of reason that he has at length ceased to be mentioned under so opprobrious a designation. Who would imagine, that in the *Mercure de Paris*, in 1741, the author sharply rebukes a certain writer for failing in the common courtesies of life, by calling this emperor Julian 'the apostate'? Not more than a hundred years ago, the man that would not have treated him as an apostate, would himself have been treated as an atheist.

What is very singular, and at the same time perfectly true, is that if you put out of consideration the various disputes between pagans and Christians, in which this emperor was engaged; if you follow him neither to the Christian churches nor idolatrous temples, but observe him attentively in his own household, in camp, in battle, in his manners, his conduct, and his writings, you will find him in every respect equal to Marcus Aurelius.*

Thus, the man who has been described as so abominable and execrable, is perhaps the first, or at least the second of mankind. Always sober, always temperate, indulging in no licentious pleasures, sleeping on a mere bear's skin, devoting only a few hours, and even those with regret to sleep; dividing his time between study and business, generous, susceptible of friendship, and an enemy to all pomp, and pride, and ostentation. Had he been merely a private individual, he must have extorted universal admiration.

If we consider him in his military character, we see him constantly at the head of his troops, establishing or restoring discipline without rigour, beloved by his soldiers and at the same time restraining their excesses, conducting his armies almost always on foot, and showing them an example of enduring every species of hardship, ever victorious in all his expeditions even to the last moment of his life, and at length dying at the glorious crisis when the Persians were routed. His death was that of a hero, and his last words were those of a philosopher: 'I submit,' says he, 'willingly to the eternal decrees of heaven, convinced that he who is captivated with life, when his last hour is arrived, is more weak and pusillanimous than he who would rush to voluntary death when it is his duty still to live.' He converses to the last moment on the immortality of the soul; manifests no regrets, shows no weakness, and speaks only of his submission to the decrees of providence. Let it be remembered that this is the death of an emperor at the age of thirty-two, and let it be then decided whether his memory should be insulted.

As an emperor, we see him refusing the title of 'Dominus', which Constantine affected; relieving his people from difficulties, diminishing taxes, encouraging the arts; reducing to the moderate amount of seventy ounces each those presents in crowns of gold, which had before been exacted from every city to the amount of three or four hundred marks; promoting the strict and general observance of the laws; restraining both his officers and ministers from oppression, and preventing as much as possible all corruption.

Ten Christian soldiers conspire to assassinate him; they are discovered, and Julian pardons them. The people of Antioch, who united insolence to voluptuousness, offer him an insult: he revenges himself only like a man of sense; and while he might have made them feel the weight of imperial power, he merely makes them feel the superiority of his mind. Compare with this conduct the executions which Theodosius (who was very near being made a saint) exhibited in Antioch, and the ever dreadful and memorable slaughter of all the inhabitants of Thessalonica, for an offence of a somewhat similar description; and then decide between these two celebrated characters.

Certain fathers of the church, Gregory of Nazianzen, and Theodoret, thought it incumbent on them to calumniate him, because he had abandoned the Christian religion. They did not consider that it was the triumph of that religion to prevail over so great a man, and even over a sage, after having resisted tyrants. One of them says, that he took a barbarous vengeance on Antioch and filled it with blood. How could a fact so public escape the knowledge of all other historians? It is perfectly known that he shed no blood at Antioch but that of the victims sacrificed in the regular services of religion. Another ventures to assert, that before his death he threw some of his own blood towards heaven, and exclaimed, 'Galilean, thou hast conquered'.* How could a tale so insipid and so improbable, even for a moment obtain credit? Was it against the Christians that he was then in combat? and is such an act, are such expressions, characteristic of the man?

Minds of a superior order to those of Julian's detractors, may perhaps inquire, how it could occur, that a statesman like him, a man of so much intellect, a genuine philosopher, could quit the Christian religion, in which he was educated, for paganism, of which he must have felt the folly and ridicule. It might be inferred, that if Julian yielded too much to the suggestions of his reason against the mysteries of the Christian religion, he ought to have yielded more readily to the same reason, when condemning the fables of paganism.

Perhaps, by attending a little to the progress of his life, and the nature of his character, we may discover what it was that inspired him with so strong an aversion to Christianity. The emperor Constantine, his great uncle, who had placed the new religion on the throne, was stained by the murder of his wife, his son, his brother-in-law, his nephew, and his father-in-law. The three children of Constantine began their bloody and baleful reign, with murdering their uncle and their cousins. From that time followed a series of civil wars and murders. The father, the brother, and all the relations of Julian, and even Julian himself, were marked down for destruction by Constantius, his uncle. He escaped this general massacre, but the first years of his life were passed in exile [. . .]

If he saw that he was in a Christian family, he saw he was in a family distinguished by parricides; if he looked at the court bishops, he perceived that they were at once audacious and intriguing, and that all anathematized each other in turn. The hostile parties of Arius and Athanasius filled the empire with confusion and carnage. The pagans, on the contrary, never had any religious quarrels. It is natural therefore that Julian, who had been educated, let it be remembered, by philosophic pagans, should have strengthened by their discourses the aversion he must necessarily have felt in his heart for the Christian religion. It is not more extraordinary to see Julian quit Christianity for false gods, than to see Constantine quit false gods for Christianity. It is highly probable, that both changed from motives of state policy, and that this policy was blended in the mind of Julian with the stern loftiness of a stoic soul.

The pagan priests had no dogmas: they did not compel men to believe that which was incredible; they required nothing but sacrifices, and even sacrifices were not enjoined under rigorous penalties; they did not form a state within a state. These might well be considered motives to induce a man of Julian's character to declare himself on their side; and if he had piqued himself upon being nothing besides a stoic, he would have had against him the priests of both religions, and all the fanatics of each. The common people would not at that time have endured a prince who was content simply with the pure worship of a pure divinity and the strict observance of justice. It was necessary to side with one of the opposing parties. We must therefore believe, that Julian submitted to the pagan ceremonies, as the majority of princes and great men attend the forms of worship in the public temples. They are led thither by the people themselves, and are often obliged to appear what in fact they are not. The Turkish sultan must bless the name of Omar. The Persian sophi must bless the name of Ali. Marcus Aurelius himself was initiated in the mysteries of Eleusis.

We ought not therefore to be surprised, that Julian should have debased his reason by condescending to the forms and usages of superstition [. . .]

Both Christians and pagans equally circulated fables concerning Julian; but the fables of the Christians, who were his enemies, were filled with calumny. Who could ever be induced to believe, that a philosopher sacrificed a woman to the moon, and tore out her entrails with his own hands? Is such atrocity compatible with the character of a rigid stoic?

He never put any Christians to death: he granted them no favours, but he never persecuted them. He permitted them, like a just sovereign, to keep their own property; and he wrote in opposition to them like a philosopher. He forbade their teaching in the schools the profane authors, whom they endeavoured to decry – this was not persecuting them; and he prevented them from tearing one another to pieces in their outrageous hatred and quarrels – this was protecting them. They had in fact therefore nothing with which they could reproach him, but with having abandoned them, and with not being of their opinion. They found means however of rendering execrable to posterity a prince, who, but for his change of religion, would have been admired and beloved by all the world.

Letters (Men of) (Lettres, Gens de lettres, ou lettrés)

First published in 1765. Voltaire often presents the positive and peaceful nature of the 'man of letters' – himself, of course! – in contrast with the destructive, intolerant or fanatical politician or priest. See also 'Philosopher', p. 178.

In barbarous times, when the Franks, Germans, Bretons, Lombards, and Spanish Mosarabians* knew neither how to read nor write, we instituted schools and universities almost entirely composed of ecclesiastics, who, knowing only their own jargon, taught this jargon to those who would learn it. Academies were not founded until long after: the latter have despised the follies of the schools, but they have not always dared to oppose them, because there are follies which we respect when they are attached to respectable things.

Men of letters who have rendered the most service to the small number of thinking beings scattered over the earth are isolated scholars, true sages shut up in their closets, who have neither publicly disputed in the universities, nor said things by halves in the academies; and such have almost all been persecuted. Our miserable race is so created, that those who walk in the beaten path always throw stones at those who would show them a new one.

Montesquieu says,* that the Scythians put out the eyes of their slaves, that they might be more attentive to the making of their butter. It is thus that the Inquisition acts, and almost every one is blinded in the countries in which this monster reigns. In England people have had two eyes for more than a hundred years. The French are beginning to open one eye – but sometimes men in place will not even permit us to be one-eyed.

These miserable statesmen are like Doctor Balouard of the Italian comedy, who will only be served by the fool Arlequin,* and who fears to have too penetrating a servant.

Compose odes in praise of lord Superbus Fadus, madrigals for his mistress; dedicate a book of geography to his porter – you will be well received. Enlighten men, and you will be crushed.

Descartes is obliged to quit his country; Gassendi is calumniated; Arnauld* passes his days in exile; all the philosophers are treated as the prophets were among the Jews.

Who would believe, that in the eighteenth century, a philosopher* has been dragged before the secular tribunals, and treated as impious by reasoning theologians, for having said, that men could not practise the arts, if they had no hands? I expect that they will soon condemn to the galleys the first who shall have the insolence to say, that a man could not think if he had no head; for a learned bachelor will say to him, the soul is a pure spirit, the head is only matter: God can place the soul in the heel as well as in the brain; therefore I denounce you as a blasphemer.

The greatest misfortune of a man of letters is not perhaps being the object of the jealousy of his brother scholars, the victim of cabals, and the contempt of the powerful of the world – it is being judged by fools. Fools sometimes go very far, particularly when fanaticism is joined to folly, and folly to the spirit of vengeance. Further, the great misfortune of a man of letters is generally to have no post. A citizen buys a little situation, and is maintained by his fellow-citizens. If any injustice is done him, he soon finds defenders. The man of letters is without aid: he resembles the flying fish: if he rises a little, the birds devour him; if he dives, the fishes eat him up.

Every public man pays tribute to malignity; but he is repaid in deniers and honours. The man of letters pays the same tribute, but receives no recompense; he himself has chosen to enter the arena; he himself has chosen to be devoured by beasts.

Philosopher (Philosophe)

One of Voltaire's more positive articles, comparable with 'Julian', 'Letters (Men of)', and 'Quakers'. First published in 1756.

Philosopher, 'lover of wisdom', that is, 'of truth'. All philosophers have possessed this two-fold character; there is not one among those of antiquity who did not give examples of virtue to mankind, and lessons of moral truth. They might be mistaken, and undoubtedly were so, on subjects of natural philosophy; but that is of comparatively so little importance to the conduct of life, that philosophers had then no need of it. Ages were required to discover a part of the laws of nature. A single day is sufficient to enable a sage to become acquainted with the duties of man.

The philosopher is no enthusiast; he does not set himself up for a prophet; he does not represent himself as inspired by the gods. I shall not therefore place in the rank of philosophers the ancient Zoroaster, or Hermes, or Orpheus, or any of those legislators in whom the nations of Chaldea, Persia, Syria, Egypt, and Greece made their boast. Those who called themselves the sons of gods were the fathers of imposture; and if they employed falsehood to inculcate truths, they were unworthy of inculcating them; they were not philosphers; they were at best only prudent liars.

By what fatality, disgraceful perhaps to the nations of the west, has it happened that we are obliged to travel to the extremity of the east, in order to find a sage of simple manners and character, without arrogance and without imposture, who taught men how to live happy six hundred years before our era, at a period when the whole of the north was ignorant of the use of letters, and when the Greeks had scarcely begun to distinguish themselves by wisdom? That sage is Confucius, who deemed too highly of his character as a legislator for mankind, to stoop to deceive them. What finer rule of conduct has ever been given since his time, throughout the earth?

'Rule a state as you rule a family; a man cannot govern his family well without giving a good example.

'Virtue should be common to the labourer and the monarch.

'Be active in preventing crimes, that you may lessen the trouble of punishing them.

'Under the good kings Yao and Xu, the Chinese were good; under the bad kings Kie and Chu, they were wicked.

'Do to another as to thyself.

'Love mankind in general, but cherish those who are good. Forget injuries, but never benefits.

'I have seen men incapable of the sciences, but never any incapable of virtue.'

Let us acknowledge, that no legislator ever announced to the world more useful truths.

A multitude of Greek philosophers taught afterwards a morality equally pure. Had they distinguished themselves only by their vain systems of natural philosophy, their names would be mentioned at the present day only in derision. If they are still respected, it is because they were just, and because they taught mankind to be so.

It is impossible to read certain passages of Plato, and particularly the admirable introduction to the laws of Zaleucus,* without experiencing an ardent love of honourable and generous actions. The Romans have their Cicero, who alone is perhaps more valuable than all the philosophers of Greece. After him come men more respectable still, but whom we may almost despair of imitating; these are Epictetus in slavery, and the Antonines and Julian upon a throne.*

Where is the citizen to be found among us who would deprive

himself, like Julian, Antoninus, and Marcus Aurelius, of all the refined accommodations of our delicate and luxurious modes of living? Who would, like them, sleep on the bare ground? Who would restrict himself to their frugal habits? Who would, like them, march bare-headed and bare-footed at the head of the armies, exposed sometimes to the burning sun, and at other times to the freezing blast? Who would, like them, keep perfect mastery of all his passions? We have among us pious people, but where are the sages? where are the souls just and tolerant, serene and undaunted?

There have been some private philosphers in France; and all of them, with the exception of Montaigne, have been persecuted. It seems to me the last degree of malignity that our nature can exhibit, to attempt to oppress those who devote their best endeavours to correct and improve it.

I can easily conceive of the fanatics of one sect slaughtering those of another sect; that the Franciscans should hate the Dominicans, and that a bad artist should cabal and intrigue for the destruction of an artist that surpasses him; but that the sage Charron should have been menaced with the loss of life; that the learned and noble-minded Ramus should have been actually assassinated; that Descartes should have been obliged to withdraw to Holland in order to escape the rage of ignorance; that Gassendi* should have been often compelled to retire to Digne, far distant from the calumnies of Paris – these are events that load a nation with eternal opprobrium.

One of the philosophers who were most persecuted, was the immortal Bayle,* the honour of human nature. I shall be told that the name of Jurieu, his slanderer and persecutor, is become execrable; I acknowledge that it is so; that of the Jesuit Le Tellier is become so likewise; but is it the less true that the great men whom he oppressed ended their days in exile and penury?

One of the pretexts made use of for reducing Bayle to poverty, was his article *David*, in his valuable dictionary. He was reproached with not praising actions which were in themselves unjust, sanguinary, atrocious, contrary to good faith, or grossly offensive to decency.

Bayle certainly has not praised David for having, according to Hebrew historians, collected six hundred vagabonds over-whelmed with debts and crimes; for having pillaged his countrymen at the head of these banditti; for having resolved to destroy Nabal and his whole family, because he refused paying contributions to him; for having hired out his services to King Achish, the enemy of his country; for having afterwards betrayed Achish, notwithstanding his kindness to him; for having sacked the villages in alliance with that King; for having massacred in these villages every human being, including even infants at the breast, that no one might be found on a future day to give testimony of his depredations, as if an infant could have possibly disclosed his villainy; for having destroyed all the inhabitants of some other villages under saws, and harrows, and axes, and in brick-kilns; for having wrested the throne from Ishbosheth, the son of Saul, by an act of perfidy; for having despoiled of his property and afterwards put to death Mephibosheth, the grandson of Saul, and son of his own peculiar friend and generous protector Jonathan; or for having delivered up to the Gibeonites two other sons of Saul, and five of his grandsons who perished by the gallows.

I say nothing of the extreme incontinence of David, his numerous concubines, his adultery with Bathsheba, or his murder of Uriah.

What then! is it possible that the enemies of Bayle should have expected or wished him to praise all these cruelties and crimes? Ought he to have said 'Go, ye princes of the earth, and imitate the man after God's own heart; massacre without pity the allies of your benefactor; destroy or deliver over to destruction the whole family of your king; appropriate to your own pleasures all the women, while you are pouring out the blood of the men; and you will thus exhibit models of human virtue, especially if you composed a book of psalms?'

Was not Bayle perfectly correct in his observation, that if David was the man after God's own heart, it must have been by his penitence, and not by his misdeeds? Did not Bayle perform a service to the human race when he said, that God, who undoubtedly dictated the Jewish history, has not consecrated all the crimes recorded in that history?

However, Bayle was in fact persecuted, and by whom? By the very men who had been elsewhere persecuted themselves; by refugees, who in their own country would have been delivered over to the flames; and these refugees were opposed by other refugees called Jansenists, who had been driven from their own country by the Jesuits; who have at length been themselves driven from it in their turn.

Thus all the persecutors declare against each other mortal war, while the philosopher, oppressed by them all, contents himself with pitying them.

It is not generally known, that Fontenelle,* in 1713, was on the point of losing his pensions, place, and liberty, for having published in France, twenty years before, the learned Van Dale's *Treatise on Oracles*, in which he had taken particular care to retrench and modify the original work, so as to give no unnecessary offence to fanaticism. A Jesuit had written against Fontenelle, and he had not deigned to make him any reply; and that was enough to induce the Jesuit Le Tellier, confessor to Louis XIV, to accuse Fontenelle to the king of atheism [...]

It is so easy for a confessor to seduce his penitent, that we ought to bless God that Le Tellier did no more harm than is justly imputed to him. There are two situations in which seduction and calumny cannot easily be resisted – the bed and the confessional.

We have always seen philosophers persecuted by fanatics. But can it be really possible, that men of letters should be seen mixed up in a business so odious; and that they should often be observed sharpening the weapons against their brethren, by which they are themselves almost universally destroyed or wounded in their turn? [...]

How inexpressible is the meanness of being a hypocrite! how horrible is it to be a mischievous and malignant hypocrite! There were no hypocrites in ancient Rome, which reckoned us a small portion of its innumerable subjects. There were impostors, I admit, but not religious hypocrites, which are the most profligate and cruel species of all. Why is it that we see none such in England, and whence does it arise that there still are such in France? Philosophers, you will solve this problem with ease.

Quakers

First published in 1772, this item was then printed in company with the first four of the Letters Concerning the English Nation, *and is clearly an addition to the fourth of these, describing the foundation of Pennsylvania by the Quaker William Penn.*

Quaker, primitive, member of the primitive Christian church, Pennsylvanian or Philadelphian.

Of all these titles, the one which I like best is that of Philadelphian, *friend of the brothers*. There are many kinds of vanities, but the finest is that which, not arrogating to itself any title, renders almost all others ridiculous.

I soon accustom myself to see a good Philadelphian treat me as a friend and brother: these words reanimate charity in my heart, which freezes too easily. But that two monks should call and write themselves 'your reverence', that they should cause their hands to be kissed in Italy and Spain, is the greatest degree of insane pride; the greatest degree of folly in those who kiss, and ought to excite the greatest degree of surprise and laughter in those who are witnesses to their fooleries. The simplicity of the Philadelphians is the continual satire of bishops, who *my lord* themselves.

'Are you not ashamed to call yourself lord and prince?' said a layman to the son of a labourer become a bishop; 'Is it thus that Barnabas, Philip, and Jude styled themselves?' 'Go to,' said the prelate; 'If Barnabas, Philip, and Jude, could have done so, they would; the proof of which is, that their successors did so as soon as they could.'

Another, who had one day several Gascons at his table, said 'I must be monseigneur, since all these gentlemen are marquises.' *Vanitas vanitatum.*

I have already spoken of Quakers in the article 'Church (primitive)', for which reason I again speak of them. I beg, my dear reader, you will not say that I repeat myself, for if there are two or three pages repeated in this Dictionary, it is not my fault, it is that of the editors. I am ill at Mount Krapack,* and cannot see to everything. I have associates who labour like myself in the vineyard of the Lord;* who seek to inspire peace and tolerance, horror for fanaticism, persecution, calumny, harshness of manners, and insolent ignorance.

I tell you, without repetition, that I love Quakers. Yes, if the sea did not disagree with me, it should be in thy bosom, Oh Pennsylvania! that I would finish the rest of my career; if there be any remaining. Thou art situated in the fortieth degree of latitude, in the softest and most favourable climate; thy houses commodiously built; thine inhabitants industrious; thy manufactures in repute. An eternal peace reigns among thy citizens; crimes are almost unknown; and there is but a single example of a man banished from the country. He deserved it very properly, being an Anglican priest who turning Quaker, was unworthy of being so. This poor man was no doubt possessed of the devil, for he dared to preach intolerance; he was called George Keith, and they banished him. I know not where he went; but may all intolerants go with him.

Thus, of three hundred thousand inhabitants who live happily in thee, there are two hundred thousand foreigners. For twelve guineas, you may purchase an hundred acres of very good land, and in these hundred acres you are truly king, for you are free and a citizen; you can do no harm to any one, nor any one to you; you think as you please, and say what you think without being persecuted; you know not the weight of continually redoubled taxes, you fear not the insolence of an importunate subaltern. It is true, that at Mount Krapack we live nearly the same as yourselves; but we owe the tranquillity which we enjoy only to mountains covered with eternal snow, and to frightful precipices which surround our terrestrial paradise. Further, the devil, as in Milton, sometimes leaps these frightful hills and precipices, to infect the flowers of our paradise with his poisonous breath. Satan transformed himself into a toad to deceive two creatures who loved one another. He once came among us in his own shape to bring intolerance. Our innocence has triumphed over all the malice of the devil.

Theism (Théïsme)

First published in 1742, the last two paragraphs added in 1756. Like the following item, 'Theist' (first published 1765), a gentle and positive statement by Voltaire, comparable with the article 'Philosopher', and with the deist religion of Eldorado, in Candide, Ch. 18.

Theism is a religion diffused through all religions; it is a metal which mixes itself with all the others, the veins of which extend under ground to the four corners of the world. This mine is more openly worked in China; everywhere else it is hidden, and the secret is only in the hands of the adepts.

There is no country where there are more of these adepts than in England. In the last century there were many atheists in that country as well as in France and Italy. What the chancellor Bacon had said proved true to the letter, that a little philosophy makes a man an atheist, and that much philosophy leads to the knowledge of a God. When it was believed with Epicurus, that chance made everything, or with Aristotle and even with many ancient theologians, that nothing was created but through corruption, and that by matter and motion alone the world goes on, then it was impossible to believe in Providence. But since nature has been looked into, which the ancients did not perceive at all; since it is observed, that all is organised, that everything has its germ; since it is well known, that a mushroom is the work of Infinite Wisdom, as well as all the worlds; then those who thought, adored in the countries where their ancestors had blasphemed. The physicians have become the heralds of Providence; a catechist announces God to children, and a Newton demonstrates him to the learned.

Many persons ask whether theism, considered abstractedly, and without any religious ceremony, is in fact a religion? The answer is easy: he who recognises only a creating God, he who views in God only a being infinitely powerful, and who sees in his creatures only wonderful machines, is not religious towards him any more than a European, admiring the King of China, would thereby profess allegiance to that prince. But he who thinks that God has deigned to set a link between himself and mankind; that he has made them free, capable of good and evil; that he has given all of them that good sense which is the instinct of man, and on which the law of nature is founded – such a one undoubtedly has a religion, and a much better religion than all those sects who are beyond the pale of our church; for all these sects are false, and the law of nature is true. Thus, theism is good sense not yet instructed by revelation; and other religions are good sense perverted by superstition.

All sects differ, because they come from men; morality is everywhere the same, because it comes from God.

It is asked why, out of five or six hundred sects, there have scarcely been any who have not spilled blood; and why the theists, who are everywhere so numerous, have never caused the least disturbance? It is because they are philosophers. Now philosophers may reason badly, but they never intrigue. Those who persecute a philosopher, under the pretext that his opinions may be dangerous to the public, are as absurd as those who should be afraid that the study of algebra would raise the price of bread in the market: one must pity a thinking being who errs; the persecutor is frantic and horrible. We are all brethren: if one of my brothers, full of respect and filial love, inspired by the most fraternal charity, does not salute our common father with the same ceremonies as I do, ought I to cut his throat and tear out his heart?

What is a true theist? It is he who says to God: 'I adore and I serve you'; it is he who says to the Turk, the Chinese, the Indian, and the Russian: 'I love you'.

He doubts, perhaps, that Mahomet made a journey to the moon and put half of it in his pocket; he does not wish that after his death his wife should burn herself from devotion; he is sometimes tempted not to believe the story of the eleven thousand virgins, and that of St Amable, whose hat and gloves were carried by a ray of the sun from Auvergne as far as Rome. But, saving that, he is a just man. Noah would have placed him in his ark, Numa Pompilius in his councils; he would have ascended the car of Zoroaster; he would have talked philosophy with the Platos, the Aristippuses, the Ciceros, the Atticuses – but would he have drunk hemlock with Socrates?

Theist

The theist is a man firmly persuaded of the existence of a Supreme Being equally good and powerful, who has formed all extended, vegetating, sentient, and reflecting existences; who perpetuates their species, who punishes crimes without cruelty, and rewards virtuous actions with kindness.

The theist does not know how God punishes, how he rewards, how he pardons; for he is not presumptuous enough to flatter himself that he understands how God acts; but he knows that God does act and that he is just. The difficulties opposed to a Providence do not stagger him in his faith, because they are only great difficulties, not proofs: he submits himself to that Providence, although he only perceives some of its effects and some appearances; and judging of the things he does not see from those he does see, he thinks that this Providence pervades all places and all ages.

United in this principle with the rest of the universe, he does not join any of the sects, who all contradict themselves; his religion is the most ancient and the most extended: for the simple adoration of a God has preceded all the systems in the world. He speaks a language which all nations understand, while they are unable to understand each other. He has brethren from Peking to Cayenne, and he reckons all the wise his brothers. He believes that religion consists neither in the opinions of incomprehensible metaphysics, nor in vain decorations, but in adoration and justice. To do good – that is his worship: to submit oneself to God – that is his doctrine. The Mahometan cries out to him: 'Take care of yourself, if you do not make the pilgrimage to Mecca.' – 'Woe be to thee', says a Franciscan, 'if thou dost not make a journey to our Lady of Loretto'. He laughs at Loretto and Mecca; but he succours the indigent and defends the oppressed.

Vampires

First published in 1772, Voltaire's joyous mockery of the idea of vampires comes some forty years after the agitations in rural regions round Belgrade had produced a flood of documents describing vampire activity, and referring to earlier examples in the border-lands between the Austrian and Turkish empires. The 'epidemic' did not spread into Western Europe, remaining a matter for theological speculation, and later – from the late 1770s – becoming an element in pre-romantic horror tales.

What! is it in our eighteenth century that vampires exist? Is it after the reigns of Locke, Shaftesbury, Trenchard and Collins? Is it under those of d'Alembert, Diderot, Saint-Lambert, and Duclos, that we believe in vampires, and that the reverend father Dom Calmet,* benedictine priest of the congregation of St Vannes and St Hidulphe, Abbé of Senon – an abbey of an hundred thousand livres a year, in the neighbourhood of two other abbeys of the same revenue, – has printed and reprinted the history of vampires, with the approbation of the Sorbonne, signed Marcilli?*

These vampires were corpses, who went out of their graves at night to suck the blood of the living, either at their throats or stomachs, after which they returned to their cemeteries. The persons so sucked waned, grew pale, and fell into consumptions; while the sucking corpses grew fat, got rosy, and enjoyed an excellent appetite. It was in Poland, Hungary, Silesia, Moravia, Austria, and Lorraine, that the dead made this good cheer. We never heard speak of vampires in London, nor even at Paris. I confess, that in both these cities there were stock-jobbers, brokers, and men of business, who sucked the blood of the people in broad day-light; but they were not dead, though corrupted. These true suckers lived not in cemeteries, but in very agreeable palaces.

Who would believe, that we derive the idea of vampires from Greece? Not from the Greece of Alexander, Aristotle, Plato, Epicurus and Demosthenes; but from Christian Greece, unfortunately schismatic.

For a long time, Christians of the Greek rite have imagined that the bodies of Christians of the Latin church, buried in Greece, do not decay, because they are excommunicated. This is precisely the contrary idea to that of we Christians of the Latin church, who believe that corpses which do not corrupt are marked with the seal of eternal beatitide [. . .]

The Greeks are persuaded that these dead are sorcerers; they call them 'broucolacas', or 'vroucolacas', according as they pronounce the second letter of the alphabet. The Greek corpses go into houses to suck the blood of little children, to eat the supper of the fathers and mothers, drink their wine, and break all the furniture. They can only be put to rights by burning them when they are caught. But the precaution must be taken of not putting them into the fire until after their hearts are torn out, which must be burnt separately.

The celebrated Tournefort,* sent into the Levant by Louis XIV, as well as so many other virtuosos, was witness of all the acts attributed to one of these 'broucolacas', and to this ceremony.

After slander, nothing is communicated more promptly than superstition, fanaticism, sorcery, and tales of those raised from the dead. There were broucolacas in Wallachia, Moldavia, and some among the Poles, who are of the Romish church. This superstition being absent, they acquired it, and it went through all the east of Germany. Nothing was spoken of but vampires, from 1730 to 1735; they were laid in wait for, their hearts torn out and burnt. They resembled the ancient martyrs – the more they were burnt, the more they abounded.

Finally, Calmet became their historian, and treated vampires as he treated the Old and New Testaments, by relating faithfully all that has been said before him.

The most curious things, in my opinion, were the verbal suits juridically conducted, concerning the dead who went from their tombs to suck the little boys and girls of their neighbourhood. Calmet relates, that in Hungary two officers delegated by the emperor Charles VI, assisted by the bailiff of the place and an executioner, held an inquest on a vampire, who had been dead six weeks and who sucked all the neighbourhood. They found him in his coffin, fresh and jolly, with his eyes open, and asking for food. The bailiff passed his sentence; the executioner tore out the vampire's heart, and burnt it, after which he feasted no more [. . .]

You will find stories of vampires in the *Jewish Letters* of d'Argens,* whom the Jesuit authors of the *Journal de Trévoux* have accused of believing nothing. It should be observed how they triumph in the history of the vampire of Hungary; how they thanked God and the Virgin for having at last converted this poor d'Argens, the chamberlain of a king who did not believe in vampires. 'Behold', said they, 'this famous unbeliever, who dared to throw doubts on the appearance of the angel to the holy virgin; on the star which conducted the magi; on the cure of the possessed; on the immersion of two thousand swine into a lake; on an eclipse of the sun at the full moon; on the resurrection of the dead who walked in Jerusalem – his heart is softened, his mind is enlightened: he believes in vampires.'

There no longer remained any question, but to examine whether all these dead were raised by their own virtue, by the power of God, or by that of the devil [. . .]

The difficulty was to know whether it was the soul or the body of the dead which ate. It was decided that it was both. Delicate and unsubstantial things, as sweetmeats, whipped cream, and melting fruits, were for the soul, and roast beef and the like were for the body [. . .]

The result of all this is, that a great part of Europe has been infested with vampires for five or six years, and that there are now no more; that we have had convulsionaries in France for twenty years, and that we have them no longer; that we have had demoniacs for seventeen hundred years, but have them no longer; that the dead have been raised ever since the days of Hippolytus, but that they are raised no longer; and lastly, that we have had Jesuits in Spain, Portugal, France, and the two Sicilies, but that we have them no longer.

War (Guerre)

The first three paragraphs date from 1771, and were added then to replace a different introduction. The main body of the article was first published in 1764. Voltaire is one of the world's foremost anti-war campaigners. The Memoirs are punctuated by the horrors of Frederick's wars, and Voltaire's historical works all indicate his horror at the senseless cruelty and destruction achieved by war throughout man's history.

All animals are perpetually at war; every species is born to devour another. There are none, down to sheep and doves, who do not swallow a prodigious number of minute and smaller animals. Males of the same species make war for the females, like Menelaus and Paris. Air, earth, and the waters, are fields of destruction.

It seems that since God gave reason to men, this reason should teach them not to debase themselves by imitating animals, particularly when nature has given them neither arms to kill their fellow-creatures, nor instinct which leads them to suck their blood.

Yet murderous war is so much the dreadful lot of man, that except two or three nations, there are none but what their ancient histories represent as armed against one another. Towards Canada, man and warrior are synonymous; and we have seen, in our hemisphere, that thief and soldier were the same thing. Manicheans!* behold your excuse.

The most determined of flatterers will easily agree, that war always brings pestilence and famine in its train, from the little that he may have seen in the hospitals of the armies of Germany, or the few villages he may have passed through in which some great exploit of war has been performed.

It is doubtless a very fine art which desolates countries, destroys habitations, and in a common year causes the death of forty to a hundred thousand men. This invention was first cultivated by nations assembled for their common good; for instance, the diet of the Greeks declared to the diet of Phrygia and neighbouring nations, that they intended to depart on a thousand fishers' barks, to exterminate them if they could.

The assembled Roman people judged that it was to their interest to go and fight, before harvest, against the people of Veii or the Volscians. And some years after, all the Romans, being exasperated against all the Carthaginians, fought them a long time on sea and land. It is not the same at present.

A genealogist proves to a prince, that he descends directly from a count, whose parents made a family compact, three or four hundred years ago, with a house whose memory is now utterly lost. This house had distant pretentions to a province whose last possessor died of apoplexy. The prince and his council see his right at once. This province, which is some hundred leagues distant from him, protests in vain that it knows him not; that it has no desire to be governed by him; that to give laws to its people, he must at least have their consent; these discourses do not even reach the ears of the prince, whose right is incontestable. He immediately assembles a great number of men who have nothing to lose, dresses them in coarse blue cloth, borders their hats with broad white binding, makes them turn to the right and left, and marches to glory.

Other princes who hear of this enterprise take part in it, each according to his power, and cover a small extent of country with more mercenary murderers than Genghis Khan, Tamburlaine, and Bajazet employed in their train.

Distant people hear that they are going to fight, and that they may gain five or six sous a-day, if they will be of the party; they divide themselves into two bands, like reapers, and offer their services to whoever will employ them.

These multitudes fall upon one another, not only without having any interest in the affair, but without knowing the reason of it.

We see at once five or six belligerent powers, sometimes three against three, sometimes two against four, and sometimes one against five; all equally detesting one another, uniting with and attacking by turns; all agreed in a single point – that of doing all the harm possible.

The most wonderful part of this infernal enterprise is, that each chief of the murderers causes his colours to be blessed, and solemnly invokes God before he goes to exterminate his neighbours. If a chief has only the fortune to kill two or three thousand men, he does not thank God for it; but when he has exterminated about ten thousand by fire and sword, and, to complete the work, some town has been levelled with the ground, they then sing a long song in four parts,* composed in a language unknown to all who have fought, and moreover replete with barbarism. The same song serves for marriages and births as well as for murders; which is unpardonable, particularly in a nation the most famous for its new songs [. . .]

What is the sense to me, of humanity, beneficence, modesty, temperance, mildness, wisdom, and piety, whilst half a pound of lead, sent from six hundred steps away, pierces my body, and I die at twenty years of age, in inexpressible torments, in the midst of five or six thousand dying men, whilst my eyes, which open for the last time, see the town in which I was born destroyed by fire and sword, and the last sounds which reach my ears are the cries of women and children expiring under the ruins, all for the pretended interests of a man whom I know not?

What is worse, war is an inevitable scourge. If we take notice, all men have worshipped Mars. Sabaoth among the Jews signifies the god of arms; but Minerva in Homer calls Mars a furious, mad, and infernal god [. . .]

CHAPTER 12

The Encyclopaedia*
(De l'Encyclopédie)

This item does not seem to have been published until 1774, though it may have appeared a little earlier. An amiable piece, it came well after the main battles for the Encyclopédie *had been fought, and after the publication of the great work was completed in 1772. Voltaire is guilty of anachronism, since the volumes of text were not all published until 1765 – a year after Mme de Pompadour's death.*

In this piece Voltaire rightly shows the many practical *aspects of the work – it was, after all, the 'Encyclopaedia, or reasoned dictionary of the sciences, the arts and the trades'.*

I was told by a servant of Louis xv that one day, while the King his master was supping with a small company at Trianon, the conversation turned first upon hunting and then upon gunpowder. Someone said, that the best powder was made with equal parts of saltpetre, of sulphur and of charcoal. The Duke de la Vallière, better instructed, maintained that, to make good powder for shooting, you should take one single part of sulphur and one of charcoal to five parts of saltpetre, well filtered, well dried and well crystallized.

'It is droll enough,' said the Duke de Nivernois, 'that we should amuse ourselves every day by killing partridges in the park of Versailles, and sometimes by killing men, or by getting ourselves killed on the frontier, without knowing precisely what it is that does the killing.'

'Alas!' replied Madame de Pompadour, 'we are reduced to that where everything in this world is concerned. I have no idea what the rouge that I place on my cheeks is composed of, and I should be mightily put to it if any one asked me how they make the silk stockings which I wear.'

''Tis a pity,' said the Duke de la Vallière, 'that His Majesy has confiscated our encyclopaedic dictionaries, which cost each of us a hundred pistoles: we should there have quickly found the answers to all our questions.'

The King justified his confiscation; he had been advised that the twenty and one folio volumes, which were to be found on every lady's toilet table, were the most dangerous things in the world for the realm of France; and he wished to know for himself whether that was true, before he allowed people to read the book. When supper was finished, he sent three lackeys of the bed-chamber to look for a copy, and they brought him seven volumes a-piece, which they had great difficulty in carrying.

They found, from the article *Powder*, that the Duke de la Vallière was right; and Madame de Pompadour soon knew the difference between the ancient rouge of Spain, with which the ladies of Madrid used to colour their cheeks, and the rouge of the ladies of Paris. She learned that the Greek and Roman ladies were painted with purple which came from the *murex*, and that, consequently, our scarlet was the purple of the ancients; that there was more saffron in Spanish rouge, and more cochineal in the French.

She saw how they made her silk stockings for her in the work-room, and the machine for this operation ravished her with astonishment. 'Ah! the pretty book', cried she. 'Sire, you have confiscated this storehouse of all useful things to possess it yourself alone, and to be the one learned man in your kingdom?'

Each one fell upon the volumes like the daughters of Lycomedes* upon the jewels of Odysseus; each one found on the instant all that he was searching for. Those who were at law were surprised to find therein a decision on their suits. And there the King read all the rights of his crown. 'Nay, truly,' said he, 'I know not why, they have told me such ill things of this book.' 'Ah, Sire', replied the Duke de Nivernois, 'do you not see 'tis because the book is a very good one? Folk never fling out at anything which is dull or commonplace. If the women try to make a newcomer seem ridiculous, you may be sure she is prettier than they are.'

All this time, they were turning over the pages, and the Count of C . . . said out loud: 'Sire, you are but too happy that there should be found in your reign men capable of understanding all the arts and of handing them on to posterity. All is here, from the manner of making a pin to the casting and aiming of your cannon; from the infinitely small to the infinitely great. Thank God for having ordained, in your country, the birth of those who have thus been of service to the whole universe. The other nations must either buy the *Encyclopaedia* or they must copy it. Take all my wealth, if you will; but give me back my *Encyclopaedia*.'

'For all that,' replied the King, 'they say there are many faults in this work which is so necessary and so admirable.'

'Sire,' answered the Count of C—, 'there were two spoilt ragoûts at your supper; we did not eat them, and we had mighty good cheer. Would you have wished us to throw the whole supper out of the window because of those two ragoûts?' – The King felt the force of the argument; each one received his treasure back again: it was a happy day.

Envy and ignorance will not confess themselves beaten; these two immortal sisters continue to cry, to plot and to persecute: in this, ignorance is especially cunning.

What happened? – The foreigners made four editions of this French work proscribed in France, and gained about eighteen hundred thousand crowns.

Frenchmen, learn from henceforth to have a better knowledge of your own interests.

NOTES

Letters Concerning the English Nation
p. 1 **exactness:** Moland, XXXIII, letter 77. Tr. C. T.

p. 2 **Thieriot:** published in L. Foulet, *Correspondance de Voltaire, 1726–29*, 1913, pp. 53–64. *Cf. D. 303. Voltaire's sister, Madame Mignot, died in September 1726.*

p. 2 **Despreaux:** Alexander Pope's *Essay on Criticism* was first published in 1711; *The Rape of the Lock* in 1713. The latter was indeed based on Nicolas Boileau-Despreaux; *Le Lutrin* (1674).

p. 2 **London citizen:** almost certainly Everard Fawkener. His 'country house' was in – then – rural Wandsworth.

p. 2 **Tiriot:** Nicolas Claude Thieriot (1696–1792), spelt variously Thieriot, Thiriot, Tiriot. A lifelong friend of Voltaire.

p. 2 **poor Henry:** Voltaire's epic poem the *Henriade* – published at last in England in 1728.

p. 3 **Tr. C. T.** The French version first published in the 'Kehl' edition of Voltaire, XLIX, 10–21 (1785). Cf. Moland, XXII, 17–24. An annotated version is in G. Lanson's edition of the *Lettres philosophiques*, II, 257–77.

p. 5 **King and Queen:** probably soon after the coronation of George II, in the summer of 1727. The races in the following paragraph would have been at Deptford, in south-east London.

p. 6 **gladiators in London:** i.e. in the theatre.

p. 7 **the east wind was blowing:** in this period the English were generally thought to be subject to periodic, seasonal, depression, often leading to suicide.

p. 9 **letter on the fire:** Voltaire simplifies and mis-states the situation. Press-gangs were not abolished, but in May 1728, there was an Act to encourage sailors to join the navy voluntarily. Cf. Lanson, *op. cit.*, II, 275.

p. 9   most learned treatises: religious treatises by Thomas Woolston, in 1727–8. A fifth and sixth treatise led to his imprisonment. The 'wretched bookseller' was Edmund Curll, who was fined, imprisoned and later pilloried in 1728, in part for publishing *The Nun in Her Shift* (a translation of the Abbé Duprat's salacious novel, first published in 1683).

p. 9   surplices in Scotland: Charles I wished to introduce the Anglican practice into Scotland.

p. 10   printed in *Memoirs of Viscountess Sundon*, 2v., 1847, I, 177–8. Cf. L. Foulet, *op. cit.*, pp. 209–10.

p. 11   French: for the extent of Voltaire's *own* English in the *Letters*, see Harcourt Brown, 'The Composition of the *Letters* . . .' in *The Age of the Enlightenment: Studies Presented to Theodore Besterman*, ed. W. H. Barber et al., 1967, pp. 15–34.

p. 11   Quakers: Voltaire has chosen the most distinctively independent of the Protestant sects as the subject of his first four Letters – the Quakers are as different from any part of the Roman Catholic Church in France as any group he could imagine.

p. 11   visit: probably to Andrew Pitt (died 1736), who lived in Hampstead; or possibly to Edward Higginson, in Wandsworth (*see* N. Cronk, ed. Voltaire, *Letters Concerning the English Nation*, (1994), pp. 172–4).

p. 11   thou: the Quakers' use of the second person singular – thou, thee, thine – intrigued many foreigners, and continued into the mid-20th century, in the editor's own experience.

p. 12   baptised: cf. the Quaker's speech in the 'Dramatic Balderdash', *see* p. 71 below.

p. 13   Robert Barclay: Scots Quaker (1648–90). His work in Latin and in English, the *Theologiae vere christianae apologia*, and *An Apology for the Christian Divinity* (both 1675).

p. 15   the monument: built by Charles II in 1671 to record the Fire of London.

p. 16   by the Lord: belief in the possibility of immediate revelation, held by the Quakers, is comparable with that of the Huguenot refugee Fatio de Duillier in 1707 (*see* 'On Fanaticism', pp. 166–9 below).

p. 17   Malbranche: Nicolas de Malebranche (1638–1715), Cartesian philosopher, wrote *De la Recherche de la vérité* (1674).

p. 17   George Fox: (1624–90) was the founder of the Quaker movement.

p. 18   *Dove ... chiavava*: meaning 'where there was no sexual intercourse'.

p. 20   Pen: William Penn (1664–1718), founder of Pennsylvania in 1681.

p. 21   Elizabeth: James I's granddaughter, and daughter-in-law to Frederick v of the Rhine Palatinate.

p. 21   *Philosophical Romance*: Descartes's *Principes de la philosophie* (1647). Voltaire came to reject the Cartesian approach after reading Locke (*see* Letters XIII–XIV).

p. 22   to the south: in fact to the north!

p. 22   Philadelphia: *see* 'Quakers', p. 182 below.

p. 23   Nonconformists: the Declarations of Indulgence were issued in 1687 and 1688 by James II, but did not achieve the general tolerance (including that of Roman Catholics) which he desired.

p. 24   traffick: trade.

p. 24   mansions: this line from John xiv:2 is omitted from Voltaire's French version.

p. 24   established church: the Corporation Act (1661) and the Test Act (1675) made conformity with the Anglican practice necessary for those who wished to hold municipal or political office.

p. 25   Guelphs and Gibelins: in Italy between the eleventh and fourteenth centuries, the Guelphs had usually supported the Papacy, the Ghibellines the Imperial cause.

p. 25   Oxford: Robert Harley, 1st Earl of Oxford.

p. 25   Bolingbroke: Voltaire's friend and patron.

p. 25 *jure divino*: by divine right.

p. 25 B——: Bolingbroke.

p. 26 Abbé: *see* 'Abbé', pp. 161–2 below.

p. 26 as Rabelais says: from *The Third Book . . . of Pantagruel*, Ch. 22.

p. 27 Diogenes: 'Alexander . . . asked him if he lacked anything. "Yea," said he, "that I do: that you stand out of my sun a little"', Plutarch, *Life of Alexander*.

p. 27 Cato: Voltaire here refers to Cato, 'the Censor' (234–149 BC), great-grandfather of Cato of Utica, the subject of Addison's tragedy. *See* Letter XVIII.

p. 28 Royal Exchange: this new building (1669) was the commercial centre of the City of London, and Voltaire wrote of it in his *Notebooks* (I, 51) as 'the rendez vous of all foreigners', *trade* bringing people of different religious views into profitable contact. *See* also 'A Dramatic Balderdash', pp. 70–72 below.

p. 28 Arians or Socinians: two separate but, in fact, overlapping groups related by their views on the nature of the Trinity, in which both saw Christ not as equal in divinity with God, but as the highest – indeed uniquely so – form of man. The Unitarians follow the Socinian view.

p. 28 Newton: Sir Isaac Newton (1642–1727). Voltaire coupled Newton's religious views with his preeminence as a thinker and scientist. *See* Letter XIV.

p. 28 Dr Clark: Samuel Clarke (1675–1729), theologian with distinct Arian views, publicised in his *Scripture Doctrine of the Trinity* (1712).

p. 29 Luther . . . Zuinglius: Martin Luther, Jean Calvin, Ulrich Zwingli – founders of Protestant reform in the sixteenth century.

p. 29 Newton . . . Le Clerc: all Unitarians, and all to some extent concerned with the advances in science achieved in the late seventeenth and early eighteenth centuries.

p. 29 Cardinal de Retz: Jean-François Paul de Gondi, Cardinal de Retz (1614–79). He was involved in the civil disturbances of the Fronde in 1648–52.

p. 30 Shippen: William Shippen (1673–1743), a Tory member of Parliament and a supporter of the Jacobites.

p. 30 the Flamen: a priest serving one of the Roman gods.

p. 31 interested motives: by the 1770s Voltaire will have changed his views, as British colonial possessions were extended.

p. 32 Henry the seventh ... Henry the fourth: the Emperor Henry VII (who died 1313) was probably poisoned by a priest; Henry III of France (who died 1589) was murdered by a monk; Henry IV (who died 1600) was likewise assassinated.

p. 32 so little understood: Voltaire was never particularly interested in early medieval history.

p. 33 Ina ... the Heptarchy: Ina was a king of Wessex, in the eighth century, when there were seven Saxon kingdoms in England.

p. 33 John: King John, 1199–1216. He was forced by the Barons to grant Magna Carta in 1215. King Louis was ruler in England for less than a year.

p. 33 Villains: villeins or serfs. While serfdom had long been abolished in Britain, it lingered on in a few parts of France, in some ecclesiastical properties, until the Revolution.

p. 34 though it was: an error in translation from the French. It should read 'as it removed a greater tyranny'.

p. 35 a Nobleman or a Priest: Voltaire is – as throughout the *Letters* – thinking of the contrasting situation in France.

p. 36 1723: it was actually 1726.

p. 36 Prince Eugene: Eugène de Savoie (1663–1736), a noted general who fought beside Marlborough at Blenheim and other victories, and who relieved Turin in 1706. The 'five Millions' were francs – £250,000.

p. 37 a Factor in Aleppo: this was Nathaniel Harley, brother of Robert Harley, 1st Earl of Oxford. This reference to the Levant leads on to Letter XI, revolving round Lady Mary Wortley Montagu's experiences in Ottoman Turkey.

p. 37 Escutcheons: compare this with the German pride in ancestry mocked in *Candide*, Ch. 1.

p. 38 Inoculation: the process, introduced to Britain by Lady Mary Wortley Montagu, was soon abandoned after vaccination was developed by Dr Jenner in the late eighteenth century. Here the far less dangerous disease of cow-pox was the source of the inoculatory material.

p. 38 Pustle . . . Yest: read 'Pustule', 'Yeast'.

p. 39 Bassa: Pasha.

p. 39 Mountague: Lady Mary Wortley Montagu (1690–1762), wife of the British ambassador, had her son Edward Wortley Montagu (1713–76) inoculated while she was at Adrianople/Edirne in 1717. *See* her letter to Miss Sarah Chiswell, 1 April 1717, in her *Letters . . . 1709 to 1762* (Everyman, 1906), pp. 123–5.

p. 40 Queen of England: Queen Caroline, to whom Voltaire dedicated the *Henriade* in 1727.

p. 40 Daughter of Milton: Mrs Clarke – we may note that Voltaire was to exert even greater efforts to help Corneille's collateral descendant, Marie-Françoise Corneille, from the 1760s onwards.

p. 40 Beauty: Voltaire simplifies the history of inoculation in England – there were numerous opponents, many claiming that it was either medically unsound, or contrary to religion – or both. It was not generally accepted until the mid-century.

p. 41 fiftieth Year: Louis xv himself was to die of smallpox in 1774.

p. 42 Bacon: Sir Francis Bacon (1561–1626), Baron Verulam – statesman, philosopher, historian, writer.

p. 43 a parte rei: the scholastic philosophers were referring to the existence and reality of universal objects.

p. 43 Philosophers: Anaxagoras (*c*. 500–428 BC)

p. 43 Toricelli: Evangelista Torricelli (1608–47), mathematician and inventor of the barometer.

p. 44 moral Essays: Bacon's *Essays* are today read with delight; but Voltaire wishes to emphasise Bacon as a scientific thinker . . .

p. 44 Mr Locke: John Locke (1632–1704), empirical philosopher (*Essay Concerning Human Understanding* (1690), *Thoughts Concern-*

ing Education (1693)). His consistent concern with a practical, rather than an abstract approach to existence was profoundly important to the thinkers of the early eighteenth century.

p. 45   I shall leave: in the *Essay*, II, I.

p. 46   thinks or not: a truncated passage from the *Essay*, IV, 3.

p. 46   Bishop Stillingfleet: Edward Stillingfleet (1635–99), Bishop of Worcester.

p. 47   composed: for Voltaire's view of the necessity, social or otherwise, of religious belief, see the Introduction, p. xxii above.

p. 48   Mankind: Voltaire had no belief in the intellectual equality of human beings.

p. 49   Countries: in an addition made in 1756 to this passage, Voltaire includes the names of several books of travel (like his own!) such as Marana's *Turkish Spy* and Montesquieu's *Persian Letters*, which introduced French readers to the varieties of society and belief in different countries.

p. 49   much of Letter XIV, and practically all of XV has been cut, since the long references to Descartes and other French philosophers do not in fact help with understanding Voltaire's views of England.

p. 49   plenum ... vacuum: while the Aristotelian view – continued through Descartes – was that the universe was a 'full' and 'complete' creation, Newtonian physics had rejected this.

p. 50   Destroyer: Newton's main achievement was to oppose the hypothetical approach with a practical attitude – 'I do not invent hypotheses – *hypotheses non fingo*' – supported by solid evidence.

p. 50   interred him: *see* Letter XXIII.

p. 51   [Newton] despaired: thought to be the earliest reference to Newton's reflections on the falling apples. Voltaire's first English and French texts say 'fruits', but he names them as apples in his *Eléments de la philosophie de Newton* in 1738. For the origins of this anecdote, *see* J. Churton Collins, *Voltaire, Montesquieu and Rousseau in England* (1908), pp. 33–5.

p. 51   Galileo: Galileo Galilei (1564–1642), Italian astronomer.

p. 51 Shakespear: Voltaire was the first Frenchman to comment on Shakespeare at any length. From the start Voltaire presents him as a writer fundamentally at odds with the 'rules' and 'good taste' which French dramatists respected – the 'rules' proposed in Aristotle's *Poetics* and Horace's *Ars Poetica*, and further developed by French theoreticians in the seventeenth century.

p. 51 Corneille: Pierre Corneille (1606–84), French dramatist.

p. 52 de Vega: Lope Félix de Vega (1560–1635), Spanish poet and dramatist.

p. 52 Otway: Thomas Otway (1652–85), dramatist.

p. 53 Sophs: short for *sophisters*, B.A. students in the year before graduation.

p. 54 *l'hypocrisie:* Voltaire has inserted a line here, 'and bless the hypocrisy of our lying priests'. In his third line, Voltaire has also substituted 'Dieux cruels' ['cruel Gods'] for 'outrageous Fortune'. Both the change, and the addition, show that he was at this point writing with French, rather than English readers in mind.

p. 55 Fustian: bombast, pomposity.

p. 55 Cato: *Cato. A Tragedy*, by Joseph Addison, first performed and published, 1713. Many times reprinted in the eighteenth century, and still available in John Gay's *The Beggar's Opera and other Eighteenth-Century Plays* (Everyman, 1993). Addison (1672–1719) undoubtedly wrote *Cato* in an attempt to introduce tragedy in the French classical style, observing the 'rules' and keeping the 'unities' – of time, place and action – which are so obviously *not* a part of the Shakespearian tradition. Though its success in England was short-lived, it was used by J. C. Gottsched (1700–66) as the main source for his tragedy *Der sterbende Cato* ('The Death of Cato') in 1732 – a year before Voltaire's letters were published – with the avowed hope of establishing the French style of tragedy in Germany (*see* Thacker, *The Wildness Pleases*, p. 32).

p. 56 Garden of Marli: laid out from the 1680s, Marly was Louis XIV's extravagant 'hermitage' a few miles from Versailles, in which utmost formality was observed throughout the gardens, and where the trees and bushes were trained and clipped with military precision.

p. 56 Shadwell: Thomas Shadwell (1640–92), dramatist and, in 1689, Poet Laureate. Several of his plays borrowed freely from Molière.

p. 56 Wycherley: William Wycherley (1640–1716), whose *Plain Dealer* (1677) was adapted from Molière's *Misanthrope* (1666), and whose *Country Wife* (1675) came from Molière's *École des Femmes* (1662).

p. 58 Vanbrugh: Sir John Vanbrugh (1666–1726), architect, poet, dramatist. Designed the Palace at Blenheim, which Voltaire may have visited. His 'epitaph' was by Abel Evans (1679–1737). His stay in the Bastille in 1692 would have interested Voltaire who suffered two periods of internment there.

p. 59 Congreve: William Congreve (1670–1729), dramatist. After *The Way of the World* (1700), he gave up writing for the stage.

p. 60 Lully: Jean Baptiste Lully (1633–87), French composer.

p. 60 Buononcini: Giovanni Bononcini (1672–1729), Italian composer, living in London from 1720.

p. 60 Steele: Sir Richard Steele (1672–1729), dramatist and essayist.

p. 60 Cibber: Colley Cibber (1671–1757), playwright, poet and, in 1730, Poet Laureate.

p. 60 Prior: Matthew Prior (1664–1721), minor poet and politician.

p. 60 Roscommon: Wentworth Dillon, 4th Earl of Roscommon (?1633–85), minor poet.

p. 60 Dorset: Charles Sackville, 6th Earl of Dorset (1638–1706), minor poet.

p. 61 prick down: note down, as in music.

p. 61 Hudibras: long mock-heroic poem (published in three parts, 1663, '64, '68) by Samuel Butler (1612–80). It is above all a satire of the rival – and quarrelling – Nonconformist sects in the period of the Commonwealth.

p. 61 Swift: Jonathan Swift (1667–1745), Dean of St Patrick's, Dublin. Swift's satire *Gulliver's Travels* (1726) was read by Voltaire soon after his arrival in England, and Voltaire urged his friend Thieriot to translate it into French – but without success. François Rabelais'

Gargantua and *Pantagruel* (published with an additional three parts, from 1532 to 1562) likewise tells of the adventures of giants and human beings, but Voltaire found Rabelais' ebullience and earthiness altogether too crude. Swift was a continuing influence on Voltaire – his tale *Micromégas* (1752) was inspired by Swift's *Gulliver*, his tale *Pot-Pourri* (1752) was inspired by *A Tale of a Tub*, and the 'Account of the Illness ... of the Jesuit Berthier' (*see* pp. 80–87 below) goes back to Swift's *Bickerstaff Papers* of 1708–9.

p. 62 the Island: Swift was born in Ireland, in Dublin. Voltaire was aware of this – he corresponded with Swift – but never 'visited the Island' himself. In 1756, a later French edition of the *Lettres Philosophiques* included two more paragraphs praising Swift's *Tale of a Tub*.

p. 62 Nations: here Voltaire continues with an extract from Pope's *Rape of the Lock*, quoted in English and in Voltaire's translation.

p. 62 Specimens enough: Voltaire means, in the *Letters* as a whole, not simply in Letter XXII

p. 62 History: the *Histoire d'Angleterre* (1724–35), begun by Rapin de Thoyras, completed by David Durand.

p. 63 Foundations: Louis XIV established no less than five such 'academies' between 1648 and 1672.

p. 64 professes: Pope was a Roman Catholic, and was therefore debarred from government office. His translations of Homer (1715–26) brought him some £8,000.

p. 64 Mrs Oldfield ... le Couvreur: both actresses died in 1730. While Anne Oldfield was buried in Westminster Abbey, Adrienne Lecouvreur in Paris was denied Christian burial.

p. 65 Mr Prynne: William Prynne (1600–69), a Puritan fanatic, particularly virulent in attacking the theatre.

p. 65 Le Brun: Pierre Le Brun wrote a *Discours sur la comédie* (1694), attacking the theatre as Prynne had done.

p. 65 Senesino ... Cuzzoni: two Italian opera singers in London in the 1720s. This last paragraph in Letter XXIII is most clearly directed at French rather than English readers.

p. 67 with great ... Falkeners: quoted in Beer and Rousseau, ed.,

Voltaire's British Visitors, item 128, and by them from Cayrol, ed., Voltaire, *Lettres inédites*, 2 vols., 1856, I, 75. Tr. C. T.

p. 67 Sir . . . Voltaire: quoted in *Political and Social Letters of a Lady of the Eighteenth Century 1721–1771*, ed. E. F. D. Osborn, (no date), c. 1890, pp. 113–14.

p. 67 Admiral Byng: for Byng's tragedy, *see* T. H. White, *The Age of Scandal*, 1950, Ch. 10.

Fragment of a Letter . . . Holland
p. 68 tr. Morley, XIX, i, 68–9. Cf. Moland, XXIII, 127–8.

p. 69 the Abbé: Charles I. C. de Saint-Pierre (1658–1743) published his *Projet de paix perpétuelle* ('Project for Perpetual Peace') in 1713. A visionary writer, eager for reform, but not especially practical.

A Dramatic Balderdash
p. 70 tr. C. T. Cf. Moland, XXIV, 75–7.

p. 70 Escobar: Antonio Escobar y Mendoza (1589–1669), Spanish Jesuit, noted for his writings on moral theology.

p. 71 Molinist: followers of the Jesuit Louis de Molina, who stressed the value of free-will.

p. 71 in, cum, sub: the Lutheran belief that in the Eucharist the body of Christ was present *in*, *with*, and *beneath* the bread.

p. 72 chews . . . feet: cf. Deuteronomy, xiv. 7.

Wives, Submit Yourselves unto Your Husbands
p. 74 tr. C. E. Vulliamy, in Voltaire, *The White Bull and Other Stories*, 1929, pp. 149–53.

p. 74 wives . . . husbands: Ephesians v: 22.

p. 75 All . . . beard: *École des femmes*, III, 2.

How Far Should We Impose on the People?
p. 77 tr. from Morley, XIX i. 199–202. Cf. Moland, XXIV, 71–3.

p. 77 Provincial Letters: by Blaise Pascal (1623–62), published 1657.

p. 78   Boutan: Bhutan, region north of India, east of Nepal, south of Tibet.

p. 78   clutches: claws, or talons.

Account of the Illness . . . of the Jesuit Berthier
p. 80   tr. C. T. Cf. Moland, XXIV, 95–104.

p. 80   13 October 1759: D.853.

p. 81   Mead and Boerhaave: Richard Mead (1673–1754), English doctor, much admired by Voltaire. Hermann Boerhaave (1668–1738), noted Dutch doctor, under whom Voltaire's friend Théodore Tronchin had studied.

p. 83   in France: Voltaire's lists contrast works which are merely trivial or tedious, with others which he considers pernicious. While all these Jesuits have now passed into oblivion, we might note Guillaume Bougeant (1690–1743), Joseph Berruyer (1681–1758), and Thomas Sanchez (1550–1610), various of whose writings were condemned by the Church.

p. 83   Aretino: Pietro Aretino (1492–1556), Italian poet, notorious for his sonnets, accompanying a series of erotic drawings by Giulio Romano.

p. 83   the *Nouvelles ecclésiastiques*: published by the Jansenists – in many respects passionately opposed to the Jesuits – and equally odious to Voltaire.

p. 84   *Lettres . . . curieuses*: *see* Voltaire's views on religious 'convulsions' in the *Letters*, p. 15, and in 'Convulsionaries', p. 165. The *Lettres édifiantes* gave reports of the missionary activities of the Jesuits in many different countries.

p. 85   *Paradise . . . Philagie*: a volume of prayers addressed to the Virgin Mary, by Father Barry.

p. 86   the *Provincial Letters*: by the Jansenist Pascal.

p. 86   Port-Royal: the principal convent for Jansenist nuns.

p. 86   Le Tellier: Michel Le Tellier (1643–1719), Jesuit, and confessor to Louis XIV. The 'most worthy Archbishop' was the Cardinal de Noailles.

p. 87 *Année littéraire*: periodical produced by Élie Fréron (1719–76), one of Voltaire's main targets at this time.

p. 87 Malagrida: Gabriel Malagrida (1689–1761), a Portuguese Jesuit, involved in a plot to assassinate the king, Joseph I, which had led the Portuguese minister Pombal to expel the Jesuits from Portugal. Shortly after Voltaire's *Account of . . . Berthier* was published, Malagrida was condemned by the Inquisition and executed in 1761.

Memoirs Related to the Life of M. de Voltaire, Written by Himself
p. 88 1789: Kehl, LXX (1789), 257–344. Cf. Moland, I (1883), 3–65. The present translation, mainly by C. T., but including sections from the *Memoirs* as quoted in *Voltairiana*, 4 vols., 1805, selected and translated by Mary Julia Young, scattered through vol. I.

p. 89 toleration: Thomas Babington Macaulay, *Frederick the Great* (1855), pp. 68–9.

p. 89 possible? 2 September 1751 (D. 4564). Cf. 29 October 1751 (D. 4597).

p. 89 heard it: 24 July 1752 (D. 4956).

p. 90 branches of science: Gabrielle-Emilie, Marquise du Châtelet (1706–49), woman of letters, student of philosophy and science, intimate friend and supporter of Voltaire.

p. 90 Dacier: Anne Lefèvre, Mme Dacier (1654–1720), classical scholar, and in France the leader of the 'moderns', in supporting the merits and beauties of Homer.

p. 90 château: at Cirey, where her husband, the Marquis du Châtelet, encouraged his wife's interests and tolerated her friends. Voltaire stayed there, with intervals, from 1733 to 1740.

p. 90 Kœnig . . . Bernouilli: Samuel Kœnig (1712–57), German mathematician; Pierre-Louis Moreau de Maupertuis (1698–1759), French mathematician; Jacques Bernoulli (1654–1705).

p. 91 Algarotti: Count Francesco Algarotti (1712–66). Voltaire called him 'the Swan of Venice'.

p. 91 *Institutions de physique*: written by Mme du Châtelet in 1740.

Voltaire was to become less and less approving of Leibnitz and the theory of Optimism.

p. 91 commentary: published in 1759. Voltaire had introduced her to Newton's work. Cf. his praise in the *Letters Concerning the English Nation*.

p. 91 *Essay ... Present Day*: eventually published in 1756, as the *Essai sur les Moeurs*.

p. 91 Bossuet: Jacques-Bénigne Bossuet, Bishop of Condom (1627–1704).

p. 91 de Witt: John de Witt (1625–72), Grand Pensionary (Raadpensionarius) of Holland.

p. 92 Frederick-William: King of Prussia, born 1688, ruled 1713–40.

p. 92 four years: Prince Frederick's first letter to Voltaire was written in 1736.

p. 93 giants: apart from further references in the *Memoirs*, cf. *Candide*, Ch. 2.

p. 94 The prince ... France: Frederick-William's violent treatment of his son was well known.

p. 94 Katt and Keith: Hans Hermann von Katt (1704–30); Peter C. C. von Keith (b. 1711).

p. 94 Wilhelmina: Wilhelmina, Margravine of Bayreuth (1709–58), second sister of Frederick the Great, and lifelong correspondent of Voltaire.

p. 95 a soldier to serve him: this was Michel Gabriel Fredersdorf (1708–58). From a humble origin, he was raised by Frederick to a variety of posts.

p. 96 Seckendorf: Friedrich Heinrich von Seckendorf (1673–1763). Imperial Ambassador at Berlin, 1726–34.

p. 96 Brandenburg Memoirs: *Mémoires pour servir à l'histoire de Brandebourg*.

p. 96 writing ... fell on me: the correspondence with Frederick continued until Voltaire's death.

p. 97   at last: 31 May 1740.

p. 97   Camas: Paul Henri de Camas (1688–1741). He had lost his left arm in battle in 1706. The French Ambassador at Berlin (1729–50, and in 1756) was G.–L.–H. de Valori (1692–1774). He had lost two fingers of his left hand.

p. 97   Château de Meuse: the château de Moyland. Voltaire stayed there in mid-September 1740.

p. 99   Abbé Desfontaines: *see* below, pp. 102–3 and note p. 211.

p. 99   Van Duren: this is the Vanderdendur of *Candide*, Ch. 19.

p. 99   *Anti-Machiavel*: Frederick's treatise refuting Machiavelli's *Il Principe*, setting out his pacific views, which he was to contradict once he came to the throne.

p. 101   battle . . . Molwitz: on 10 April 1741.

p. 102   *History of Charles XII*: Voltaire had published this in 1731.

p. 102   *Elements of Newton's Philosophy*: first published in French in 1738.

p. 102   Saint . . . Quesnel: Saint Thomas Aquinas (1224–74); Pasquier Quesnel (1634–1719), Jansenist divine.

p. 103   son of a peasant . . . atheist: the Abbé Desfontaines made these suggestions in his *Voltairomanie*, which appeared 12 December 1738.

p. 105   Maurepas: Jean Frédéric Phélypeaux, comte de Maurepas (1701–81).

p. 105   Boyer: Jean-François Boyer (1675–1755), French clergyman, appointed Bishop of Mirepoix 1730, tutor to the Dauphin 1735.

p. 106   Podewils: Othon-Christophe, comte de Podewils, was at this point Frederick's ambassador at the Hague.

p. 107   When . . . Berlin: on 30 August 1743.

p. 108   Pesne: Antoine Pesne, French painter, studied in Italy, employed for many years by Frederick (died 1770).

p. 110   La Barberina: brought from Venice to Berlin, she later married Baron Cocceji, son of the Chancellor, and after his death became Comtesse de Campanini.

p. 111   sixpence a day: the prisoner, named Courtils, was in Spandau from 1730 to 1749.

p. 112   Poisson: Jeanne-Antoinette Poisson, Marquise de Pompadour (1721–64).

p. 112   Académie: on 25 April 1746.

p. 112   Historiographer: on 1 April 1745.

p. 112   gentleman-in-ordinary: on 22 December 1746.

p. 113   King Stanislas: Stanislas Leczinski (1677–1766), King of Poland. He lost Poland (for the second time) in 1735, and in 1738 he was given Lorraine by Louis XV, to rule for the remainder of his life.

p. 114   Bishop of Troyes: Matthias Poncet de La Rivière, Bishop of Troyes from 1742.

p. 114   died ... illness: she died in September 1749, a week after giving birth to a daughter. The father was the Marquis de Saint-Lambert (1717–1803), soldier and poet. Voltaire had discovered their liaison, quickly became reconciled, and persuaded the Marquis du Châtelet that he was the father.

p. 115   Astolphus ... Alcina: a knight from Tasso's *Jerusalem Liberated*, who visited the palace of the witch-queen Alcina, who had imprisoned Rinaldo there.

p. 115   How could ... as I shall live: Frederick's letter, dated 23 August 1750, was in fact not quite so fulsome. He wrote, not 'I promise you ...', but 'I am firmly persuaded ...' (D. 4195).

p. 116   La Mettrie: Julien Offroy de Lamettrie (1709–51), French doctor and philosopher.

p. 116   an orange ... throw it away: Voltaire was deeply disturbed by this remark. He wrote to Mme Denis 29 October 1751 'I dream continually of the *orange skin*' (D. 4597).

p. 117   Wurtemberg: Charles-Eugène, Duke of Wurtemberg (1728–93). He had married the daughter of the Markgraf and Margravine of Bayreuth in 1748. His 'lands in France' were the area of Franche-Comté.

p. 117   Atheist to the King: Voltaire also complained that he was 'tired of taking in the King's dirty linen' – *i.e.* of correcting his copious and insipid verse (letter of 24 July 1752, D. 4956).

p. 117 **Chasot:** I.–F.E. de Chasot (1716–97).

p. 117 **Maupertuis ... published:** Maupertuis's collection of twenty-three essays on different projects, included in his *Oeuvres*, 1752.

p. 118 **the only one who spoke up:** particularly with the *Histoire du docteur Akakia, médicin du pape*, mocking Maupertuis' proposals. This first edition, in 1732, was confiscated by Frederick, and a second, in December 1752, was seized by Frederick and publicly burnt, the ashes being sent to Maupertuis.

p. 119 **Pöllnitz:** Karl Ludwig, Freiherr von Pöllnitz (1692–1775). His *Mémoires* were published in 1734, enlarged in 1737.

p. 119 **d'Argens:** J. B. de Boyer, marquis d'Argens (1704–71). His *Lettres juives* were published in 1736.

p. 120 **one of my nieces:** Mme Denis.

p. 121 **Van Duren:** *see* note p. 211, above.

p. 122 **property of some ninety acres:** Voltaire had reached Geneva on 12 December 1754, and in January 1755 he bought the 'modest property', which he re-named *Les Délices*.

p. 123 **finer house:** this was 6, rue du Grand-Chêne, Lausanne, which Voltaire usually referred to as *le Chêne* ('the Oak'). He also bought another property close to Lausanne in 1755, *Monrion*, which he sold in 1757.

p. 124 **King of Prussia ... back to me:** after a few letters exchanged in 1754–5, the correspondence was begun again in 1757.

p. 124 **England ... in 1756:** the 'acres of snow' were in fact Canada, from which the French were expelled after the fall of Quebec in 1759.

p. 125 **18 June 1757:** the battle of Kolin.

p. 125 **the Caudine Forks:** the convention of Closter-Seven, signed by Marshal de Richelieu and the Duke of Cumberland, 10 September 1757. The Caudine Forks was a defile, the *Furcae Caudinae*, where the Roman army was trapped, and compelled by the Samnites to pass under the yoke.

p. 126 **long epistle in verse:** dated 23 September 1757. Voltaire's prose reply, discouraging Frederick from suicide, was in October (D. 7419).

p. 126 **And should ... and die a king:** Frederick to Voltaire, 8 October 1757 (D. 7414).

p. 128 **another victory:** the battle of Lissa, 5 December 1757.

p. 129 **I dared to suggest:** in the *Essai sur les Moeurs*, Ch. 134.

p. 129 **properties in France:** Ferney, and the manor of Tournay, acquired by Voltaire towards the end of 1758.

p. 130 **Damiens:** his attempt to wound (or kill) Louis xv was made on 5 January 1757. Cf. *Candide*, Ch. 22.

p. 131 **dictionary:** the *Encyclopédie* – *see* the introduction to *The Portable Philosophical Dictionary*, p. 161, below, and 'The Encyclopaedia', p. 193, below.

p. 132 **Helvétius:** his *De l'Esprit* had been condemned to be burnt on 6 February 1759 – at the same time that the further distribution of the *Encyclopédie* was prohibited.

p. 132 **not our fault:** *see* note on 'Malagrida', pp. 209, below.

p. 134 **Emilie, you find us now:** from Corneille's *Cinna*, Act i, scene iii. But the 'Emilie' is, of course, Mme du Châtelet.

p. 134 **three days:** slightly incorrect. Frederick's letter was dated 17 November 1759 (D. 8602). Marshal Daun's victory was at Maxen, in Saxony, on 20 November.

p. 135 *Perrette and the milk jug:* La Fontaine's fable, 'Perrette et le pot au lait' (*Fables*, vii, 10).

p. 135 **Silhouette:** Etienne de Silhouette (1709–67).

p. 136 **Cartouche:** Louis-Dominique Cartouche (1693–1721), French bandit. In French, his name now carries the sense of 'brigand', or 'highway robber'.

A Prophecy
p. 137 **I have received ... you and I:** Tr. in Morley, xxi, 223. Cf. D. 6451.

p. 138   The Philosophers: by Charles Palissot de Montenoy (1730–1814), first performed on 2 May 1759.

p. 138   the opera ... 1752: *see* Thacker, 'Rousseau's *Devin du village*', in *Das deutsche Singspiel im 18. Jahrhundert* (1981), pp. 119–124.

p. 138   I do not ... your wish: first printed in the *Second supplément à la collection des oeuvres de J.-J. Rousseau* (1789), ii. 148–52 (D. 8986). Tr. C. T.

p. 138   enthusiasm: for the eighteenth century, this term implied irrational inspiration – the opposite of the reason of the *philosophes*.

p. 138   inconsistency: in Voltaire's view, his principal weakness.

p. 138   born: Rousseau was born in Geneva.

p. 138   sciences and the arts: his *Discours sur les sciences et les arts* was published in 1750, stating unequivocally that humanity was corrupted by civilisation, and praising the 'noble savage'.

p. 138   operas and plays: notably *Le Devin du village*, 'The Village Soothsayer' (1752), for which he wrote both libretto and music. In 1758 he published a *Lettre sur les spectacles* ('Letter on the theatre') condemning the theatre for its immorality.

p. 139   French music: he earned a pittance copying music; and in 1753 published a *Lettre sur la musique française* ('Letter on French music') stating that Italian music was better than French.

p. 139   a romance: the novel *Julie, ou la Nouvelle Héloïse*, in which the heroine, Julie, is seduced by Saint-Preux, her tutor, and becomes pregnant.

p. 139   nobleman: 'Milord Edouard Bomston' (Part I, letters 45, 56–7).

p. 139   Paris: Part II, letter 26.

p. 139   The man: Part II, letter 18. Julie marries M. de Wolmar.

p. 139   tour of the world: Saint-Preux goes off round the world for several years, having joined the British naval expedition commanded by George Anson.

p. 140   elysium: Julie's garden is described at length in Part IV, letter 11.

A Short Account of the Death of John Calas
p. 141   the text is from *A Treatise on Religious Toleration* (1764), Ch.
1. Cf. Moland, XXV, 113–18.

p. 141   You may . . . worse than us: D. 10382. Tr. C. T.

p. 142   It interests . . . opera: D. 10387. Tr. C. T.

p. 142   True . . . shred them: D. 10943. Tr. C. T.

Discourse Addressed to the Welsh
p. 153   the text is from Morley, XIX. i. 89–99. Cf. Moland, XXV,
229–39.

p. 153   **Welsh!:** Voltaire uses the English word, for which the French
is 'gallois' – or, therefore, confusingly, 'from Gaul'.

p. 153   *infundens . . . butyro*: from Sidonius Apollinaris (*c.* 438–84),
Christian poet – and a native of Gaul.

p. 155   **a king:** François I (1494–1547).

p. 157   **factories:** trading-stations. The French had been expelled by
the British from their Indian station at Pondicherry in 1761.

p. 157   **Newton:** yet another echo of the *Letters Concerning the
English Nation.*

p. 158   **inoculation:** cf. the *Letters*, pp. 37–41.

p. 159   **foundation of Robert Sorbon:** i.e., the Sorbonne in Paris, still
largely controlled in Voltaire's day by ecclesiastics.

p. 159   **Duchapt:** Mlle Duchapt was a celebrated dress-designer in the
mid-eighteenth century. Her shop in Paris was close to the Opéra.

The Portable Philosophical Dictionary
p. 161   apart from 'On Fanaticism' (tr. C. T.), the English translations
are all from Voltaire, *A Philosophical Dictionary* (6 volumes, 1824),
and the French versions are all in Moland, XVII–XX.

p. 161   **Twenty . . . established:** D. 13235 to Jean Le Rond d'Alembert
(tr. C. T.). For the genesis of Voltaire's *Dictionary*, see Besterman,
Voltaire, pp. 433–9.

p. 163   **Juvenal relates:** *Satires*, XV, v. 83.

p. 163   In 1725 ... conversing: elsewhere (letter to Frederick, c. 15 October 1737, D. 1376) Voltaire says that this meeting was in 1723.

p. 164   Well ... beings: this paragraph was added in 1772.

p. 165   One word ... dead: this paragraph was added in 1774. Voltaire's source for this Irish anecdote is not known.

p. 167   resurrection ... year: Dr Thomas Emes died on 22 December 1707, and was buried in the cemetery at Bunhill Fields. His resurrection was predicted for 25 May 1708. Many broadsheets or articles were published about this – including items by Shaftesbury and Swift. Before this Fatio had already been condemned to the pillory for supporting such prophecies.

p. 167   accurate: for details of this event, and of Fatio de Duillier's part in it, see Hillel Schwartz, The French Prophets (1980), pp. 73–4, 109–11, 117–123.

p. 167   witnesses: on 25 May, some 20,000 people gathered to see the event, where one John Lacy (not Fatio) was expected to resurrect the dead man. Fatio was one of the Huguenots' appointed witnesses.

p. 169   God: this section, comparable in form to many of Voltaire's 'philosophic dialogues' (like 'A Dramatic Balderdash'), gives yet another view of contrasting attitudes to the Deity. Here, Logomachos ('word-battler') fails to understand Dondindac's – to us – simple point of view. Dondindac's happy rustic life is close to that of the 'Old Turk' whose existence so impresses Candide at the end of his adventures.

p. 169   Arcadius: ruler of the Eastern Roman Empire from 395.

p. 172   Julian: the Emperor Julian, 331–63, ruled from 361 to 363. Known to some as 'Julian the Apostate', since he rejected Christianity and returned to the religion of pagan Greece.

p. 172   little farm ... 1758–9: see Thacker, 'The Misplaced Garden ...', Studies on Voltaire, XLI, 189–202.

p. 173   Marcus Aurelius: Marcus Aurelius Antoninus, Roman emperor, philosopher, writer (born 121, ruled 161–80).

p. 174   Galilean ... conquered: an exclamation invented by the Christian theologian Theodoret (c. 386–c. 455), long after Julian's death.

Julian died, victorious, after battle with the Persians, on the eastern side of the Tigris.

p. 176 Mosarabians: those Spanish who lived in Spain under Moorish rule.

p. 177 Montesquieu says: in the *Esprit des lois* (1748).

p. 177 Doctor Balouard ... Arlequin: stock characters in the Italian *commedia dell'arte*.

p. 177 Descartes ... Arnauld: René Descartes (1596–1650), French philosopher and mathematician; Abbé Pierre Gassendi (1592–1655), French astronomer; Antoine Arnauld (1612–94), French theologian.

p. 177 a philosopher: Helvétius, following the publication of his *De l'Esprit* in 1758.

p. 179 Zaleucus: Greek lawgiver, fl. *c.* 660 BC.

p. 179 Julian upon a throne: cf. 'Julian', above.

p. 180 Charron ... Gassendi: Pierre Charron (1541–1603), Pierre Ramus (1515–72), Descartes and Gassendi – all French thinkers who were persecuted by the Church for their opinions.

p. 180 Bayle: Pierre Bayle (1647–1706), French philosopher. His great *Dictionary* was published in 1695–97. He was attacked by the Church for sceptical and irreligious statements, particularly by the French theologian Pierre Jurieu (1637–1713) and by Michel Le Tellier (1643–1719), the Jesuit confessor of Louis XIV, and obliged to leave France for the Netherlands. His article 'David' enumerates – as Voltaire says – numerous inadmissible aspects of David's behaviour.

p. 182 Fontenelle: Bernard de Fontenelle (1657–1757), French man of letters. His *Histoire des oracles* appeared in 1687, based on a work by Anthony Van Dale (1638–1708).

p. 183 Mount Krapack: term used by Voltaire in the 1760s and later to describe his situation, far away from the world's centres of activity – an exaggeration comparable with his repeated statements that he was at death's door. Voltaire is alluding to Passo Crap, high up on the Greina Pass, in the south-central Alps.

p. 183 the vineyard of the Lord: 'La vigne du Seigneur', the Lord's

vineyard (Matthew xx:21), whose cultivation (like Candide's 'garden')
is the duty of all true believers. *See* the Introduction, p. xxiii.

p. 187 Calmet: Dom Augustin Calmet (1672–1757), *Dissertation sur
les apparitions ...* (1746). For the events of 1732 and slightly before
concerning vampires, *see* Thacker, 'The Year of the Vampire: An
Undying Memory', in *Essays for Peter Mayer*, ed. Thacker, 1980,
pp. 165–71.

p. 187 Marcilli: for de Marcilly's 'approbation' from the Sorbonne,
16 December 1745, *see* Moland, xx, 547.

p. 188 Tournefort: Joseph Pitton de Tournefort (1658–1708), *Relation d'un voyage au Levant* (3 volumes, 1717), I, 155ff.

p. 189 d'Argens: J. B. Boyer, Marquis d'Argens (1704–71), *Lettres
juives*, Letter 137 (2nd. ed., 6 volumes, 1738).

p. 190 Manichaean: one who believes that the world is divided
between two opposed and eternal forces – good and evil.

p. 192 song in four parts: the *Te Deum*, sung or chanted to give
thanks to God for some fortunate happening. In his *Age of Louis xiv*
Voltaire notes several battles where the leaders of *both* sides had the *Te
Deum* sung after the combat. Cf. *Candide*, Ch. 3.

The Encyclopaedia
p. 193 tr. C. E. Vulliamy, in Voltaire, *The White Bull and Other
Stoties* (1929), pp. 183–5.

p. 194 Lycomedes: King of Scyros. The young warrior Achilles was
hidden, disguised as a girl, among his daughters, and discovered when
Odysseus offered them jewels, which Achilles disdained, and a sword
and a helmet, which he seized with delight.

SUGGESTIONS FOR FURTHER READING

Voltaire's Writings in English Translation

Collected Works, ed. Lord Morley, tr. T. Smollett, rev. W. F. Fleming, 22 volumes, London and New York: 1901, 1927.

The Calas Affair, ed. and tr. B. Masters, London: Folio Society, 1994. Voltaire's texts with thoughtful commentary.

Candide, ed. and tr. C. Thacker, ill. Angela Barrett, Marlborough: Libanus Press, 1995. Parallel French and English texts.

Letters Concerning the English Nation (facsimile of the 1733 ed.), ed. and intr. C. Whibley, London: Peter Davies, 1926.

Letters Concerning the English Nation (facsimile of the 1733 ed.), ed. and intro. N. Cronk, Oxford: World's Classics, OUP, 1994.

Philosophical Dictionary, tr. T. Besterman, Harmondsworth: Penguin, 1972.

Works on Voltaire in English, or in English and French

Besterman, T., *Voltaire*, London: Longman, 1969. The most detailed modern biography.

Mason, H. T., *Voltaire: A Biography*, London: 1981. A balanced and perceptive study.

Thacker, C., *Voltaire*, London: Profiles in Literature, Routledge, 1971.

Studies on Voltaire and the Eighteenth Century, 1953–. The principal forum for writings on Voltaire and on the Enlightenment in general.

Works by Voltaire in French

Oeuvres complètes, ed. L. Moland, 52 volumes, Paris: Garnier, 1877–85.

Complete Works, ed. T. Besterman et al., Geneva: Institut et Museé Voltaire, 1968–.

Correspondance, ed. T. Besterman, 51 volumes, Geneva and Oxford:

1968–77. The definitive edition, the letters being numbered D1 onwards.

Dialogues philosophiques, ed. R. Naves, Paris: 1961 and later.

Dictionnaire philosophique, ed. J. Benda, R. Naves, Paris: 1961 and later.

Lettres philosophiques, ed. F. A. Taylor, Bristol Classical Press, 1992 (intr. and notes in English)

Mélanges, ed. J. Van den Heuvel, Paris: Bibliothèque de la Pléiade, Gallimard, 1961 and later.

Mémoires pour servir à la vie de M. de Voltaire, ed. J. Brenner, Paris: Mercure de France, 1965.

Candide, ed. C. Thacker, Geneva: Textes Littéraires Français, Droz, 1968.

Romans et contes, ed. H. Bénac, Paris: Classiques Garnier, 1960 and later.

Among the many editions of works by Voltaire, those issued by Bibliothèque de la Pléiade, Classiques Garnier, Classiques Larousse and Librairie Droz are generally reliable.

INDEX

PHILOSOPHY AND RELIGIOUS
WRITING IN EVERYMAN

A SELECTION

Ethics
SPINOZA
Spinoza's famous discourse on the
power of understanding **£4.99**

Critique of Pure Reason
IMMANUEL KANT
The capacity of the human intellect
examined **£6.99**

A Discourse on Method,
Meditations, and Principles
RENÉ DESCARTES
Takes the theory of mind over
matter into a new dimension **£4.99**

Philosophical Works
including the Works
on Vision
GEORGE BERKELEY
An eloquent defence of the power
of the spirit in the physical world
£4.99

Utilitarianism, On Liberty,
Considerations on
Representative Government
J. S. MILL
Three radical works which trans-
formed political science **£5.99**

Utopia
THOMAS MORE
A critique of contemporary ills
allied with a visionary ideal for
society **£3.99**

An Essay Concerning
Human Understanding
JOHN LOCKE
A central work in the development
of modern philosophy **£5.99**

Hindu Scriptures
The most important ancient Hindu
writings in one volume **£6.99**

Apologia Pro Vita Sua
JOHN HENRY NEWMAN
A moving and inspiring account of
a Christian's spiritual journey **£5.99**

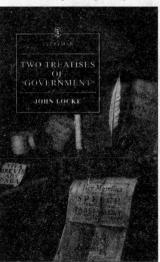

£3.99

AVAILABILITY
All books are available from your local bookshop or direct from
**Littlehampton Book Services Cash Sales, 14 Eldon Way, Lineside Estate,
Littlehampton, West Sussex BN17 7HE.** PRICES ARE SUBJECT TO CHANGE.

To order any of the books, please enclose a cheque (in £ sterling) made payable to
Littlehampton Book Services, or phone your order through with credit card details (Access,
Visa or Mastercard) on 0903 721596 (24 hour answering service) stating card number and
expiry date. Please add £1.25 for package and postage to the total value of your order.

In the USA, for further information and a complete catalogue call 1-800-526-2778.

ESSAYS, CRITICISM AND HISTORY IN EVERYMAN

A SELECTION

The Embassy to Constantinople and Other Writings
LIUDPRAND OF CREMONA
An insider's view of political machinations in medieval Europe **£5.99**

Speeches and Letters
ABRAHAM LINCOLN
A key document of the American Civil War **£4.99**

Essays
FRANCIS BACON
An excellent introduction to Bacon's incisive wit and moral outlook **£3.99**

Puritanism and Liberty: Being the Army Debates (1647-49) from the Clarke Manuscripts
A fascinating revelation of Puritan minds in action **£7.99**

Biographia Literaria
SAMUEL TAYLOR COLERIDGE
A masterpiece of criticism, marrying the study of literature with philosophy **£4.99**

Essays on Literature and Art
WALTER PATER
Insights on culture and literature from a major voice of the 1890s **£3.99**

Chesterton on Dickens: Criticisms and Appreciations
A landmark in Dickens criticism, rarely surpassed **£4.99**

Essays and Poems
R. L. STEVENSON
Stevenson's hidden treasures in a new selection **£4.99**

THE NATURAL HISTORY OF SELBORNE

GILBERT WHITE

£3.99

AVAILABILITY

All books are available from your local bookshop or direct from
Littlehampton Book Services Cash Sales, 14 Eldon Way, Lineside Estate, Littlehampton, West Sussex BN17 7HE. PRICES ARE SUBJECT TO CHANGE.

To order any of the books, please enclose a cheque (in £ sterling) made payable to Littlehampton Book Services, or phone your order through with credit card details (Access, Visa or Mastercard) on 0903 721596 (24 hour answering service) stating card number and expiry date. Please add £1.25 for package and postage to the total value of your order.

In the USA, for further information and a complete catalogue call 1-800-526-2778.